BENJAMIN KARLSTEIN

2,500+ Marketing Ideas for Bakeries

Digital Marketing, Social Media Marketing, Brand Marketing, Content Marketing, and Product Marketing

CONTENTS

Page 1: Best Practices

Page 3: Digital Marketing Ideas

Page 49: Social Media Marketing Ideas

Page 95: Brand Marketing Ideas

Page 141: Content Marketing Ideas

Page 187: Product Marketing Ideas

Page 232: Closing Words

Copyright © 2024 Benjamin Karlstein, Karlstein Publishing. All rights reserved.

COPYRIGHT AND DISCLAIMER

Book Title: 2,500+ Marketing Ideas for Bakeries
First Edition, 2024
Published by Benjamin Karlstein, Karlstein Publishing

Copyright © 2024 by Benjamin Karlstein, Karlstein Publishing. All rights reserved. No part of this publication may be reproduced, distributed, or transmitted in any form or by any means, including photocopying, recording, or other electronic or mechanical methods, without the prior written permission of the publisher, except in the case of brief quotations embodied in critical reviews and certain other noncommercial uses permitted by copyright law. For permission requests, write to the publisher, addressed "Attention: Permissions Coordinator," at the address below.

Disclaimer: The information in this book is meant to supplement, not replace, proper digital marketing practice. Approaches described in this book may involve risk. The author and publisher advise readers and clients to take full responsibility for their safety and know their limits. Before practicing the techniques described in this book, be sure that your equipment is well maintained, and do not take risks beyond your level of experience, aptitude, training, and comfort level.

Contact: www.karlstein-publishing.com/contact

Best Practices For Using This Book

Congratulations on acquiring our marketing ideas paperback edition! The following chapters contain over 2,500 carefully crafted marketing ideas designed to enhance your marketing practice and boost your sales. To make the most out of this valuable tool, it's essential to follow best practices that can help you unlock its full potential. Here are some best practices to consider:

1. Apply the Content: The content of this book is designed to be applied in real-world marketing scenarios. Reflect on how each concept or strategy can be integrated into your personal or professional life. Practical application is key to internalizing and benefiting from the material.

2. Learn Continuously: As you work through the book, view each section as a step in your continuous learning journey. Revisit sections as needed, and feel free to update your responses or notes as your understanding deepens over time.

3. Setting a Regular Schedule: Consistency is key to maximizing the benefits of this book. Set aside regular time slots for engaging with the content. Whether it's a daily short session or a longer weekly deep-dive, a regular schedule will help you build and maintain momentum in your marketing journey.

4. Tracking Your Progress: Keep track of your marketing progress through the book. Celebrate small victories and milestones to maintain motivation. This could be completing a section, successfully applying a concept in real life, or having a breakthrough in understanding.

5. Share and Discuss: Use the content of the book as a basis for discussion with peers, mentors, or colleagues. Sharing marketing insights and experiences can enhance your understanding and offer new perspectives.

Sincerely, Benjamin Karlstein, Karlstein Publishing

500+ Digital Marketing Ideas for Bakeries

SECTIONS IN THIS CHAPTER:

1. Identifying Your Bakery's Unique Value Proposition – Page 4
2. Building an Engaging Bakery Website – Page 6
3. SEO Strategies for Bakeries – Page 8
4. Crafting the Perfect Email Marketing Campaigns – Page 10
5. Leveraging Social Media to Showcase Bakery Offerings – Page 12
6. Utilizing Video Marketing for Bakery Promotions – Page 14
7. Implementing an Online Ordering System – Page 16
8. Developing a Loyalty Program for Online Customers – Page 18
9. Engaging with Customers Through Blogging – Page 20
10. Pay-Per-Click Advertising for Bakeries – Page 22
11. Managing Online Reviews and Feedback – Page 24
12. Influencer Marketing Strategies for Bakeries – Page 26
13. Creating Eye-Catching Online Advertisements – Page 28
14. Hosting Virtual Bakery Events – Page 30
15. Using Analytics to Track Marketing Performance – Page 32
16. Mobile Marketing for On-the-Go Customers – Page 34
17. Collaborating with Other Local Businesses Online – Page 36
18. Utilizing Geo-Targeting for Local Promotions – Page 38
19. Creating Interactive Content for Engagement – Page 40
20. Planning Seasonal Marketing Campaigns – Page 42
21. Enhancing Customer Service with Chatbots – Page 44
22. Sustainable and Ethical Marketing Practices for Bakeries – Page 46

DIGITAL MARKETING IDEAS

Identifying Your Bakery's Unique Value Proposition

- Begin by conducting thorough market research to understand your bakery's target audience, including their preferences, needs, and pain points.
- Analyze your competitors' digital presence to identify gaps and opportunities where your bakery can stand out.
- Create customer personas based on demographic, psychographic, and behavioral data to tailor your unique value proposition to specific audience segments.
- Highlight your bakery's heritage, tradition, or family recipes to evoke a sense of authenticity and nostalgia among customers.
- Emphasize the quality of your ingredients and the artisanal craftsmanship behind your baked goods to differentiate yourself from mass-produced alternatives.
- Showcase any certifications or awards your bakery has received for excellence in baking, food safety, or sustainability practices.
- Leverage user-generated content such as customer reviews, testimonials, and photos to demonstrate social proof and build trust with potential customers.
- Offer exclusive promotions or discounts to reward loyal customers and incentivize repeat purchases.
- Partner with local influencers or food bloggers to generate buzz and increase visibility for your bakery on social media platforms.
- Develop a unique selling proposition (USP) that succinctly communicates what sets your bakery apart from competitors in a compelling and memorable way.
- Create a visually appealing website that showcases your bakery's products, story, and values to engage visitors and encourage exploration.
- Optimize your website for search engines (SEO) to improve your bakery's visibility in organic search results and attract relevant traffic.
- Utilize email marketing campaigns to keep customers informed about new products, special offers, and upcoming events at your bakery.
- Collaborate with complementary businesses such as coffee shops, florists, or event planners to cross-promote each other's products and services.
- Host virtual baking classes or workshops to educate and engage your audience while promoting your bakery's expertise and products.
- Develop a loyalty program that rewards customers for their continued support with perks such as discounts, freebies, or exclusive access to events.
- Create branded merchandise such as t-shirts, tote bags, or mugs featuring your bakery's logo or iconic baked goods to increase brand visibility and generate additional revenue.
- Engage with your audience on social media platforms by sharing behind-the-scenes content, responding to comments and messages, and participating in relevant conversations.
- Partner with local charities or community organizations to sponsor events or fundraisers and demonstrate your bakery's commitment to giving back.

- Experiment with interactive content formats such as polls, quizzes, or contests to encourage participation and foster a sense of community around your bakery.
- Invest in professional photography and videography to showcase your bakery's products in the most appetizing and enticing way possible.
- Offer customization options for your baked goods, allowing customers to personalize their orders for special occasions or dietary preferences.
- Create educational content such as blog posts, recipe videos, or baking tips to position your bakery as a trusted authority in the industry.
- Monitor and analyze key performance indicators (KPIs) such as website traffic, social media engagement, and sales conversions to measure the effectiveness of your digital marketing efforts and make data-driven adjustments as needed.

DIGITAL MARKETING IDEAS

Building an Engaging Bakery Website

- Design your bakery website with a user-friendly interface, intuitive navigation, and clear calls-to-action to guide visitors through the site and encourage interaction.
- Utilize high-quality images of your baked goods to showcase their visual appeal and entice visitors to explore further.
- Ensure your website is mobile-responsive to provide a seamless browsing experience for users accessing it from smartphones and tablets.
- Incorporate an online ordering system to allow customers to place orders for pickup or delivery directly through your website, streamlining the purchasing process.
- Implement an easy-to-use reservation system for customers to book tables or pre-order specialty items for pickup at your bakery.
- Include detailed product descriptions and pricing information to help customers make informed purchasing decisions and reduce the need for inquiries.
- Integrate customer reviews and testimonials into your website to build trust and credibility with potential customers.
- Feature a blog or news section on your website to share updates, behind-the-scenes stories, recipes, and baking tips to engage visitors and encourage repeat visits.
- Offer a virtual tour of your bakery, providing a glimpse into your kitchen, production process, and ambiance to create a sense of transparency and authenticity.
- Incorporate interactive elements such as polls, quizzes, or surveys to encourage visitor engagement and gather feedback about their preferences and experiences.
- Create a dedicated section on your website for special promotions, discounts, and seasonal offerings to incentivize purchases and drive sales.
- Include an FAQ page to address common inquiries and provide helpful information to customers, reducing the need for direct communication and enhancing the user experience.
- Integrate social media buttons and sharing options throughout your website to encourage visitors to connect with your bakery on various platforms and share content with their networks.
- Optimize your website for search engines (SEO) by incorporating relevant keywords, meta tags, and descriptive titles to improve visibility and attract organic traffic.
- Implement live chat support or a contact form to enable real-time communication with customers and address any questions or concerns they may have.
- Create a gallery or portfolio section on your website to showcase custom cakes, wedding desserts, and other specialty creations to inspire potential customers and showcase your bakery's capabilities.
- Offer downloadable resources such as recipe cards, baking guides, or e-books as incentives for visitors to join your email list or follow your bakery on social media.
- Incorporate video content such as tutorials, recipe demonstrations, or customer testimonials to enhance engagement and provide valuable content to your audience.

- Utilize customer data and analytics to track website performance, user behavior, and conversion metrics to identify areas for improvement and optimize the user experience.
- Implement security measures such as SSL encryption and secure payment gateways to protect customer information and instill confidence in online transactions.
- Integrate a newsletter signup form on your website to capture leads and nurture relationships with potential customers through targeted email marketing campaigns.
- Utilize storytelling techniques to share the history, values, and passion behind your bakery, creating an emotional connection with visitors and fostering brand loyalty.
- Collaborate with local photographers, designers, or videographers to create custom multimedia content that showcases your bakery's unique personality and offerings.
- Regularly update your website with fresh content, promotions, and seasonal offerings to keep visitors engaged and encourage them to return to your bakery both online and offline.

SEO Strategies for Bakeries

- Begin by conducting keyword research to identify relevant search terms and phrases that potential customers may use when looking for bakery products or services online.
- Optimize your website's meta titles, meta descriptions, and headers to include target keywords and attract clicks from search engine results pages (SERPs).
- Create high-quality, informative content that addresses common questions, concerns, and interests related to baking, such as recipes, baking tips, and ingredient guides.
- Incorporate long-tail keywords and localized terms into your content to capture specific queries and attract traffic from users in your bakery's target geographic area.
- Utilize structured data markup such as schema.org markup to enhance the visibility and relevance of your bakery's website in search engine results.
- Optimize your website's loading speed and mobile-friendliness to improve user experience and satisfy search engine ranking criteria.
- Build high-quality backlinks from reputable websites and directories within the food, hospitality, and local business sectors to increase your bakery's authority and credibility in the eyes of search engines.
- Create a Google My Business listing for your bakery to enhance its visibility in local search results and provide essential information such as business hours, location, and contact details to potential customers.
- Encourage satisfied customers to leave positive reviews and ratings on your Google My Business listing to improve your bakery's reputation and attract more customers.
- Leverage social media platforms such as Facebook, Instagram, and Pinterest to showcase your bakery's products, engage with customers, and drive traffic to your website.
- Publish blog posts or articles on your website regularly to keep content fresh and relevant, demonstrating to search engines that your bakery is active and authoritative within its niche.
- Monitor your bakery's online reputation and respond promptly and professionally to customer reviews, comments, and inquiries across various digital channels.
- Optimize your bakery's website for local search by including location-specific keywords in your content, meta tags, and anchor text, especially if you serve a specific geographic area.
- Partner with local influencers, food bloggers, and community organizations to generate buzz and increase visibility for your bakery online, both through their networks and yours.
- Utilize online directories and review platforms relevant to the food and hospitality industry to ensure your bakery is listed accurately and consistently across the web.
- Regularly audit your website for technical SEO issues such as broken links, duplicate content, and crawl errors, and address them promptly to maintain optimal performance.
- Monitor and analyze your bakery's website traffic, keyword rankings, and other SEO metrics using tools like Google Analytics and Google Search Console to track progress and identify areas for improvement.

- Implement a content marketing strategy that focuses on creating valuable, shareable content that attracts links and social media engagement, thereby boosting your bakery's SEO efforts.
- Develop partnerships with local businesses, such as cafes, restaurants, and event venues, to cross-promote each other online and increase visibility within the community.
- Create an FAQ page on your bakery's website to address common queries and provide helpful information to both customers and search engines.
- Conduct regular competitor analysis to identify opportunities and gaps in your bakery's SEO strategy, allowing you to stay ahead of the competition and capitalize on emerging trends.
- Utilize local SEO tactics such as optimizing your bakery's Google Maps listing, acquiring local citations, and participating in community events to improve your visibility in local search results.
- Invest in ongoing SEO training and education for your bakery's marketing team to stay updated on industry best practices and algorithm changes that may affect your search rankings.
- Continuously monitor and adapt your bakery's SEO strategy based on performance data, customer feedback, and changes in search engine algorithms to maintain a competitive edge and drive sustainable growth.

Crafting the Perfect Email Marketing Campaigns

- Begin by segmenting your email list based on factors such as purchase history, demographics, and engagement levels to tailor your campaigns to specific audience segments.
- Personalize your email content by addressing recipients by name and incorporating dynamic content blocks that reflect their preferences and behaviors.
- Craft attention-grabbing subject lines that are concise, compelling, and relevant to the content of your emails to increase open rates and engagement.
- Use a responsive email design that renders well on various devices and screen sizes to ensure optimal readability and user experience for recipients.
- Provide valuable and relevant content in your emails, such as special offers, product updates, recipe ideas, or baking tips, to keep subscribers engaged and interested.
- Include clear and prominent calls-to-action (CTAs) in your emails to guide recipients toward desired actions, such as making a purchase, signing up for an event, or visiting your bakery.
- Incorporate visually appealing images and graphics that showcase your bakery's products and brand aesthetic to capture recipients' attention and convey your message effectively.
- Experiment with different email formats, such as newsletters, product updates, event invitations, or automated drip campaigns, to keep your email marketing efforts fresh and engaging.
- A/B test various elements of your email campaigns, including subject lines, CTAs, imagery, and email copy, to identify what resonates best with your audience and optimize performance.
- Utilize email automation tools to schedule and send targeted campaigns at the optimal times based on recipients' time zones, past engagement behavior, and other relevant factors.
- Implement an email preference center that allows subscribers to customize their email preferences, such as frequency and content types, to ensure they receive relevant and desired communications.
- Leverage user-generated content such as customer reviews, testimonials, and photos in your emails to add social proof and authenticity to your messaging.
- Encourage recipients to engage with your emails by asking questions, soliciting feedback, or inviting them to participate in polls or surveys.
- Include social sharing buttons in your emails to make it easy for recipients to share your content with their networks and expand your reach organically.
- Offer exclusive discounts, promotions, or early access to new products or events as incentives for subscribers to stay engaged with your email communications.
- Utilize email personalization techniques beyond just addressing recipients by name, such as recommending products based on past purchases or browsing behavior.
- Incorporate storytelling elements into your email content to create emotional connections with recipients and showcase the people, processes, and stories behind your bakery.

- Monitor key email metrics such as open rates, click-through rates, conversion rates, and unsubscribe rates to evaluate the effectiveness of your campaigns and make data-driven optimizations.
- Segment your email list further based on factors such as geographic location, preferences, or engagement history to deliver even more targeted and relevant content to subscribers.
- Implement email list hygiene practices such as regularly removing inactive subscribers, correcting typos and formatting errors, and ensuring compliance with anti-spam regulations.
- Develop a consistent sending cadence for your email campaigns to maintain top-of-mind awareness with subscribers without overwhelming their inboxes.
- Create compelling email content that provides value to recipients beyond just promotional messages, such as educational resources, insider tips, or exclusive behind-the-scenes content.
- Use storytelling and visual elements to create engaging email campaigns that resonate with recipients emotionally and leave a lasting impression.
- Continuously analyze and optimize your email marketing campaigns based on performance data and subscriber feedback to ensure they remain effective and impactful over time.

DIGITAL MARKETING IDEAS

Leveraging Social Media to Showcase Bakery Offerings

- Establish a presence on popular social media platforms such as Instagram, Facebook, Pinterest, and Twitter to reach a wide audience of potential customers and engage with existing ones.
- Create visually appealing content that showcases your bakery's products in an enticing and appetizing way, utilizing high-quality images and videos to capture attention and drive engagement.
- Develop a content calendar to plan and schedule your social media posts in advance, ensuring a consistent and cohesive presence across all platforms.
- Use hashtags strategically to increase the visibility and discoverability of your social media posts, targeting both broad and niche hashtags relevant to your bakery and its offerings.
- Engage with your audience by responding to comments, messages, and mentions promptly and authentically, fostering a sense of community and building relationships with customers.
- Collaborate with local influencers, food bloggers, and other businesses to expand your reach and tap into new audiences through sponsored posts, giveaways, or joint promotions.
- Share behind-the-scenes content that gives followers a glimpse into your bakery's kitchen, production process, and the people behind the scenes, humanizing your brand and adding authenticity.
- Showcase customer testimonials, reviews, and user-generated content (UGC) on your social media channels to build trust and credibility with potential customers and encourage user engagement.
- Run social media contests, challenges, or giveaways to incentivize engagement, reward loyal followers, and generate buzz around your bakery's products and promotions.
- Utilize Instagram Stories, Facebook Live, or other live streaming features to provide real-time updates, demonstrations, or Q&A sessions, allowing followers to interact with your bakery in an immediate and interactive way.
- Develop themed content series or recurring features, such as "Recipe of the Week" or "Behind the Bake," to provide regular value to your audience and encourage repeat engagement.
- Leverage seasonal trends, holidays, and special occasions to create timely and relevant content that resonates with your audience and drives traffic to your bakery.
- Collaborate with local businesses, organizations, or events to cross-promote each other's social media accounts and expand your reach within the community.
- Utilize social media advertising options such as boosted posts, sponsored content, or targeted ads to reach specific demographics, interests, and geographic locations with your bakery's messaging.
- Monitor social media analytics and insights to track the performance of your posts, understand audience behavior, and identify opportunities for optimization and improvement.

- Experiment with different content formats, such as carousels, slideshows, videos, and interactive polls, to keep your social media feed dynamic and engaging.
- Share educational content, tips, and tutorials related to baking, decorating, or using your bakery's products to provide value to your audience and position your brand as a helpful resource.
- Encourage user-generated content by inviting customers to share photos of their bakery purchases or creations using a branded hashtag, then reshare and highlight the best submissions on your own social media channels.
- Develop a consistent brand aesthetic and voice across all your social media profiles, reflecting your bakery's personality, values, and unique selling points to create a cohesive and memorable impression.
- Monitor social media conversations and trends related to baking, food, and local events to identify opportunities for timely and relevant engagement with your audience.
- Offer exclusive promotions, discounts, or special offers to your social media followers as a reward for their loyalty and engagement, driving traffic to your bakery and encouraging repeat purchases.
- Create shareable content that taps into nostalgia, humor, or emotional appeal to resonate with your audience and encourage them to share your posts with their own networks.
- Showcase your bakery's involvement in community events, fundraisers, or charitable initiatives on social media to demonstrate your commitment to giving back and foster positive sentiment among followers.
- Continuously monitor and adapt your social media strategy based on performance data, audience feedback, and changes in platform algorithms to ensure your efforts remain effective and impactful over time.

DIGITAL MARKETING IDEAS

Utilizing Video Marketing for Bakery Promotions

- Create short, visually appealing videos showcasing your bakery's products being prepared, decorated, and enjoyed to capture viewers' attention and showcase your offerings in an engaging way.
- Develop recipe videos featuring step-by-step instructions for baking your signature treats, offering viewers valuable content while showcasing your expertise and enticing them to visit your bakery.
- Produce behind-the-scenes videos that provide a glimpse into your bakery's kitchen, introducing viewers to your team, processes, and commitment to quality, fostering transparency and building trust with potential customers.
- Collaborate with local influencers, food bloggers, or chefs to create sponsored content or cooking demos featuring your bakery's products, leveraging their audience and credibility to expand your reach and credibility.
- Host live cooking demonstrations or baking classes on platforms like Facebook Live, Instagram Live, or YouTube, allowing viewers to interact in real-time, ask questions, and learn from your bakery's experts.
- Create "meet the baker" videos introducing viewers to the talented individuals behind your bakery's creations, sharing their stories, passion for baking, and favorite recipes to humanize your brand and forge connections with customers.
- Produce customer testimonial videos featuring satisfied patrons sharing their experiences, favorite products, and reasons for choosing your bakery, providing social proof and inspiring trust among potential customers.
- Develop video tutorials showcasing creative ways to decorate cakes, cupcakes, or pastries using your bakery's products, offering viewers inspiration and encouraging them to try their hand at baking at home.
- Host virtual events such as baking contests, taste tests, or product launches, streaming the festivities live and engaging viewers with interactive elements like polls, Q&A sessions, and giveaways to drive excitement and participation.
- Partner with local businesses, such as coffee shops, event venues, or wedding planners, to create collaborative video content promoting joint offerings or events, reaching new audiences and reinforcing community ties.
- Produce "day in the life" videos highlighting a typical day at your bakery, from early morning dough preparation to bustling lunchtime sales, providing viewers with an immersive glimpse into your bakery's daily operations and atmosphere.
- Share customer success stories or special occasions, such as birthdays, weddings, or anniversaries, captured on video, celebrating memorable moments and showcasing your bakery's role in creating cherished memories.
- Produce seasonal video content featuring holiday-themed treats, decorations, and recipes, tapping into seasonal trends and inspiring viewers to visit your bakery for festive treats and gifts.

- Create educational videos addressing common baking questions, techniques, or troubleshooting tips, positioning your bakery as a knowledgeable resource and building credibility with viewers.
- Produce cinematic brand videos that capture the essence of your bakery's brand identity, values, and unique selling points, evoking emotion and leaving a lasting impression on viewers.
- Utilize user-generated content by encouraging customers to share videos of themselves enjoying your bakery's products, then reshare and amplify the best submissions on your own social media channels.
- Develop video testimonials from satisfied customers, featuring their authentic praise and recommendations for your bakery's products and services, adding credibility and persuasive power to your marketing efforts.
- Host virtual bakery tours, allowing viewers to explore your bakery's facilities, equipment, and offerings from the comfort of their own homes, generating interest and familiarity with your brand.
- Produce interactive video content such as polls, quizzes, or interactive hotspots that engage viewers and encourage them to participate actively with your bakery's brand and offerings.
- Share fun and lighthearted videos featuring baking challenges, taste tests, or behind-the-scenes bloopers, showcasing your bakery's personality and fostering a sense of connection and relatability with viewers.
- Produce informative videos addressing topics related to baking trends, ingredient sourcing, sustainability practices, or nutrition information, positioning your bakery as an industry leader and trusted authority.
- Create video ads or promotional clips highlighting special offers, seasonal promotions, or limited-time deals at your bakery, compelling viewers to take action and visit your store or website.
- Develop video testimonials or endorsements from local influencers, chefs, or celebrities, lending their credibility and influence to your bakery's brand and products, and reaching new audiences through their networks.
- Analyze video performance metrics such as views, engagement, and watch time to evaluate the effectiveness of your video marketing efforts and make data-driven optimizations to improve results over time.

DIGITAL MARKETING IDEAS

Implementing an Online Ordering System

- Choose a user-friendly online ordering system that seamlessly integrates with your bakery's website, allowing customers to browse your menu, select items, customize orders, and complete transactions with ease.
- Customize your online ordering platform to reflect your bakery's branding, colors, and imagery, providing a cohesive and immersive experience for customers that aligns with your brand identity.
- Optimize your website for search engines (SEO) to ensure that your online ordering platform ranks prominently in search results when potential customers are looking for bakery products in your area.
- Prominently feature your online ordering platform on your website's homepage and navigation menu, making it easy for visitors to find and access when they're ready to place an order.
- Offer incentives such as discounts, promotions, or loyalty rewards for customers who place orders through your online ordering system, encouraging repeat purchases and driving adoption.
- Utilize targeted email marketing campaigns to promote your online ordering platform to existing customers, highlighting the convenience, speed, and safety of ordering from your bakery online.
- Leverage social media channels to showcase your bakery's products and drive traffic to your online ordering platform, using mouth-watering images, enticing captions, and compelling calls-to-action to encourage engagement and conversion.
- Partner with local influencers, food bloggers, or community organizations to promote your online ordering platform to their followers, leveraging their credibility and reach to expand your audience and generate buzz.
- Invest in professional food photography and videography to create visually stunning images and videos of your bakery's products, enticing customers to place orders online.
- Implement user-friendly navigation and search functionality on your online ordering platform, allowing customers to easily find and filter menu items based on categories, dietary preferences, or special requests.
- Offer a variety of payment options on your online ordering platform, including credit/debit cards, mobile wallets, and cash on delivery, to accommodate different customer preferences and increase convenience.
- Provide detailed product descriptions, including ingredients, allergen information, and serving sizes, to help customers make informed decisions and reduce the likelihood of returns or complaints.
- Implement a streamlined checkout process on your online ordering platform, minimizing the number of steps required to complete a transaction and reducing friction for customers.
- Offer contactless delivery and curbside pickup options through your online ordering platform, providing customers with a safe and convenient way to receive their bakery

orders during times of heightened health concerns.

- Leverage customer data and analytics from your online ordering platform to gain insights into customer preferences, order patterns, and purchasing behavior, informing future marketing strategies and menu optimizations.

- Encourage customers to create accounts on your online ordering platform, enabling you to track order history, offer personalized recommendations, and provide targeted marketing communications based on their preferences and habits.

- Implement a referral program on your online ordering platform, rewarding customers who refer friends and family with discounts, freebies, or other incentives, incentivizing word-of-mouth marketing and customer acquisition.

- Monitor online reviews and feedback from customers who use your online ordering platform, responding promptly and professionally to address any concerns or issues and maintain a positive reputation.

- Utilize email and SMS notifications to keep customers informed about the status of their orders, from confirmation and preparation to delivery or pickup, providing transparency and peace of mind.

- Leverage seasonal promotions, limited-time offers, and holiday specials on your online ordering platform to drive excitement and urgency among customers, encouraging them to place orders and try new products.

- Implement upselling and cross-selling techniques on your online ordering platform, suggesting complementary items or add-ons during the checkout process to increase order value and maximize revenue.

- Offer catering and bulk ordering options through your online ordering platform, catering to larger groups and events and expanding your bakery's customer base beyond individual consumers.

- Utilize targeted advertising campaigns on search engines, social media platforms, and local directories to promote your online ordering platform to potential customers in your area, driving traffic and generating sales.

- Continuously monitor and optimize your online ordering platform based on customer feedback, technological advancements, and industry trends, ensuring that it remains a valuable and competitive asset for your bakery's digital marketing efforts.

Developing a Loyalty Program for Online Customers

- Design a tiered loyalty program that rewards customers with points, discounts, or exclusive perks based on their level of engagement and spending on your bakery's online ordering platform.
- Offer a sign-up bonus or welcome reward to new members of your loyalty program, incentivizing customers to join and start earning rewards from their very first purchase.
- Implement a points-based system where customers earn points for every dollar spent on your online ordering platform, with the ability to redeem points for discounts, free products, or special rewards.
- Provide additional incentives for customers to engage with your bakery's online ordering platform, such as bonus points for writing reviews, referring friends, or sharing their purchases on social media.
- Personalize rewards and offers based on each customer's purchase history, preferences, and behavior, tailoring the loyalty program experience to their individual needs and interests.
- Create exclusive member-only events, promotions, or product releases for loyalty program members, making them feel valued and appreciated for their continued support and patronage.
- Offer birthday rewards or anniversary gifts to loyalty program members, celebrating special occasions and fostering a sense of personal connection and loyalty with your bakery.
- Utilize gamification elements such as challenges, milestones, and badges to make earning and redeeming rewards more engaging and enjoyable for loyalty program members.
- Communicate regularly with loyalty program members through email, SMS, or push notifications, keeping them informed about their rewards balance, upcoming promotions, and exclusive offers.
- Provide a seamless and user-friendly interface for members to track their rewards balance, view available offers, and redeem rewards on your bakery's online ordering platform.
- Offer bonus points or rewards for members who consistently engage with your bakery's online ordering platform over time, encouraging long-term loyalty and repeat purchases.
- Partner with other local businesses or brands to offer joint rewards or cross-promotional opportunities for loyalty program members, expanding the value and appeal of your program.
- Solicit feedback and suggestions from loyalty program members on ways to improve the program and enhance their experience, demonstrating your commitment to customer satisfaction and continuous improvement.
- Reward customers for engaging with your bakery's social media channels, such as following, liking, or sharing posts, to increase visibility and engagement while also fostering loyalty.
- Provide VIP treatment for top-tier members of your loyalty program, such as early access to sales, priority customer service, or exclusive gifts, to incentivize higher spending and retention.

- Offer seasonal or limited-time promotions exclusively for loyalty program members, such as double points, bonus rewards, or free shipping, to drive engagement and increase loyalty during key periods.
- Create a referral program within your loyalty program, rewarding members who refer friends and family with bonus points, discounts, or other incentives, while also attracting new customers to your bakery.
- Showcase success stories and testimonials from satisfied loyalty program members, highlighting the value they've received and the benefits of joining your bakery's loyalty program.
- Implement a tiered rewards structure where members can unlock higher levels and greater rewards based on their cumulative spending or engagement over time, incentivizing continued loyalty and patronage.
- Provide convenient redemption options for loyalty program rewards, such as online ordering credits, digital gift cards, or exclusive products, to ensure a seamless and rewarding experience for members.
- Encourage members to share their loyalty program experiences and rewards on social media, using branded hashtags and user-generated content to increase awareness and attract new members.
- Analyze data and insights from your loyalty program to understand member behavior, preferences, and trends, allowing you to tailor your marketing efforts and offerings to better meet their needs.
- Host special events or appreciation days for loyalty program members at your bakery, providing opportunities for members to connect with each other and with your team while enjoying exclusive perks and treats.
- Continuously evaluate and iterate on your loyalty program based on feedback, performance metrics, and industry trends, ensuring that it remains a valuable and compelling incentive for online customers to choose your bakery.

DIGITAL MARKETING IDEAS

Engaging with Customers Through Blogging

- Start a bakery blog on your website to share valuable content, insights, and updates with your audience, positioning your bakery as a trusted authority in the industry.
- Develop a content strategy for your bakery blog that aligns with your target audience's interests, preferences, and needs, ensuring that your content resonates with readers and provides them with genuine value.
- Share behind-the-scenes stories and anecdotes about your bakery's history, team members, and creative process, giving readers a glimpse into the personalities and passion behind your brand.
- Write blog posts featuring recipes for your bakery's signature treats, offering step-by-step instructions, tips, and variations to inspire readers to try baking at home and showcase your bakery's expertise.
- Create educational content addressing common baking questions, techniques, and troubleshooting tips, providing readers with valuable information and positioning your bakery as a helpful resource.
- Share updates and announcements about new products, seasonal offerings, or special promotions at your bakery through your blog, keeping readers informed and engaged with your brand.
- Interview local suppliers, artisans, or experts in related fields such as food, agriculture, or sustainability, sharing their insights and perspectives on topics of interest to your audience.
- Write blog posts featuring customer testimonials, success stories, or special occasions celebrated with your bakery's products, showcasing the positive impact your bakery has on people's lives.
- Share stories and photos from community events, fundraisers, or charitable initiatives your bakery participates in, highlighting your commitment to giving back and fostering goodwill with readers.
- Provide baking tips, tricks, and hacks to help readers improve their skills and achieve better results in the kitchen, establishing your bakery as a valuable source of expertise and guidance.
- Share insights and trends from the baking industry, such as new ingredients, techniques, or flavor combinations, keeping readers informed and inspired by the latest developments.
- Write blog posts featuring interviews with your bakery's customers, allowing them to share their experiences, favorite products, and reasons for choosing your bakery, building trust and credibility with potential customers.
- Create thematic blog series or recurring features, such as "Recipe of the Month" or "Baker's Spotlight," to provide regular content that keeps readers coming back for more.
- Share tips and ideas for hosting events, parties, or special occasions featuring your bakery's products, offering readers inspiration and practical advice for planning memorable gatherings.

- Collaborate with local influencers, food bloggers, or chefs to create guest blog posts or joint content featuring their unique perspectives, expertise, and experiences with your bakery.
- Share stories and photos from your bakery's travels, events, or adventures, giving readers an insider's view of your brand's journey and adding personality to your blog content.
- Write blog posts addressing common dietary preferences and restrictions, such as gluten-free, vegan, or keto baking, providing readers with options and alternatives that cater to their needs.
- Share tutorials and how-to guides for decorating cakes, cupcakes, or pastries using your bakery's products, offering readers inspiration and practical tips for creating beautiful and delicious treats at home.
- Solicit feedback and suggestions from readers through comments, polls, or surveys, using their input to inform future blog topics, content formats, and improvements to your bakery's offerings.
- Showcase your bakery's commitment to quality, sustainability, and community involvement through blog posts highlighting your sourcing practices, environmental initiatives, and philanthropic efforts.
- Share stories and photos from your bakery's history, milestones, and achievements, celebrating your journey and the people who have contributed to your success along the way.
- Write blog posts addressing common baking myths, misconceptions, or challenges, debunking myths and providing readers with accurate information and expert advice.
- Encourage reader engagement and interaction through contests, giveaways, or challenges hosted on your blog, rewarding participation and fostering a sense of community among your audience.
- Monitor blog analytics and track metrics such as traffic, engagement, and conversions to evaluate the performance of your blog content and make data-driven decisions to optimize future efforts.

DIGITAL MARKETING IDEAS

Pay-Per-Click Advertising for Bakeries

- Launch targeted pay-per-click (PPC) advertising campaigns on search engines like Google and Bing, bidding on keywords relevant to your bakery's products, services, and location to appear in search results when potential customers are actively looking for what you offer.
- Utilize keyword research tools to identify high-volume, low-competition keywords related to baking, desserts, pastries, and other relevant terms to incorporate into your PPC campaigns, maximizing your visibility and reach.
- Create compelling ad copy that highlights your bakery's unique selling points, such as artisanal ingredients, specialty offerings, or convenient online ordering options, to entice searchers to click on your ads and visit your website.
- Utilize ad extensions such as location extensions, call extensions, and sitelink extensions to provide additional information and opportunities for engagement within your PPC ads, increasing their effectiveness and relevance to searchers.
- Implement ad scheduling to target your PPC ads to appear during peak times when potential customers are most likely to be searching for bakery products or services, such as mornings, weekends, or holidays.
- Develop highly targeted PPC campaigns for specific geographic areas or neighborhoods served by your bakery, using location targeting settings to ensure that your ads are shown to users within your desired radius or target market.
- Leverage remarketing or retargeting campaigns to reconnect with website visitors who have previously interacted with your bakery's website or online ordering platform, encouraging them to return and complete a purchase.
- Experiment with different ad formats and placements beyond traditional search ads, such as display ads, video ads, or shopping ads, to diversify your PPC strategy and reach customers across different channels and platforms.
- Utilize audience targeting options such as demographics, interests, or behaviors to refine your PPC campaigns and ensure that your ads are shown to the most relevant and valuable audience segments for your bakery.
- Monitor and optimize your PPC campaigns regularly, adjusting bids, targeting parameters, ad copy, and landing pages based on performance data and insights to maximize return on investment (ROI) and achieve your advertising goals.
- Develop customized landing pages for your PPC ads that provide a seamless and optimized experience for users, ensuring that they find relevant information and clear calls-to-action to encourage conversions and purchases.
- Incorporate conversion tracking and attribution modeling into your PPC campaigns to measure the impact of your ads on key performance metrics such as website visits, online orders, and revenue generated for your bakery.
- Utilize ad testing features to experiment with different ad variations, headlines, images, and calls-to-action to identify the most effective messaging and creative elements for driving clicks and conversions.

- Set up conversion tracking for phone calls generated from your PPC ads, allowing you to measure the effectiveness of your campaigns in driving inbound calls to your bakery and track the return on your advertising investment.
- Leverage ad automation tools and bidding strategies offered by PPC platforms to streamline campaign management, optimize performance, and maximize efficiency in budget allocation and bid adjustments.
- Monitor competitive trends and industry insights to identify new opportunities and emerging keywords or market segments to target with your PPC advertising efforts, staying ahead of competitors and capturing market share.
- Implement ad copy testing strategies such as A/B testing or split testing to compare different ad variations and determine which messages, offers, and CTAs resonate most effectively with your target audience.
- Use ad scheduling and dayparting features to adjust bid adjustments and targeting parameters based on day of the week, time of day, or other factors that may impact ad performance and customer behavior.
- Develop PPC campaigns specifically tailored to seasonal trends, holidays, or special occasions relevant to your bakery, such as Valentine's Day, Easter, or Thanksgiving, to capitalize on increased demand and drive sales during peak periods.
- Leverage dynamic ad features and ad customizers to create personalized and relevant ad experiences for users based on their search queries, location, device, or other contextual factors, increasing engagement and conversions.
- Implement ad extensions such as callout extensions, review extensions, and promotion extensions to enhance your PPC ads with additional information and incentives that encourage clicks and conversions.
- Utilize geo-targeting options to adjust bids and targeting settings based on the proximity of users to your bakery's physical locations, ensuring that your ads are shown more prominently to users in your immediate vicinity.
- Experiment with different bidding strategies such as manual bidding, automated bidding, or enhanced CPC to find the most cost-effective approach for maximizing ROI and achieving your advertising objectives with PPC.
- Continuously monitor and analyze performance metrics such as click-through rate (CTR), conversion rate, cost per click (CPC), and return on ad spend (ROAS) to assess the effectiveness of your PPC campaigns and make data-driven optimizations to improve results over time.

DIGITAL MARKETING IDEAS

Managing Online Reviews and Feedback

- Monitor online review platforms and social media channels regularly to stay informed about what customers are saying about your bakery online, including platforms such as Google My Business, Yelp, Facebook, and Instagram.
- Respond promptly to both positive and negative reviews to show customers that you value their feedback and are committed to providing excellent service, aiming to respond within 24-48 hours whenever possible.
- Personalize your responses to online reviews by addressing reviewers by name and addressing their specific comments or concerns, demonstrating empathy and a genuine desire to address their feedback.
- Thank customers for leaving positive reviews and express appreciation for their support and patronage, reinforcing positive sentiment and encouraging repeat business and referrals.
- Apologize sincerely to customers who leave negative reviews and acknowledge any issues or shortcomings they experienced, demonstrating accountability and a willingness to make things right.
- Offer to resolve any issues or concerns raised in negative reviews offline, such as through direct messaging or contacting the reviewer privately, to address their concerns in a more private and personalized manner.
- Provide explanations or context when responding to negative reviews, such as detailing any extenuating circumstances or explaining the steps you've taken to prevent similar issues from occurring in the future.
- Encourage satisfied customers to leave reviews and feedback online by including calls-to-action in your marketing materials, email communications, and receipts, making it easy for them to share their experiences.
- Monitor and respond to customer inquiries and messages received through social media channels, chat platforms, or email promptly and professionally, providing helpful assistance and addressing any concerns they may have.
- Implement reputation management tools or software to streamline the process of monitoring, managing, and responding to online reviews and feedback across multiple platforms from a centralized dashboard.
- Encourage constructive feedback and suggestions from customers by actively soliciting their input through surveys, polls, or feedback forms, demonstrating a commitment to continuous improvement and customer satisfaction.
- Analyze trends and patterns in online reviews and feedback to identify common themes, areas for improvement, and opportunities to enhance the customer experience at your bakery.
- Share positive reviews and customer testimonials on your bakery's website, social media channels, and marketing materials to showcase social proof and build trust with potential customers.

- Train staff members to handle customer interactions and feedback professionally and empathetically, providing them with guidelines and resources for responding to online reviews and managing customer relationships effectively.
- Monitor and address fake or malicious reviews by reporting them to the relevant platforms and providing evidence to support your claims, taking steps to protect your bakery's reputation and credibility.
- Implement a system for tracking and documenting customer feedback and complaints internally, allowing you to identify recurring issues, track resolutions, and measure improvements over time.
- Encourage customers to leave detailed and specific feedback when they leave reviews, asking them to provide details about their experience, the products they purchased, and any specific aspects they liked or disliked.
- Offer incentives or rewards for customers who leave reviews or provide feedback, such as discounts, freebies, or entries into prize drawings, to incentivize participation and engagement.
- Share updates and improvements made in response to customer feedback publicly, demonstrating your commitment to listening to customers and taking action to address their concerns and suggestions.
- Monitor online review platforms for mentions of your bakery's brand, products, or services beyond formal reviews, such as in social media posts, blog articles, or forums, and respond as appropriate to engage with customers and manage your reputation.
- Use feedback received from online reviews to inform business decisions and strategic initiatives, such as menu changes, operational improvements, or marketing campaigns, aligning your efforts with customer preferences and priorities.
- Monitor your bakery's overall online reputation score or rating across multiple review platforms to track changes over time, benchmark performance against competitors, and identify areas for improvement.
- Leverage positive reviews and customer testimonials in your marketing materials and advertising campaigns to build credibility and trust with potential customers and differentiate your bakery from competitors.
- Continuously evaluate and refine your approach to managing online reviews and feedback based on evolving customer expectations, industry trends, and changes in online review platforms and algorithms, ensuring that your efforts remain effective and impactful over time.

Influencer Marketing Strategies for Bakeries

- Identify relevant influencers in the food, baking, and lifestyle niches whose audience demographics and interests align with your bakery's target market and brand values.
- Research potential influencers' reach, engagement rates, and content quality to ensure they have a genuine and engaged following that is likely to resonate with your bakery's offerings.
- Reach out to selected influencers with personalized pitches introducing your bakery, explaining why you believe they would be a good fit for collaboration, and outlining potential partnership opportunities.
- Offer influencers complimentary products, samples, or experiences from your bakery to try and share with their audience, allowing them to experience your offerings firsthand and create authentic content.
- Collaborate with influencers to create sponsored content such as product reviews, recipe features, or behind-the-scenes tours of your bakery, providing them with creative freedom to showcase your products in a way that feels natural and authentic to their audience.
- Host influencer events or tastings at your bakery, inviting local influencers to sample your products, meet your team, and create content to share with their followers, generating buzz and excitement around your brand.
- Leverage influencer-generated content across your bakery's social media channels, website, and marketing materials to amplify reach and engagement, and provide social proof of your bakery's quality and popularity.
- Partner with micro-influencers who have smaller but highly engaged followings within your local community or niche audience segments, offering them incentives to promote your bakery to their loyal followers.
- Collaborate with macro-influencers or celebrity chefs to create high-impact campaigns that reach a broader audience and lend credibility and prestige to your bakery's brand and products.
- Negotiate mutually beneficial terms and compensation arrangements with influencers, taking into account factors such as reach, engagement, exclusivity, and deliverables to ensure a fair and successful partnership.
- Encourage influencers to disclose sponsored content and partnerships transparently to their audience, adhering to relevant regulations and guidelines to maintain trust and credibility with their followers.
- Track and measure the performance of influencer marketing campaigns using key metrics such as reach, engagement, website traffic, and conversions to evaluate ROI and inform future strategies.
- Foster long-term relationships with influencers who align closely with your bakery's brand values and objectives, cultivating ongoing partnerships and collaborations that deliver sustained results and mutual benefits.

- Explore opportunities for co-branded or co-created products with influencers, leveraging their creativity, expertise, and audience insights to develop unique offerings that resonate with their followers and drive sales for your bakery.
- Amplify influencer content through paid promotion or sponsored posts on social media platforms, extending its reach to a broader audience and maximizing the impact of your influencer marketing efforts.
- Host influencer takeovers on your bakery's social media channels, allowing influencers to temporarily control your account and share their perspective, content, and experiences with your audience.
- Collaborate with influencers to host giveaways, contests, or challenges featuring your bakery's products, encouraging user participation, engagement, and brand awareness.
- Provide influencers with exclusive discounts, perks, or VIP experiences as a token of appreciation for their collaboration and support, fostering goodwill and strengthening relationships over time.
- Leverage influencer insights and feedback to inform product development, marketing strategies, and customer experience enhancements, tapping into their expertise and perspective to drive innovation and growth.
- Feature influencers prominently on your bakery's website, social media profiles, and marketing materials, showcasing their endorsements and testimonials to build credibility and trust with potential customers.
- Collaborate with influencers to create sponsored content series or ongoing partnerships that provide consistent exposure and engagement over time, reinforcing your bakery's presence and messaging with their audience.
- Monitor influencer mentions, tags, and conversations related to your bakery on social media platforms, engaging with influencers and their followers in real-time to build relationships and amplify positive sentiment.
- Provide influencers with exclusive access to new products, menu items, or events before they are available to the public, allowing them to create anticipation and excitement among their followers.
- Continuously evaluate and adjust your influencer marketing strategies based on performance data, feedback from influencers, and changes in industry trends and consumer behavior, ensuring that your efforts remain effective and aligned with your bakery's goals and objectives.

Creating Eye-Catching Online Advertisements

- Use high-quality, visually appealing images or videos of your bakery's products as the focal point of your online advertisements, showcasing their freshness, deliciousness, and mouth-watering appeal.
- Incorporate vibrant colors, appetizing textures, and enticing compositions in your ad creative to capture viewers' attention and evoke cravings and desire for your bakery's offerings.
- Highlight special promotions, discounts, or limited-time offers in your online advertisements to create a sense of urgency and encourage viewers to take immediate action and visit your bakery.
- Utilize eye-catching typography and design elements such as bold fonts, catchy slogans, and compelling calls-to-action to make your ad copy stand out and effectively communicate your message.
- Tailor your online advertisements to resonate with your target audience's preferences, interests, and lifestyles, using imagery, language, and messaging that speaks directly to their needs and desires.
- Experiment with different ad formats and placements across various digital channels such as search engines, social media platforms, display networks, and mobile apps to maximize reach and exposure.
- Create interactive or multimedia ads that engage viewers and encourage them to interact with your content, such as quizzes, polls, or gamified experiences that entertain and educate while promoting your bakery.
- Implement dynamic remarketing ads that dynamically adjust content and messaging based on users' browsing behavior and preferences, delivering personalized and relevant ad experiences that drive conversions.
- Incorporate user-generated content such as customer reviews, testimonials, or social media posts into your online advertisements to build credibility, trust, and social proof with potential customers.
- Leverage social proof elements such as star ratings, awards, certifications, or endorsements in your ad creative to instill confidence and reassure viewers of your bakery's quality, reliability, and reputation.
- Target your online advertisements geographically to reach customers in your local area or target market, using location-based targeting settings to ensure that your ads are seen by relevant audiences.
- Create seasonal or holiday-themed advertisements that capitalize on relevant cultural moments, traditions, or celebrations, resonating with viewers and aligning your bakery with the spirit of the season.
- Utilize data-driven insights and audience segmentation techniques to tailor your ad targeting and messaging to different audience segments based on factors such as demographics, interests, and purchasing behavior.

- A/B test different ad creatives, headlines, offers, and calls-to-action to identify the most effective combinations and optimize your online advertisements for maximum engagement and conversion.
- Incorporate social media engagement features such as likes, comments, shares, and reactions into your ad creative to encourage viewer interaction and amplify the reach and impact of your ads.
- Leverage contextual targeting to place your online advertisements alongside relevant content or topics that are related to baking, food, cooking, or lifestyle interests, reaching audiences when they are most receptive to your message.
- Use retargeting or remarketing ads to re-engage users who have previously visited your bakery's website or interacted with your brand online, reminding them of your products and encouraging them to return and make a purchase.
- Optimize your ad creative and messaging for mobile devices, ensuring that your advertisements are visually appealing, easy to read, and quick to load on smartphones and tablets, which are increasingly the primary devices used for online browsing and shopping.
- Leverage video advertising to tell compelling stories, showcase your bakery's products in action, and create immersive experiences that captivate viewers and drive engagement and conversion.
- Collaborate with influencers or brand ambassadors to co-create online advertisements that leverage their credibility, authenticity, and reach to expand your bakery's audience and attract new customers.
- Use geo-fencing or location-based targeting to deliver hyper-targeted ads to users when they are in close proximity to your bakery's physical locations, prompting them to visit and make a purchase.
- Incorporate social proof elements such as customer testimonials, reviews, or user-generated content into your ad creative to build trust and credibility with potential customers and increase the effectiveness of your advertisements.
- Utilize ad sequencing or storytelling techniques to deliver a series of ads that progressively engage and persuade viewers over time, guiding them through the customer journey from awareness to conversion.
- Continuously monitor and optimize your online advertisements based on performance data and insights, adjusting targeting, creative, and messaging as needed to maximize ROI and achieve your advertising goals.

Hosting Virtual Bakery Events

- Organize virtual baking classes or workshops where participants can learn how to make your bakery's signature recipes from the comfort of their own kitchens, led by experienced bakers or pastry chefs from your team.
- Host live baking demonstrations or tutorials on social media platforms such as Instagram, Facebook, or YouTube, showcasing your bakery's products and techniques while engaging with viewers in real-time.
- Collaborate with influencers, food bloggers, or chefs to co-host virtual baking events or cook-along sessions, leveraging their expertise, creativity, and audience reach to attract participants and generate excitement around your bakery.
- Create themed virtual baking challenges or competitions where participants can submit photos or videos of their creations for a chance to win prizes, encouraging participation and community engagement.
- Offer virtual tasting experiences where participants can sample your bakery's products from home, either through curated tasting kits delivered to their doorsteps or digital tasting sessions conducted via video conferencing platforms.
- Partner with local businesses or organizations to co-host virtual events such as wine and dessert pairing nights, holiday baking workshops, or charity fundraisers, expanding your reach and connecting with new audiences.
- Host virtual tours of your bakery's facilities, giving participants an insider's look at your kitchen, production processes, and behind-the-scenes operations, while sharing insights and stories about your brand and products.
- Organize online Q&A sessions or AMA (Ask Me Anything) events with your bakery's founders, chefs, or staff members, allowing participants to ask questions, share feedback, and learn more about your bakery's history, values, and offerings.
- Create interactive polls, quizzes, or trivia games related to baking, desserts, or your bakery's products, engaging participants and encouraging them to interact with your brand while having fun and learning new things.
- Host virtual birthday parties, bridal showers, or other special occasions where participants can celebrate and enjoy your bakery's treats together with friends and family, either through virtual gatherings or by ordering party packages for delivery.
- Offer exclusive discounts, promotions, or special offers to participants of your virtual events as a way to incentivize attendance, reward engagement, and drive sales for your bakery's products.
- Provide downloadable recipes, baking tips, or instructional guides to participants of your virtual events as valuable takeaways that they can use to recreate your bakery's treats at home and share with others.
- Invite guest speakers or industry experts to present educational sessions or panel discussions on topics relevant to baking, food trends, or entrepreneurship, adding value and diversity to your virtual event lineup.

- Incorporate interactive elements such as polls, surveys, or live chats into your virtual events to encourage participation, gather feedback, and facilitate conversations among participants and presenters.
- Partner with local schools, community centers, or libraries to offer virtual baking classes or educational programs for children, teens, or adults, providing opportunities for learning and skill development in a fun and engaging format.
- Collaborate with other businesses or brands to co-host cross-promotional virtual events, such as bake-offs, recipe exchanges, or themed challenges, leveraging each other's audiences and resources to enhance the event experience.
- Create branded event hashtags and encourage participants to share photos, videos, and experiences from your virtual events on social media, increasing visibility, engagement, and user-generated content for your bakery.
- Provide interactive ingredient kits or baking bundles for participants to purchase in advance of your virtual events, containing all the necessary ingredients and supplies to follow along with the recipes or activities.
- Host virtual focus groups or tasting panels to gather feedback and insights from participants on new product ideas, flavors, or menu concepts, leveraging their input to inform future decisions and innovations for your bakery.
- Offer customizable virtual event packages for corporate team-building activities, client appreciation events, or employee wellness initiatives, providing a unique and memorable experience that promotes teamwork and camaraderie.
- Collaborate with local influencers, bloggers, or media outlets to promote your virtual events and reach new audiences through guest blog posts, social media shoutouts, or sponsored content partnerships.
- Provide options for participants to purchase gift certificates, merchandise, or branded merchandise during your virtual events, offering additional revenue streams and opportunities for participants to support your bakery.
- Host follow-up engagement activities or post-event discussions to continue the conversation and maintain momentum after your virtual events, fostering ongoing relationships and community engagement with participants.
- Monitor and analyze key metrics such as attendance, engagement, feedback, and sales generated from your virtual events, using data-driven insights to evaluate their success and inform future event planning and strategy.

DIGITAL MARKETING IDEAS

Using Analytics to Track Marketing Performance

- Implement website analytics tools such as Google Analytics to track key metrics such as website traffic, user behavior, and conversion rates, gaining insights into how visitors interact with your bakery's website.
- Set up goal tracking in your analytics platform to monitor specific actions or outcomes on your website, such as form submissions, online orders, or newsletter sign-ups, to measure the effectiveness of your marketing efforts.
- Utilize UTM parameters in your marketing URLs to track the source, medium, and campaign associated with website visits, enabling you to attribute traffic and conversions to specific marketing channels and campaigns.
- Analyze audience demographics and interests data in your analytics reports to understand the characteristics and preferences of your website visitors, informing your targeting and messaging strategies for future marketing campaigns.
- Monitor website engagement metrics such as bounce rate, average session duration, and pages per session to assess the quality and relevance of your website content and user experience.
- Track conversion funnels in your analytics platform to identify drop-off points and optimize the user journey, streamlining the path to conversion and maximizing the effectiveness of your website's conversion process.
- Use event tracking to monitor user interactions such as clicks, downloads, or video views on your website, providing deeper insights into user engagement and behavior beyond standard pageviews and sessions.
- Set up e-commerce tracking if your bakery's website includes an online store, allowing you to monitor sales performance, revenue, and product performance metrics to evaluate the effectiveness of your e-commerce efforts.
- Monitor website performance and page load times using website speed reports in your analytics platform, ensuring that your website delivers a fast and seamless experience for users across devices and platforms.
- Analyze referral traffic reports to identify external websites, social media platforms, or online directories that drive traffic to your bakery's website, enabling you to assess the impact of external partnerships and promotions.
- Track email marketing performance metrics such as open rates, click-through rates, and conversion rates using email analytics tools or integrations with your email marketing platform, optimizing your email campaigns for engagement and conversion.
- Monitor social media analytics to track key metrics such as reach, engagement, and follower growth across your bakery's social media profiles, identifying top-performing content and audience preferences.
- Use social media listening tools to monitor mentions, comments, and conversations about your bakery on social media platforms, gaining insights into customer sentiment, feedback, and brand perception.

- Analyze paid advertising performance metrics such as impressions, clicks, and conversion rates in advertising platforms such as Google Ads, Facebook Ads, or Instagram Ads, optimizing your ad campaigns for maximum ROI.
- Set up call tracking to monitor phone call conversions generated from your marketing campaigns, attributing phone calls to specific marketing channels and campaigns to measure their impact on lead generation and sales.
- Utilize customer relationship management (CRM) software to track and analyze customer interactions and conversions across multiple channels and touchpoints, gaining a holistic view of the customer journey and lifetime value.
- Implement A/B testing or multivariate testing to experiment with different marketing strategies, messaging, or creative elements and measure their impact on key performance metrics such as conversion rates and ROI.
- Use cohort analysis to track the behavior and performance of specific groups of users over time, such as new customers, returning customers, or customers segmented by acquisition channel, enabling you to identify trends and patterns in customer behavior.
- Monitor customer retention and churn rates to assess the effectiveness of your marketing efforts in retaining existing customers and reducing customer attrition, implementing strategies to improve customer loyalty and lifetime value.
- Analyze geographic data to identify regions or locations with high concentrations of website traffic, customers, or potential market opportunities, informing your targeting and expansion strategies for future marketing initiatives.
- Set up custom dashboards or automated reports in your analytics platform to regularly monitor key metrics and performance indicators, providing actionable insights and facilitating data-driven decision-making for your marketing team.
- Conduct regular performance reviews and analysis of your marketing campaigns, channels, and tactics to identify areas for optimization and improvement, iterating on your strategies based on data-driven insights and lessons learned.
- Collaborate with cross-functional teams such as sales, product development, and customer service to share insights and align marketing efforts with broader business objectives and priorities.
- Continuously iterate and refine your analytics strategy and measurement framework based on evolving business goals, market dynamics, and technological advancements, ensuring that your marketing performance tracking remains relevant and effective over time.

DIGITAL MARKETING IDEAS

Mobile Marketing for On-the-Go Customers

- Develop a mobile-responsive website for your bakery that is optimized for viewing and navigation on smartphones and tablets, ensuring a seamless and user-friendly experience for mobile visitors.
- Implement click-to-call functionality on your bakery's website, allowing mobile users to easily contact your bakery with a single tap to place orders, make reservations, or inquire about products and services.
- Create a mobile app for your bakery that provides customers with convenient access to your menu, online ordering, loyalty program, location information, and special offers directly from their mobile devices.
- Utilize SMS marketing to send targeted messages, promotions, and reminders to customers' mobile phones, driving engagement, loyalty, and repeat business for your bakery.
- Implement mobile-friendly email campaigns that are optimized for viewing and interaction on smartphones, using responsive design techniques and concise messaging to capture and hold recipients' attention.
- Leverage location-based marketing techniques such as geofencing or beacon technology to target mobile users with relevant promotions, offers, or reminders when they are in close proximity to your bakery's physical locations.
- Use mobile advertising platforms such as Google Ads or Facebook Ads to target mobile users with tailored ads and promotions based on their demographics, interests, and browsing behavior on mobile devices.
- Optimize your bakery's listings on mobile search and mapping platforms such as Google Maps, Apple Maps, and Yelp, ensuring accurate and up-to-date information about your locations, hours, contact details, and customer reviews.
- Incorporate mobile-friendly QR codes into your marketing materials, packaging, or signage to provide customers with easy access to additional information, promotions, or online ordering options from their smartphones.
- Offer mobile-exclusive promotions, discounts, or rewards to incentivize customers to engage with your bakery through their mobile devices, driving traffic, sales, and app downloads.
- Enable mobile payments and digital wallets such as Apple Pay, Google Pay, or PayPal on your bakery's website, app, or point-of-sale system, providing customers with convenient and secure payment options while reducing friction in the checkout process.
- Implement mobile-friendly loyalty programs that reward customers for repeat purchases, referrals, or engagement with your bakery's brand through their mobile devices, fostering customer loyalty and retention.
- Create mobile-friendly content such as recipe videos, cooking tips, or behind-the-scenes glimpses of your bakery's operations to engage and entertain mobile users on social media platforms like Instagram, TikTok, or Snapchat.

- Partner with food delivery apps and aggregators such as Uber Eats, DoorDash, or Grubhub to offer delivery and takeout services for your bakery's products, reaching mobile users who prefer the convenience of ordering food on their smartphones.
- Use push notifications to send timely and relevant messages, reminders, or promotions to users who have opted in to receive updates from your bakery's mobile app or website, keeping your brand top-of-mind and driving engagement.
- Create mobile-friendly landing pages or microsites for specific marketing campaigns, promotions, or events, providing mobile users with targeted and optimized experiences that encourage conversion and action.
- Optimize your bakery's social media profiles and content for mobile viewing and interaction, using visually compelling images, videos, and stories to engage and entertain mobile users while promoting your bakery's offerings.
- Offer mobile-friendly ordering options such as curbside pickup, drive-thru, or contactless delivery for customers who prefer to order and pay for their bakery purchases directly from their smartphones.
- Utilize augmented reality (AR) or virtual reality (VR) experiences to create immersive and interactive mobile marketing campaigns that showcase your bakery's products, facilities, or brand story in innovative and engaging ways.
- Host mobile-friendly events or promotions such as flash sales, pop-up shops, or tasting events that cater to on-the-go customers and encourage spontaneous visits and purchases from mobile users.
- Monitor and analyze mobile traffic, engagement, and conversion metrics using analytics tools such as Google Analytics or mobile app analytics platforms, gaining insights into mobile user behavior and preferences to inform your marketing strategy.
- Conduct usability testing and optimization on your bakery's mobile website and app to identify and address any usability issues, friction points, or performance bottlenecks that may detract from the user experience on mobile devices.
- Stay informed about emerging trends and technologies in mobile marketing, such as voice search, chatbots, or progressive web apps, and explore opportunities to integrate these innovations into your bakery's digital marketing strategy.
- Continuously iterate and refine your mobile marketing efforts based on feedback, performance data, and evolving customer preferences, ensuring that your bakery remains accessible, engaging, and relevant to on-the-go customers in an increasingly mobile-centric world.

Collaborating with Other Local Businesses Online

- Partner with local coffee shops or cafes to cross-promote each other's products and services through joint marketing initiatives such as social media shoutouts, co-branded promotions, or collaborative events.
- Collaborate with nearby restaurants or eateries to create themed dining experiences or food tours that highlight the culinary diversity and offerings of your local community, attracting visitors and generating buzz for both businesses.
- Join forces with neighboring retailers or boutique shops to organize shopping events, pop-up markets, or sidewalk sales that encourage foot traffic and support local businesses while providing exposure for your bakery's products.
- Host joint contests or giveaways with complementary businesses in your area, such as florists, gift shops, or event venues, offering prizes or gift baskets featuring products from each participating business to incentivize participation and engagement.
- Partner with local breweries or wineries to create pairing events or tasting experiences that showcase the harmonious flavors and combinations of your bakery's treats with craft beers, wines, or spirits produced by nearby producers.
- Collaborate with fitness studios, gyms, or wellness centers to offer healthy eating workshops, nutrition seminars, or post-workout snack options featuring your bakery's nutritious and wholesome products, promoting a balanced lifestyle.
- Team up with local farmers' markets or artisanal food vendors to participate in joint events or festivals celebrating local food and culture, showcasing your bakery's handmade, artisanal products alongside other local producers.
- Establish partnerships with nearby hotels, bed and breakfasts, or tourist attractions to offer special packages or promotions that include vouchers or discounts for your bakery's products as part of the guest experience, enhancing their stay and promoting local tourism.
- Collaborate with local event planners, wedding venues, or caterers to provide custom dessert options, wedding cakes, or catering services for special events and celebrations, leveraging each other's expertise and networks to serve clients effectively.
- Partner with local schools, community centers, or libraries to host educational workshops, baking classes, or hands-on activities for children, families, or community groups, fostering community engagement and promoting lifelong learning.
- Organize charity or fundraising events in collaboration with local nonprofit organizations, shelters, or community groups, donating a portion of proceeds from sales or event ticket sales to support important causes and give back to the community.
- Collaborate with local influencers, bloggers, or content creators to co-create sponsored content, reviews, or social media campaigns that showcase your bakery's products and reach new audiences through their platforms and networks.
- Participate in local food festivals, fairs, or tasting events as a vendor or exhibitor, showcasing your bakery's specialties and engaging directly with attendees to build brand awareness and loyalty within the community.

- Form alliances with local food delivery services, meal subscription boxes, or online marketplaces to expand your bakery's reach and accessibility to customers who prefer ordering food online or having it delivered to their doorstep.
- Collaborate with local culinary schools, colleges, or vocational training programs to offer internships, apprenticeships, or hands-on learning opportunities for aspiring bakers and pastry chefs, nurturing talent and fostering industry partnerships.
- Host joint workshops or networking events with other local businesses, industry associations, or chambers of commerce to share insights, best practices, and resources for business growth and development within the community.
- Create collaborative content such as city guides, neighborhood maps, or online directories featuring recommendations and listings for local businesses, attractions, and points of interest, promoting community pride and supporting economic growth.
- Partner with local media outlets, newspapers, or bloggers to secure press coverage, interviews, or features about your bakery and its contributions to the local community, raising awareness and generating positive publicity.
- Collaborate with local artists, designers, or artisans to create custom packaging, branded merchandise, or promotional materials for your bakery's products, adding a unique and personal touch that resonates with customers.
- Form alliances with nearby healthcare providers, wellness practitioners, or nutritionists to develop healthy eating initiatives, wellness programs, or educational resources that promote balanced nutrition and lifestyle choices within the community.
- Participate in local business networking groups, industry associations, or chambers of commerce to connect with other business owners, share referrals, and explore collaborative opportunities for mutual benefit and growth.
- Sponsor or support community events, youth sports teams, or cultural festivals as a way to give back to the community and raise visibility for your bakery's brand, aligning with local values and interests.
- Collaborate with local transportation services, tour operators, or travel agencies to offer culinary tours, foodie experiences, or destination packages that showcase your bakery's products and highlight the culinary delights of your area.
- Establish ongoing partnerships and alliances with other local businesses that share your values, target audience, or business objectives, building a supportive network of allies and collaborators that strengthen the local economy and enrich the community as a whole.

Utilizing Geo-Targeting for Local Promotions

- Begin by creating customized social media ads that target users based on their location, ensuring that your bakery's promotions are seen by those within a specific radius of your store.
- Develop interactive online maps on your website, allowing potential customers to easily locate your bakery and view special promotions or discounts available only to those in the vicinity.
- Utilize geofencing techniques to send push notifications or mobile ads to smartphones within a defined geographic area, enticing nearby individuals with exclusive offers or limited-time deals.
- Collaborate with popular location-based apps such as Yelp or Google Maps to highlight your bakery as a top local destination, showcasing promotions to users searching for nearby dining options.
- Implement location-specific landing pages on your website, optimizing them with relevant keywords to attract local search traffic and drive conversions through targeted promotions.
- Host geographically-targeted events or pop-up shops in areas with high foot traffic, using social media and online advertisements to generate buzz and attract local customers.
- Partner with local influencers or bloggers to promote your bakery's offerings to their followers within your target area, leveraging their credibility and reach to increase brand awareness.
- Utilize location-based targeting in email marketing campaigns, segmenting your subscriber list by geographic location and sending personalized promotions or event invitations tailored to each area.
- Offer special incentives or discounts to customers who check in on social media platforms like Facebook or Instagram when visiting your bakery, encouraging them to share their experience with friends and followers.
- Create hyper-localized content on social media, such as behind-the-scenes videos or staff spotlights, to foster a sense of community and connect with customers in your bakery's immediate vicinity.
- Utilize location-based retargeting ads to re-engage users who have previously visited your bakery's website or social media profiles, reminding them of promotions or special offers available in their area.
- Collaborate with neighboring businesses to cross-promote each other's products or services to local customers, expanding your reach within the community.
- Implement QR code campaigns in physical signage or printed materials, directing users to exclusive promotions or online ordering options tailored to their location.
- Leverage local SEO strategies to ensure that your bakery appears prominently in search engine results for relevant queries within your geographic area, driving organic traffic and visibility for your promotions.

- Create targeted Facebook or Instagram groups for customers in specific neighborhoods or communities, providing them with exclusive access to promotions, events, and behind-the-scenes content.
- Utilize location-based analytics tools to track foot traffic and customer behavior in real-time, allowing you to optimize your marketing efforts and promotions based on local trends and preferences.
- Offer delivery or pickup options through third-party platforms like Uber Eats or DoorDash, leveraging their geotargeting capabilities to reach customers within your bakery's delivery radius.
- Sponsor local events or community initiatives to increase brand visibility and goodwill, ensuring that your bakery remains top-of-mind when nearby residents are seeking baked goods or dining options.
- Implement geotargeted advertising campaigns on streaming platforms like Spotify or Pandora, reaching users within your bakery's vicinity with audio ads promoting special promotions or seasonal offerings.
- Host interactive online contests or giveaways targeted specifically to residents in your bakery's surrounding neighborhoods, encouraging engagement and word-of-mouth referrals.
- Collaborate with local tourism boards or visitor centers to promote your bakery as a must-visit destination for tourists and travelers passing through the area, offering special discounts or incentives to encourage visits.
- Utilize geolocation features on social media platforms like Snapchat or Instagram to create custom filters or augmented reality experiences that promote your bakery's promotions to users within your target area.
- Implement geographically-targeted digital signage or outdoor advertising near your bakery's location, capturing the attention of passersby with compelling visuals and enticing offers.
- Monitor and respond to online reviews and feedback from customers within your bakery's geographic area, demonstrating your commitment to customer satisfaction and fostering positive relationships within the local community.

DIGITAL MARKETING IDEAS

Creating Interactive Content for Engagement

- Develop a series of interactive recipe videos featuring your bakery's signature treats, allowing viewers to follow along step-by-step and engage with the content by voting on ingredient variations or sharing their own baking tips.
- Launch a digital scavenger hunt on social media platforms, where followers must visit your bakery's website or social profiles to find clues or hidden messages, encouraging active participation and driving traffic to your online platforms.
- Create a quiz or trivia game related to baking or your bakery's history, inviting followers to test their knowledge and compete for prizes or discounts on your products.
- Host live Q&A sessions or virtual baking classes on platforms like Facebook Live or Instagram Live, where viewers can interact in real-time, ask questions, and receive personalized tips from your bakery's experts.
- Develop an interactive online tool or calculator that helps customers determine the perfect cake size or flavor combination for their upcoming celebrations, providing personalized recommendations based on their preferences and guest count.
- Launch a user-generated content campaign encouraging customers to share photos of their favorite bakery treats on social media using a branded hashtag, with the chance to be featured on your bakery's profiles or win prizes for the best submissions.
- Create a digital storytelling series highlighting the journey of your bakery's ingredients from farm to table, incorporating interactive elements such as polls or quizzes to educate and engage your audience.
- Host a virtual taste-testing event where participants can sample new menu items or seasonal flavors from the comfort of their own homes, sharing their feedback and reviews in real-time on social media.
- Develop a mobile app for your bakery that offers interactive features such as virtual loyalty cards, augmented reality experiences, or gamified challenges to incentivize repeat visits and engagement.
- Collaborate with local artists or illustrators to create interactive coloring pages featuring your bakery's logo or iconic desserts, encouraging customers of all ages to unleash their creativity and share their artwork online.
- Launch a digital photo booth experience on your website or social media profiles, allowing users to upload photos of themselves enjoying your bakery's treats and customize them with fun filters or stickers before sharing with friends.
- Create a choose-your-own-adventure-style story on social media or your website, where followers can vote on different paths or outcomes to unlock exclusive discounts or promotions at your bakery.
- Host a themed online baking competition or challenge, where participants must recreate a specific recipe or design using your bakery's products and share their creations on social media for a chance to win prizes.

- Develop an interactive map showcasing the locations of your bakery's storefronts or pop-up events, allowing customers to easily find the nearest location and explore nearby attractions or points of interest.
- Launch a digital loyalty program that rewards customers for engaging with your bakery's content on social media, such as liking posts, sharing reviews, or referring friends, with points redeemable for discounts or freebies.
- Partner with local influencers or food bloggers to create interactive taste tests or blindfolded challenges featuring your bakery's products, capturing the reactions and excitement on video to share with your audience.
- Create a digital cookbook featuring exclusive recipes from your bakery's chefs or staff, with interactive elements such as embedded videos, cooking tips, and user-generated reviews to enhance the reading experience.
- Host a virtual baking competition or bake-off between different teams or influencers, livestreaming the event on social media and allowing viewers to vote for their favorite creations in real-time.
- Develop a branded mobile game or app featuring your bakery's characters or mascots, with interactive levels or challenges centered around baking-themed puzzles or activities to entertain and engage users.
- Launch a series of interactive polls or surveys on social media to gather feedback from customers about their favorite flavors, menu suggestions, or preferences for future promotions, demonstrating your commitment to listening to their input.
- Create a digital scavenger hunt or geocaching adventure that leads participants to hidden treasures or special discounts at your bakery's locations, encouraging exploration and engagement within the local community.
- Host a virtual baking masterclass or workshop series on platforms like Zoom or YouTube, inviting guest chefs or industry experts to share their tips and techniques with your audience in an interactive format.
- Develop an interactive taste test experience on your website, where visitors can answer a series of questions about their flavor preferences and dietary restrictions to receive personalized recommendations for products or menu items to try.
- Launch a digital memory lane campaign celebrating milestones or anniversaries for your bakery, inviting customers to share their favorite memories or photos from past visits and rewarding them with exclusive discounts or nostalgic treats.

DIGITAL MARKETING IDEAS

Planning Seasonal Marketing Campaigns

- Begin by analyzing past sales data and customer feedback to identify which seasonal trends or holidays have the greatest impact on your bakery's revenue and customer engagement, allowing you to prioritize your marketing efforts accordingly.
- Develop a content calendar outlining key dates and themes for upcoming seasonal campaigns, ensuring that your marketing materials are planned and executed in advance to capitalize on peak consumer interest.
- Create seasonal-themed email marketing campaigns featuring exclusive promotions, new product launches, or limited-time offers tailored to each holiday or occasion, targeting different segments of your subscriber list based on their preferences and purchase history.
- Utilize social media platforms to showcase your bakery's seasonal specials and decorations, encouraging followers to share photos of their holiday celebrations featuring your products using a branded hashtag to increase visibility and engagement.
- Collaborate with local influencers or food bloggers to create sponsored content promoting your bakery's seasonal offerings, reaching new audiences and generating buzz around your products through authentic endorsements.
- Launch targeted online advertising campaigns using keywords and ad copy related to seasonal trends or holidays, optimizing your messaging and visuals to resonate with consumers searching for festive treats or gift ideas.
- Host seasonal-themed events or tastings at your bakery's storefront, such as cookie decorating workshops or pumpkin spice latte tastings, to attract foot traffic and drive sales while providing a memorable experience for customers.
- Partner with other local businesses or community organizations to cross-promote each other's seasonal offerings or events, expanding your reach within the community and fostering goodwill through collaborative marketing efforts.
- Create seasonal gift guides or curated product bundles on your website, making it easy for customers to find the perfect treats for upcoming holidays or special occasions and encouraging upsells through bundled promotions.
- Develop interactive social media contests or giveaways centered around seasonal themes or traditions, encouraging followers to participate by sharing their favorite holiday recipes, memories, or photos for a chance to win prizes or discounts.
- Implement geotargeted advertising campaigns to reach consumers in your bakery's local area with targeted promotions or reminders about upcoming seasonal events or specials, maximizing your marketing ROI by focusing on your most relevant audience.
- Leverage user-generated content by showcasing photos or testimonials from satisfied customers enjoying your bakery's seasonal treats on your website or social media profiles, providing social proof and inspiring others to indulge in holiday indulgence.
- Collaborate with local media outlets or bloggers to feature your bakery's seasonal offerings in holiday gift guides, recipe roundups, or editorial content, increasing brand visibility and credibility through earned media coverage.

- Offer seasonal catering or bulk ordering options for holiday parties and gatherings, promoting these services through targeted email campaigns or digital ads to attract customers planning events during peak celebration periods.
- Create seasonal-themed landing pages on your website featuring curated collections of products or recipes for each holiday or occasion, optimizing them for search engines to attract organic traffic from consumers searching for festive inspiration or gift ideas.
- Develop seasonal packaging or branding elements for your bakery's products, such as holiday-themed labels, boxes, or ribbons, to enhance their visual appeal and create a sense of anticipation and excitement among customers.
- Host virtual cooking or baking classes featuring seasonal recipes and techniques, allowing participants to learn from your bakery's chefs or experts from the comfort of their own homes while promoting your products and services.
- Collaborate with local charities or nonprofit organizations to launch seasonal fundraising campaigns or donation drives, aligning your bakery's marketing efforts with a worthy cause to drive engagement and goodwill within the community.
- Create seasonal-themed social media filters or stickers featuring your bakery's logo or products, allowing followers to add a festive touch to their photos and videos while promoting your brand organically to their networks.
- Launch a loyalty program with seasonal rewards or incentives for repeat customers, such as bonus points or exclusive discounts during peak holiday shopping periods, to encourage repeat visits and drive customer loyalty throughout the year.
- Host virtual tastings or pairing events showcasing seasonal flavors and ingredients, partnering with local suppliers or producers to highlight the freshness and quality of your bakery's seasonal offerings while educating participants about the culinary heritage behind each product.
- Collaborate with local hotels, event venues, or tourist attractions to offer special packages or promotions for visitors during peak travel seasons, positioning your bakery as a must-visit destination for tourists seeking authentic local experiences.
- Create seasonal blog content or video tutorials featuring holiday baking tips, recipe ideas, or entertaining inspiration, positioning your bakery as a trusted resource for consumers seeking guidance and inspiration during the festive season.
- Monitor and analyze the performance of your seasonal marketing campaigns in real-time, tracking key metrics such as website traffic, sales conversions, and social media engagement to identify areas for optimization and inform future marketing strategies.

DIGITAL MARKETING IDEAS

Enhancing Customer Service with Chatbots

- Implement a chatbot on your bakery's website to provide instant answers to frequently asked questions about your products, services, and operating hours, improving customer satisfaction and reducing the need for manual support.
- Develop a personalized ordering experience through your chatbot, allowing customers to customize their orders, specify dietary preferences, and receive real-time updates on order status or delivery estimates.
- Integrate your chatbot with popular messaging platforms such as Facebook Messenger or WhatsApp to provide seamless customer support across multiple channels, meeting customers where they already spend their time online.
- Utilize AI-powered chatbots to analyze customer inquiries and provide tailored recommendations for products or menu items based on their preferences, purchase history, and dietary restrictions.
- Implement chatbots for proactive customer engagement, sending automated messages or notifications to remind customers of upcoming promotions, events, or order deadlines, increasing brand awareness and driving sales.
- Offer virtual assistance through your chatbot for customers planning special events or catering orders, guiding them through the menu selection process, estimating quantities, and providing pricing quotes based on their requirements.
- Develop a chatbot-driven loyalty program that allows customers to earn rewards or discounts for engaging with your bakery's chatbot, such as placing orders, leaving reviews, or referring friends, incentivizing repeat purchases and customer retention.
- Integrate your chatbot with your bakery's CRM system to provide personalized customer support, allowing your chatbot to access past interactions and order history to provide more contextually relevant assistance.
- Create a chatbot for post-purchase support, allowing customers to track their orders, request refunds or exchanges, and provide feedback on their experience, streamlining the customer service process and reducing friction for resolution.
- Utilize chatbots to gather customer feedback and insights through surveys or polls, asking about their experience with your bakery's products, services, and overall satisfaction, enabling you to identify areas for improvement and measure customer sentiment.
- Implement a chatbot-driven reservation system for customers looking to book tables or place orders for pickup or delivery, streamlining the booking process and reducing wait times for in-store or online transactions.
- Offer proactive assistance through your chatbot during peak hours or busy periods, such as holidays or weekends, providing estimated wait times, recommending alternative products, or offering discounts to encourage patience and loyalty.
- Develop a chatbot for educational purposes, providing customers with tips, tutorials, and recipes for baking at home, positioning your bakery as a trusted resource for baking enthusiasts and building brand credibility.

- Integrate your chatbot with your bakery's social media profiles to provide automated responses to comments, messages, and mentions, ensuring timely engagement and consistent communication with your online community.
- Create a chatbot for pre-ordering or prepayment, allowing customers to reserve their favorite items in advance and streamline the pickup process, reducing wait times and improving overall convenience.
- Offer live chat support through your chatbot during business hours, allowing customers to connect with a human representative for more complex inquiries or assistance, while still providing automated responses for common questions.
- Develop a chatbot for event management, allowing customers to inquire about hosting private events or ordering custom cakes for special occasions, guiding them through the planning process and collecting necessary details for fulfillment.
- Implement chatbots for multilingual support, allowing customers to interact with your bakery's chatbot in their preferred language, catering to a diverse customer base and improving accessibility for non-native speakers.
- Offer exclusive deals or promotions through your chatbot, such as limited-time discounts or freebies for customers who engage with the chatbot or refer friends to your bakery, driving engagement and word-of-mouth marketing.
- Utilize chatbots for order tracking and delivery updates, sending automated notifications to customers with real-time updates on their order status, estimated delivery time, and delivery confirmation upon arrival.
- Develop a chatbot for troubleshooting common issues or technical support, providing step-by-step guidance for resolving common problems with online ordering, payment processing, or website navigation.
- Offer personalized recommendations through your chatbot based on the customer's location, weather, or time of day, suggesting seasonal specials, warm beverages on cold days, or refreshing treats on hot summer afternoons.
- Implement chatbots for scheduling appointments or consultations with your bakery's staff, such as cake tastings, wedding consultations, or custom cake design sessions, streamlining the booking process and ensuring availability.
- Utilize chatbots for upselling and cross-selling opportunities, suggesting complementary products or add-ons to customers based on their current order or browsing history, maximizing sales potential and customer satisfaction.

Sustainable and Ethical Marketing Practices for Bakeries

- Source locally grown and organic ingredients for your bakery's products, showcasing your commitment to sustainability and supporting local farmers and producers in your community.
- Reduce food waste by implementing portion control measures, offering smaller serving sizes or creating products with longer shelf lives, and donating excess food to local charities or food banks.
- Use eco-friendly packaging materials such as biodegradable containers, compostable bags, or recycled paper products, minimizing your bakery's environmental footprint and promoting responsible waste management.
- Partner with suppliers who share your commitment to sustainability and ethical practices, ensuring that your bakery's supply chain aligns with your values and standards for environmental and social responsibility.
- Educate customers about the importance of sustainable eating habits and conscious consumer choices through your bakery's marketing channels, such as social media, email newsletters, or in-store signage.
- Offer plant-based or vegan options on your bakery's menu to cater to customers with dietary preferences or ethical considerations, expanding your customer base and promoting animal welfare.
- Implement energy-efficient practices in your bakery's operations, such as using energy-saving appliances, LED lighting, or renewable energy sources, to reduce your carbon footprint and lower utility costs.
- Participate in local sustainability initiatives or events, such as farmer's markets, green fairs, or community clean-up efforts, to demonstrate your bakery's commitment to environmental stewardship and community engagement.
- Create partnerships with environmental organizations or advocacy groups to raise awareness and support for key issues related to sustainability, such as climate change, deforestation, or waste reduction.
- Offer incentives or discounts for customers who bring their own reusable containers or bags when purchasing bakery items, encouraging sustainable behavior and reducing single-use plastic waste.
- Host workshops or educational events at your bakery to teach customers about sustainable baking techniques, such as using organic ingredients, reducing food waste, or incorporating alternative flours and grains.
- Showcase your bakery's sustainability efforts and achievements on your website or social media profiles, sharing updates about your eco-friendly practices, partnerships, and initiatives with your online audience.
- Implement a waste reduction program in your bakery's operations, such as composting organic waste, recycling packaging materials, or repurposing leftover ingredients into new products or recipes.

- Collaborate with local environmental experts or influencers to co-create content or campaigns promoting sustainable living and conscious consumption, leveraging their expertise and credibility to amplify your message.
- Participate in certification programs or labels that verify your bakery's commitment to sustainability and ethical practices, such as Fair Trade, Organic, or Green Business certifications, to build trust and credibility with customers.
- Host farm-to-table events or tasting experiences at your bakery, featuring locally sourced ingredients and highlighting the farmers and producers behind your bakery's products, fostering transparency and connection with your supply chain.
- Engage with your local community through volunteerism and philanthropy, supporting environmental causes or initiatives that align with your bakery's values and mission.
- Develop partnerships with sustainable brands or businesses in your area to co-promote each other's products or services, fostering a network of like-minded businesses committed to ethical and eco-friendly practices.
- Offer educational resources or guides on your bakery's website for customers interested in learning more about sustainable living, such as tips for reducing waste at home, supporting local agriculture, or shopping ethically.
- Host sustainability-focused events or workshops for your bakery's staff to raise awareness and inspire action towards reducing environmental impact in your daily operations and decision-making processes.
- Encourage employee participation in sustainability initiatives through incentives or recognition programs for ideas or actions that contribute to your bakery's sustainability goals, fostering a culture of environmental stewardship among your team.
- Advocate for policy changes or legislation that support sustainability and ethical practices in the food industry, such as reducing plastic pollution, promoting regenerative agriculture, or incentivizing renewable energy adoption.
- Conduct regular audits or assessments of your bakery's environmental performance and progress towards sustainability goals, tracking key metrics such as energy usage, waste diversion rates, and carbon emissions.
- Continuously seek feedback from customers, employees, and stakeholders on your bakery's sustainability efforts, soliciting suggestions for improvement and demonstrating your commitment to transparency and accountability in your sustainability journey.

500+ Social Media Marketing Ideas for Bakeries

SECTIONS IN THIS CHAPTER:

1. Setting Up Your Bakery's Social Media Profiles – Page 50
2. Defining Your Target Audience on Social Media – Page 52
3. Crafting Your Bakery's Brand Voice – Page 54
4. Content Planning and Calendar Management – Page 56
5. Creating Mouth-Watering Visual Content – Page 58
6. Video Marketing Tips for Bakeries – Page 60
7. Engaging With Your Audience Effectively – Page 62
8. Leveraging Instagram Stories and Reels – Page 64
9. Running Successful Social Media Contests – Page 66
10. Utilizing User-Generated Content – Page 68
11. Influencer Partnerships for Bakeries – Page 70
12. Promoting Your Bakery's Events on Social Media – Page 72
13. Effective Use of Hashtags – Page 74
14. Paid Advertising Strategies on Social Platforms – Page 76
15. Analyzing Social Media Analytics – Page 78
16. Managing Negative Feedback Online – Page 80
17. Collaborations with Food Bloggers – Page 82
18. Behind-the-Scenes Content Creation – Page 84
19. Seasonal and Holiday Campaigns – Page 86
20. Leveraging Pinterest for Bakery Inspiration – Page 88
21. Utilizing Facebook Groups for Community Building – Page 90
22. Social Media Tips for Launching New Products – Page 92

SOCIAL MEDIA MARKETING IDEAS

Setting Up Your Bakery's Social Media Profiles

- Begin by choosing the most relevant social media platforms for your bakery. Consider platforms like Instagram, Facebook, Twitter, and Pinterest, where visual content performs exceptionally well.
- Craft a compelling and consistent bio for each social media profile, reflecting your bakery's unique identity, values, and offerings. Ensure that your profile information is complete and up-to-date.
- Use high-quality, visually appealing images of your bakery products as profile pictures and cover photos across all social media platforms to create a strong visual presence.
- Optimize your usernames/handles to be easily recognizable and searchable, ideally using your bakery's name or a variation of it.
- Incorporate relevant keywords and hashtags related to baking, desserts, and your locality in your profile descriptions to enhance discoverability.
- Include essential contact information such as your bakery's address, phone number, and website URL in your social media profiles to make it easy for customers to reach you.
- Link your social media profiles to each other and to your bakery's website for seamless navigation and increased traffic.
- Utilize Instagram's business profile features to access insights, promote posts, and add contact buttons, making it easier for customers to connect with you.
- Create Facebook business pages for your bakery to engage with customers, share updates, and collect reviews and recommendations.
- Customize your Twitter profile with relevant branding elements and use tweets to share quick updates, promotions, and interact with your audience in real-time.
- Set up a Pinterest business account to showcase your bakery's products, recipes, and inspiration boards, driving traffic to your website.
- Implement a consistent posting schedule across all social media platforms to maintain audience engagement and visibility.
- Experiment with different types of content, including photos, videos, behind-the-scenes glimpses, customer testimonials, and user-generated content, to keep your audience interested and entertained.
- Engage with your followers by responding to comments, messages, and mentions promptly, fostering a sense of community and loyalty.
- Encourage user-generated content by running contests, featuring customer photos, and sharing testimonials, showcasing your bakery's popularity and satisfaction.
- Collaborate with local influencers, food bloggers, and other businesses to expand your reach and attract new followers.
- Use location-based tags and hashtags to target potential customers in your area and drive foot traffic to your bakery.

- Share exclusive promotions, discounts, and special offers on your social media profiles to incentivize followers to visit your bakery.
- Leverage Instagram Stories, Facebook Live, and Twitter Fleets to share real-time updates, behind-the-scenes content, and interactive polls, fostering a sense of immediacy and authenticity.
- Utilize Instagram's IGTV feature to showcase longer-form video content such as tutorials, interviews, and product demonstrations, highlighting your bakery's expertise and creativity.
- Monitor social media analytics regularly to track your performance, identify trends, and adjust your strategy accordingly to maximize your bakery's online presence.
- Collaborate with local photographers, food stylists, and influencers to create professional and enticing visual content for your social media profiles.
- Implement a branded hashtag for your bakery and encourage customers to use it when posting about their experiences or sharing photos of your products.
- Stay updated on social media trends, algorithm changes, and best practices to ensure that your bakery remains relevant and competitive in the digital landscape.

Defining Your Target Audience on Social Media

- Start by conducting market research to identify the demographics, interests, and preferences of your bakery's target audience. Consider factors such as age, gender, location, income level, lifestyle, and buying behavior.
- Analyze your existing customer base to gain insights into who is already engaging with your bakery on social media platforms. Look for patterns and commonalities among your most loyal customers.
- Utilize social media analytics tools to gather data on the demographics, interests, and behavior of your current social media followers. Platforms like Facebook Insights, Instagram Insights, and Twitter Analytics provide valuable audience insights.
- Create buyer personas representing your ideal customers based on the information gathered from your research. Develop detailed profiles that include demographic information, motivations, pain points, and preferred social media platforms.
- Consider the specific needs and preferences of different segments within your target audience. For example, you may have different messaging and content strategies for busy professionals looking for quick breakfast options versus families seeking custom celebration cakes.
- Identify the social media platforms where your target audience is most active and engaged. Focus your efforts on these platforms to maximize your reach and impact.
- Tailor your messaging and content to resonate with the interests, values, and aspirations of your target audience. Speak their language and address their pain points to establish a connection and build trust.
- Use audience targeting features offered by social media advertising platforms to reach specific segments of your target audience based on demographics, interests, behaviors, and location.
- Monitor social media conversations and engage with your target audience by responding to comments, messages, and mentions. Show genuine interest in their opinions and feedback to strengthen your relationship with them.
- Conduct surveys and polls on social media to gather feedback from your audience and understand their preferences, opinions, and needs better.
- Leverage user-generated content by encouraging your customers to share their experiences with your bakery on social media. Repost their content and acknowledge their contributions to foster a sense of community and belonging.
- Collaborate with influencers and brand advocates who have a following that aligns with your target audience. Partnering with influencers can help you reach new audiences and build credibility and trust among your target demographic.
- Experiment with different types of content, formats, and messaging styles to see what resonates best with your target audience. Analyze the performance of your posts and adjust your strategy accordingly.

- Use social media listening tools to monitor conversations and trends related to your industry, products, and competitors. Stay informed about the topics and issues that matter most to your target audience.
- Create customized landing pages and lead magnets to capture the contact information of your social media followers and nurture them through targeted email marketing campaigns.
- Offer exclusive promotions, discounts, and special offers to your social media followers as a way to reward their loyalty and incentivize engagement.
- Host virtual events, live streams, and Q&A sessions on social media to connect with your target audience in real-time and provide valuable insights, tips, and entertainment.
- Showcase testimonials, reviews, and user-generated content from satisfied customers on your social media profiles to build social proof and credibility with your target audience.
- Collaborate with complementary businesses and organizations to cross-promote each other's products and services to shared audiences.
- Keep track of industry trends, changes in consumer behavior, and emerging technologies to stay ahead of the curve and adapt your social media strategy accordingly.
- Continuously monitor and analyze your social media performance metrics to evaluate the effectiveness of your efforts in reaching and engaging your target audience.
- Stay responsive and adaptable to changes in the social media landscape, including algorithm updates, platform features, and user preferences.
- Solicit feedback from your audience regularly to ensure that your social media strategy remains relevant and resonates with their evolving needs and preferences.
- Iterate and refine your social media strategy based on ongoing insights and feedback to maintain a strong connection with your target audience and drive business results.

Crafting Your Bakery's Brand Voice

- Begin by defining your bakery's brand personality and values. Consider attributes such as friendly, authentic, creative, and approachable that align with your bakery's identity and resonate with your target audience.
- Determine the tone of voice that best reflects your brand personality and appeals to your target demographic. Whether it's casual and conversational, formal and informative, or playful and whimsical, ensure consistency across all your social media communications.
- Study your competitors' brand voices to identify gaps and opportunities for differentiation. Aim to carve out a unique and memorable position in the minds of your audience through your brand voice.
- Incorporate storytelling into your social media content to humanize your bakery and connect with your audience on a deeper level. Share anecdotes, behind-the-scenes stories, and personal experiences that showcase your bakery's values, passion, and expertise.
- Use humor and wit strategically in your social media posts to entertain and engage your audience. However, be mindful of cultural sensitivities and ensure that your humor aligns with your brand identity and values.
- Infuse your brand voice with empathy and authenticity to build trust and rapport with your audience. Show genuine interest in their needs, preferences, and concerns, and demonstrate that your bakery is listening and responsive.
- Develop a style guide outlining guidelines for language usage, vocabulary, grammar, and punctuation to maintain consistency in your brand voice across all social media channels and content types.
- Incorporate visual elements such as colors, fonts, and imagery that complement your brand personality and reinforce your brand voice. Consistent visual branding helps enhance brand recognition and recall.
- Tailor your brand voice to resonate with the cultural nuances and sensibilities of your target audience, especially if you operate in diverse markets or serve multicultural communities.
- Solicit feedback from your audience to gauge their perception of your brand voice and adjust your approach accordingly. Pay attention to comments, messages, and reviews to understand how your communication resonates with your audience.
- Use language and terminology that reflects your bakery's commitment to quality, freshness, and craftsmanship. Highlight the artisanal techniques, premium ingredients, and attention to detail that set your bakery apart from the competition.
- Showcase your bakery's personality and values through user-generated content, customer testimonials, and employee spotlights. Let your loyal customers and dedicated staff members become ambassadors for your brand.
- Engage with your audience in meaningful conversations, asking questions, soliciting feedback, and responding to comments and inquiries promptly. Foster a sense of community and belonging around your bakery's brand.

- Align your brand voice with your bakery's overall marketing objectives and business goals. Whether you're aiming to increase sales, launch new products, or raise brand awareness, ensure that your brand voice supports your strategic objectives.
- Stay true to your brand identity and values while adapting your brand voice to fit the context and nuances of different social media platforms. Tailor your messaging and tone to suit the platform's audience and communication style.
- Experiment with different content formats, such as videos, memes, infographics, and GIFs, to express your brand voice creatively and capture your audience's attention.
- Collaborate with influencers, content creators, and brand ambassadors who embody your bakery's brand values and can help amplify your brand voice to their followers.
- Use customer feedback, reviews, and testimonials to reinforce your brand voice and build credibility and trust with your audience. Share positive experiences and testimonials to showcase the value and satisfaction your bakery provides.
- Incorporate seasonal themes, holidays, and cultural events into your social media content to stay relevant and engage your audience in timely conversations. Customize your brand voice to fit the mood and context of each occasion.
- Empower your employees to embody your bakery's brand voice in their interactions with customers, both online and offline. Provide training and guidelines to ensure that everyone on your team represents your brand consistently and authentically.
- Monitor social media conversations and trends to stay informed about topics and issues that matter to your audience. Use your brand voice to contribute to relevant conversations and demonstrate your bakery's thought leadership and expertise.
- Be transparent and honest in your communication, admitting mistakes and addressing concerns openly and respectfully. Authenticity builds trust and loyalty with your audience, even in challenging situations.
- Regularly review and refine your brand voice based on feedback, audience insights, and evolving market trends. Stay adaptable and responsive to changes in consumer preferences and industry dynamics.
- Continuously reinforce your bakery's brand voice through consistent messaging, visuals, and interactions across all touchpoints. Build a strong and cohesive brand identity that resonates with your audience and sets your bakery apart in the competitive market.

Content Planning and Calendar Management

- Showcase behind-the-scenes footage of the bakery, including baking processes, decorating techniques, and staff interactions to give followers an insider's view of the bakery's daily operations.
- Introduce a "Recipe of the Week" series featuring step-by-step tutorials of popular bakery items, encouraging followers to try baking at home and share their results.
- Host live baking sessions on platforms like Instagram or Facebook, allowing followers to ask questions in real-time and engage with the bakery staff.
- Share customer testimonials and reviews to build credibility and trust with potential customers, highlighting their positive experiences with the bakery's products and services.
- Create visually appealing infographics or videos showcasing fun facts about baking, ingredients, or the history of the bakery to educate and entertain followers.
- Collaborate with local influencers or food bloggers to feature the bakery's products in their content, reaching a wider audience and leveraging their followers' trust.
- Launch a weekly or monthly themed photo contest where followers can submit their own bakery-inspired creations for a chance to win discounts or free treats.
- Share mouthwatering photos and videos of freshly baked goods, emphasizing their quality, freshness, and unique flavors to entice followers to visit the bakery.
- Highlight seasonal specials and promotions through visually appealing graphics or videos, creating a sense of urgency and excitement among followers to try limited-time offerings.
- Create interactive polls or quizzes asking followers about their favorite bakery treats, flavor preferences, or baking tips to encourage engagement and gather valuable insights.
- Collaborate with other local businesses or organizations for cross-promotional opportunities, such as featuring their products in the bakery or hosting joint events.
- Share fun and lighthearted baking memes or jokes to entertain followers and add personality to the bakery's social media presence.
- Provide baking tips, tricks, and hacks through short video tutorials or carousel posts, positioning the bakery as a helpful resource for aspiring bakers.
- Celebrate holidays and special occasions with themed content, promotions, and limited-edition treats to capitalize on seasonal trends and drive sales.
- Share behind-the-scenes stories or interviews with the bakery's founder or head pastry chef, offering insights into their passion for baking and the inspiration behind their creations.
- Create interactive Instagram or Facebook Stories featuring polls, quizzes, or "ask me anything" sessions to foster two-way communication with followers in real-time.
- Showcase the bakery's commitment to sustainability and locally sourced ingredients through educational posts, videos, or partnerships with eco-friendly initiatives.
- Highlight community involvement and charitable efforts, such as donating baked goods to local shelters or participating in fundraising events, to showcase the bakery's values and impact.

- Share user-generated content, such as photos or reviews from satisfied customers, to foster a sense of community and appreciation among followers.
- Collaborate with local photographers or artists to create visually stunning content featuring the bakery's products in unique settings or compositions.
- Offer exclusive discounts or promotions to followers who engage with the bakery's social media posts or refer friends to follow the page, incentivizing loyalty and word-of-mouth marketing.
- Host virtual baking classes or workshops for followers to learn new skills and techniques from the bakery's expert staff, generating additional revenue streams and brand awareness.
- Create a content calendar outlining upcoming posts, promotions, and events to ensure consistency and alignment with the bakery's marketing objectives and seasonal trends.
- Analyze social media metrics and customer feedback regularly to optimize content strategy and identify opportunities for improvement, ensuring that the bakery's social media efforts continue to drive engagement and sales.

Creating Mouth-Watering Visual Content

- Capture high-quality photos of the bakery's signature products, such as cakes, pastries, and bread, using professional photography equipment or smartphones with excellent camera capabilities to showcase their visual appeal.
- Experiment with different angles, lighting techniques, and compositions to highlight the texture, colors, and intricate details of the bakery's creations, making them irresistible to viewers.
- Utilize close-up shots to capture the delicious layers, fillings, and toppings of bakery items, allowing followers to see every mouth-watering aspect up close.
- Incorporate vibrant and eye-catching props, such as fresh fruits, flowers, or vintage kitchen utensils, to enhance the visual appeal of bakery products and create an inviting atmosphere in photos.
- Showcase the baking process from start to finish through captivating time-lapse videos or series of photos, providing followers with a behind-the-scenes look at how their favorite treats are made.
- Experiment with different backgrounds and settings to create visually stunning contrasts and textures that complement the bakery items and make them stand out in social media feeds.
- Incorporate seasonal elements, such as fall leaves, spring flowers, or holiday decorations, into photo shoots to evoke a sense of nostalgia and capture the spirit of the season.
- Collaborate with talented food stylists or influencers to create stylized photoshoots featuring the bakery's products in creative and visually appealing ways that resonate with followers.
- Use props and accessories that reflect the bakery's brand identity and values, such as rustic wooden boards, vintage plates, or branded packaging, to reinforce brand recognition and consistency in visual content.
- Experiment with flat lay photography to arrange bakery items, ingredients, and accessories in an aesthetically pleasing manner, creating visually appealing compositions that tell a story and spark cravings.
- Incorporate dynamic elements into photos and videos, such as pouring chocolate ganache over a cake or sprinkling powdered sugar on pastries, to add movement and excitement to visual content.
- Showcase the bakery's diverse range of products and flavors through visually engaging collages or grids, allowing followers to discover new favorites and menu offerings.
- Highlight the sensory experience of enjoying bakery items by capturing close-up shots of melted chocolate, flaky pastry layers, or steam rising from freshly baked bread, triggering cravings and enticing followers to visit the bakery.
- Experiment with unconventional perspectives and angles, such as overhead shots or close-ups from unique angles, to create visually striking compositions that capture the essence of the bakery's products.

- Incorporate user-generated content into visual content strategy by featuring photos and reviews from satisfied customers enjoying bakery treats, adding authenticity and social proof to the bakery's brand story.
- Showcase the versatility of bakery items by styling them in different settings and occasions, such as brunch gatherings, afternoon tea parties, or cozy winter nights, to inspire followers and drive sales.
- Experiment with playful props and decorations, such as confetti, sprinkles, or colorful napkins, to add a touch of whimsy and personality to visual content, making it more engaging and shareable.
- Utilize Instagram's carousel feature to showcase multiple images or videos in a single post, allowing followers to swipe through a series of mouth-watering visuals and discover more about the bakery's offerings.
- Incorporate interactive elements into visual content, such as polls, quizzes, or countdowns, to encourage engagement and create a sense of anticipation among followers.
- Collaborate with local artists or illustrators to create custom artwork or illustrations featuring the bakery's products, adding a unique and artistic touch to visual content that sets it apart from competitors.
- Create visually cohesive feeds by maintaining a consistent color palette, editing style, and theme across all visual content, creating a visually appealing and professional brand image that resonates with followers.
- Experiment with stop motion animation techniques to bring bakery products to life in playful and engaging ways, adding a sense of movement and personality to visual content.
- Incorporate storytelling elements into visual content by sharing anecdotes, recipes, or behind-the-scenes insights that resonate with followers and create emotional connections with the bakery's brand.
- Analyze performance metrics and feedback from followers regularly to refine visual content strategy, identify top-performing posts, and optimize future content for maximum engagement and impact.

Video Marketing Tips for Bakeries

- Create short recipe tutorial videos showcasing how to bake some of the bakery's most popular items, providing step-by-step instructions that viewers can easily follow along with.
- Host live baking sessions on platforms like Facebook or Instagram, allowing viewers to interact with the bakery staff in real-time, ask questions, and learn new techniques.
- Produce behind-the-scenes videos that offer a glimpse into the bakery's kitchen, highlighting the craftsmanship and dedication that goes into creating each delicious treat.
- Share customer testimonial videos featuring satisfied patrons expressing their love for the bakery's products, helping to build trust and credibility among potential customers.
- Showcase the bakery's unique story and heritage through engaging storytelling videos, allowing viewers to connect with the brand on a deeper level and understand its values and mission.
- Collaborate with local influencers or food bloggers to create sponsored content videos featuring the bakery's products, reaching new audiences and leveraging their credibility and influence.
- Highlight seasonal specials and promotions through visually appealing video advertisements, creating a sense of urgency and excitement among viewers to try limited-time offerings.
- Produce educational videos that offer baking tips, tricks, and techniques, positioning the bakery as an expert resource for aspiring home bakers and building trust and authority in the industry.
- Create mouth-watering "food porn" videos featuring close-up shots of bakery items being sliced, frosted, or decorated, triggering cravings and enticing viewers to visit the bakery.
- Showcase the bakery's catering services through videos that highlight beautifully arranged dessert platters, wedding cakes, or event setups, inspiring viewers to consider the bakery for their next special occasion.
- Collaborate with other local businesses or organizations to create joint promotional videos, such as featuring the bakery's desserts at a local cafe or restaurant, expanding reach and driving traffic to both businesses.
- Produce video interviews with the bakery's founder, head pastry chef, or staff members, offering insights into their passion for baking, creative process, and favorite recipes, humanizing the brand and building rapport with viewers.
- Create visually appealing "day in the life" videos that follow a bakery staff member throughout their day, showcasing the hustle and bustle of the bakery's operations and the teamwork that goes into delivering fresh, delicious treats to customers.
- Host virtual tasting events where viewers can join live video sessions to sample and review new bakery products, creating a sense of exclusivity and excitement around new menu offerings.

- Produce "behind-the-menu" videos that delve into the inspiration behind the bakery's creations, such as sourcing locally grown ingredients or experimenting with unique flavor combinations, educating viewers about the bakery's commitment to quality and innovation.
- Utilize video testimonials from satisfied customers to showcase their positive experiences with the bakery's products and services, providing social proof and encouraging others to give the bakery a try.
- Create video slideshows featuring mouth-watering photos of bakery items set to upbeat music or narration, providing a visually captivating overview of the bakery's menu offerings and enticing viewers to visit the bakery.
- Produce video content that addresses frequently asked questions from customers, such as allergy information, ingredient sourcing, or custom order inquiries, providing valuable information and building trust with potential customers.
- Host virtual baking classes or workshops where viewers can join live video sessions to learn new recipes and techniques from the bakery's expert staff, generating additional revenue streams and establishing the bakery as a go-to destination for baking education.
- Create "how-to" videos showcasing creative ways to use bakery products, such as turning leftover croissants into decadent bread pudding or transforming cupcakes into festive cake pops, inspiring viewers to get creative in the kitchen.
- Produce video content that highlights the bakery's commitment to sustainability and eco-friendly practices, such as using compostable packaging or donating leftover baked goods to local shelters, educating viewers about the bakery's efforts to reduce its environmental impact.
- Create visually stunning stop-motion animation videos featuring bakery items coming to life in playful and whimsical ways, adding a touch of creativity and personality to the bakery's video content.
- Experiment with interactive video elements, such as polls, quizzes, or clickable links, to engage viewers and encourage them to take action, such as voting for their favorite dessert or visiting the bakery's website to place an order.
- Analyze video performance metrics, such as views, engagement, and watch time, to identify top-performing content and optimize future video marketing efforts for maximum impact and effectiveness.

SOCIAL MEDIA MARKETING IDEAS

Engaging With Your Audience Effectively

- Respond promptly to comments, messages, and mentions from followers on social media platforms to demonstrate responsiveness and foster a sense of community and engagement.
- Encourage followers to share their own baking creations or experiences with the bakery by creating branded hashtags and hosting user-generated content contests or challenges.
- Host interactive Q&A sessions on social media platforms where followers can ask questions about the bakery's products, services, or baking techniques, providing valuable information and building rapport with the audience.
- Show appreciation for loyal customers and followers by acknowledging their support publicly through shoutouts, reposts, or exclusive discounts or perks.
- Initiate conversations with followers by asking open-ended questions, soliciting feedback, or inviting them to share their thoughts and opinions on bakery-related topics.
- Personalize interactions with followers by addressing them by name, responding to their comments with personalized messages, and acknowledging their individual interests and preferences.
- Create polls or surveys on social media platforms to gather insights from followers about their favorite bakery treats, flavor preferences, or suggestions for new menu items, demonstrating that their opinions are valued and taken into consideration.
- Host virtual events, such as live tastings, baking workshops, or Q&A sessions with the bakery's staff, to provide an interactive and immersive experience for followers and foster deeper connections with the brand.
- Showcase customer testimonials and reviews on social media platforms to build credibility and trust with potential customers and encourage others to share their own positive experiences with the bakery.
- Incorporate user-generated content into social media marketing efforts by featuring photos, videos, or reviews from satisfied customers enjoying bakery treats, creating a sense of community and appreciation among followers.
- Share behind-the-scenes stories, anecdotes, or fun facts about the bakery's history, staff members, or creative process to humanize the brand and foster emotional connections with followers.
- Create interactive quizzes, trivia contests, or caption competitions on social media platforms to entertain followers and encourage them to engage with the bakery's content in a fun and interactive way.
- Utilize Instagram's question sticker feature or Facebook's polls feature to solicit feedback and suggestions from followers about new product offerings, promotions, or upcoming events, involving them in the decision-making process.
- Collaborate with micro-influencers or brand ambassadors who have a genuine affinity for the bakery's products and values to amplify reach and engagement among their followers.
- Host social media-exclusive giveaways or contests where followers can enter to win prizes such as free bakery items, gift cards, or branded merchandise, incentivizing engagement

and rewarding loyal followers.
- Create a dedicated community group or forum on social media platforms where followers can connect with each other, share baking tips and recipes, and discuss their favorite bakery treats, fostering a sense of belonging and camaraderie.
- Utilize social media listening tools to monitor conversations and sentiment around the bakery's brand and industry keywords, allowing for proactive engagement with followers and timely responses to inquiries or concerns.
- Provide value-added content to followers through educational posts, tutorials, or how-to guides that share baking tips, tricks, and techniques, positioning the bakery as a helpful and reliable resource for aspiring bakers.
- Celebrate milestones, anniversaries, or special occasions with followers by hosting virtual parties, offering exclusive promotions, or sharing behind-the-scenes insights and reflections on the bakery's journey.
- Host regular "Ask Me Anything" (AMA) sessions on social media platforms where followers can submit questions in advance or ask questions in real-time, providing transparency and fostering open communication with the audience.
- Create interactive stories or polls on Instagram and Facebook to solicit feedback from followers about potential new menu items, flavor combinations, or packaging designs, involving them in the product development process.
- Showcase customer-generated content on the bakery's social media platforms by featuring photos, videos, or reviews from satisfied patrons enjoying bakery treats, demonstrating appreciation for their support and building social proof.
- Encourage followers to share their own baking successes or challenges by creating themed hashtags or weekly prompts that inspire them to showcase their culinary creations and engage with the bakery's brand.
- Analyze social media metrics and engagement data regularly to identify trends, preferences, and opportunities for improvement in audience engagement strategies, ensuring that the bakery's social media marketing efforts are effective and resonating with the target audience.

Leveraging Instagram Stories and Reels

- Use Instagram Stories to provide a behind-the-scenes look at the bakery's daily operations, showcasing the baking process, decorating techniques, and interactions with customers to give followers an insider's view of the business.
- Utilize the "Swipe Up" feature in Instagram Stories to drive traffic to the bakery's website, online ordering platform, or blog posts, making it easy for followers to take action and engage with the brand.
- Create interactive polls or quizzes in Instagram Stories to solicit feedback from followers about their favorite bakery treats, flavor preferences, or suggestions for new menu items, fostering engagement and gathering valuable insights.
- Host live baking demonstrations or tutorials on Instagram Stories, allowing followers to tune in and interact with the bakery staff in real-time, ask questions, and learn new techniques.
- Share user-generated content in Instagram Stories by featuring photos, videos, or reviews from satisfied customers enjoying bakery treats, showcasing social proof and building credibility with potential customers.
- Highlight limited-time promotions, discounts, or flash sales in Instagram Stories to create a sense of urgency and excitement among followers, encouraging them to take advantage of special offers before they expire.
- Create visually appealing carousel posts in Instagram Stories featuring multiple images or videos that showcase the bakery's menu offerings, seasonal specials, or behind-the-scenes moments, providing a comprehensive overview of the brand.
- Collaborate with local influencers or food bloggers to create sponsored content in Instagram Stories featuring the bakery's products, reaching new audiences and leveraging their credibility and influence.
- Use Instagram Stories to share announcements, updates, or sneak peeks of upcoming events, product launches, or collaborations with followers, building anticipation and excitement around the brand.
- Incorporate interactive stickers such as polls, quizzes, or countdowns in Instagram Stories to engage followers and encourage them to interact with the bakery's content in a fun and interactive way.
- Showcase customer testimonials and reviews in Instagram Stories by featuring screenshots of positive feedback or video testimonials from satisfied patrons, adding social proof and credibility to the bakery's brand story.
- Create visually stunning animations or graphics in Instagram Stories to promote seasonal specials, holiday offerings, or new menu items, capturing attention and enticing followers to visit the bakery.
- Utilize Instagram Reels to showcase quick, engaging videos of the bakery's products, staff members, or behind-the-scenes moments, leveraging the platform's algorithm to reach a wider audience and increase brand visibility.

- Create entertaining and informative "how-to" videos in Instagram Reels that demonstrate baking tips, decorating techniques, or creative recipe ideas, positioning the bakery as a helpful resource for aspiring bakers.
- Experiment with trendy audio tracks, effects, and filters in Instagram Reels to make content more engaging and shareable, staying current with popular trends and capturing the attention of younger audiences.
- Collaborate with local influencers or content creators to co-create engaging and entertaining content in Instagram Reels featuring the bakery's products, leveraging their creativity and audience reach to amplify brand visibility.
- Use Instagram Reels to share user-generated content by featuring videos from satisfied customers enjoying bakery treats, adding authenticity and social proof to the bakery's brand story.
- Host fun and interactive challenges or contests in Instagram Reels, encouraging followers to participate by creating their own videos showcasing their baking skills or favorite bakery treats, fostering engagement and community-building.
- Incorporate storytelling elements into Instagram Reels by sharing anecdotes, recipes, or behind-the-scenes insights about the bakery's products, staff members, or creative process, adding depth and personality to the brand.
- Showcase the bakery's commitment to sustainability and eco-friendly practices in Instagram Reels by highlighting initiatives such as using locally sourced ingredients, reducing food waste, or implementing eco-friendly packaging solutions, educating followers and building brand loyalty.
- Utilize Instagram Reels to share quick recipe tutorials or baking hacks that showcase the bakery's expertise and creativity, providing value-added content that resonates with followers and positions the brand as a trusted authority in the industry.
- Create visually appealing stop-motion animations in Instagram Reels featuring bakery items coming to life in playful and whimsical ways, adding a touch of creativity and personality to the brand's content.
- Experiment with different video formats, lengths, and styles in Instagram Reels to determine what resonates most with the audience and optimize content strategy accordingly, ensuring that the bakery's videos are engaging and effective.
- Analyze performance metrics and audience feedback regularly to assess the effectiveness of Instagram Stories and Reels content, identify top-performing posts, and optimize future content for maximum engagement and impact.

Running Successful Social Media Contests

- Host a photo contest where followers can submit photos of their favorite bakery treats for a chance to win a gift card or free desserts, encouraging user-generated content and engagement.
- Create a recipe contest where followers can submit their original baking recipes using a specific ingredient or theme, with the winner receiving recognition and their recipe featured on the bakery's menu.
- Host a caption contest where followers can submit creative captions for a photo or video posted by the bakery, encouraging witty and engaging responses while building brand awareness and personality.
- Organize a scavenger hunt contest where followers must visit the bakery's social media profiles to find clues or hidden messages, with the first person to solve the puzzle winning a prize.
- Run a "share to win" contest where followers must share a post or tag friends in the comments to enter, increasing the reach and visibility of the bakery's social media content.
- Create a trivia contest where followers can test their knowledge about baking, the bakery's history, or famous desserts, with prizes awarded to those who answer correctly.
- Host a guessing game contest where followers must guess the number of chocolate chips in a jar or the weight of a giant cake, with the closest guess winning a prize.
- Run a "spot the difference" contest where followers must identify differences between two similar photos of bakery items, with winners randomly selected from correct entries.
- Organize a themed costume contest where followers can dress up as their favorite bakery treats or characters, with prizes awarded for the most creative and festive costumes.
- Host a review contest where followers can leave reviews or testimonials about their favorite bakery products or experiences, with prizes awarded to randomly selected participants.
- Create a video contest where followers can submit short videos showcasing their baking skills, favorite recipes, or creative dessert decorations, with prizes awarded to the most impressive entries.
- Organize a bingo contest where followers must complete a bingo card by engaging with the bakery's social media content in various ways, such as liking posts, sharing photos, or commenting on videos, with prizes awarded to those who complete a row or column.
- Run a "guess the flavor" contest where followers must identify the flavors of mystery desserts or ingredients hidden in a photo, with prizes awarded to those who guess correctly.
- Host a story contest where followers can submit their own baking-related anecdotes or memories, with prizes awarded to the most heartwarming or entertaining stories.
- Create a puzzle contest where followers must solve a crossword puzzle or word search related to baking terms or bakery products, with prizes awarded to those who complete the puzzle correctly.
- Organize a "fan of the week" contest where followers can nominate themselves or others for recognition as the bakery's biggest fan, with winners featured on the bakery's social

media profiles and receiving special discounts or perks.
- Run a "recipe swap" contest where followers can share their favorite baking recipes in the comments, with prizes awarded to randomly selected participants and the best recipes featured on the bakery's website or social media pages.
- Host a voting contest where followers can vote for their favorite bakery products or menu items, with prizes awarded to randomly selected voters and the winning items featured as "fan favorites" on the bakery's menu.
- Create a themed art contest where followers can submit their own drawings, paintings, or digital artwork inspired by the bakery's products or logo, with prizes awarded to the most creative and visually appealing entries.
- Organize a pet photo contest where followers can submit photos of their pets enjoying bakery treats, with prizes awarded to the cutest or most adorable entries and winning photos featured on the bakery's social media profiles.
- Run a "loyalty challenge" contest where followers must complete a series of tasks or challenges related to the bakery's products or social media profiles, with prizes awarded to those who successfully complete all tasks.
- Host a "best customer photo" contest where followers can submit photos of themselves enjoying bakery treats at the bakery's storefront or events, with prizes awarded to the most enthusiastic and loyal customers.
- Create a themed holiday contest where followers can submit photos, recipes, or stories related to holiday baking traditions, with prizes awarded to entries that capture the spirit of the season and spread joy to others.
- Analyze contest performance metrics, such as engagement, participation, and follower growth, to assess the success of each contest and identify opportunities for improvement in future social media marketing efforts.

Utilizing User-Generated Content

- Launch a branded hashtag campaign encouraging followers to share photos of themselves enjoying bakery treats using a specific hashtag, allowing the bakery to easily track and showcase user-generated content.
- Create a dedicated Instagram highlight reel featuring user-generated content, such as photos or videos of satisfied customers enjoying bakery products, to showcase social proof and build credibility with potential customers.
- Host a user-generated content contest where followers can submit photos or videos of their favorite bakery creations for a chance to win prizes or be featured on the bakery's social media profiles, encouraging engagement and participation.
- Share user-generated content on the bakery's social media profiles by reposting photos, videos, or reviews from satisfied customers, acknowledging their support and fostering a sense of community and appreciation.
- Encourage customers to tag the bakery in their social media posts and stories when visiting the storefront or enjoying bakery treats at home, making it easy for the bakery to discover and share user-generated content with their audience.
- Create a dedicated section on the bakery's website or social media profiles showcasing user-generated content, such as a photo gallery or testimonials page, to highlight the positive experiences and feedback from satisfied customers.
- Collaborate with local influencers or brand ambassadors to create sponsored content featuring the bakery's products, encouraging them to share their experiences with their followers and generate user-generated content that aligns with the bakery's brand values.
- Host a "customer spotlight" series on social media profiles where the bakery highlights a different customer each week and shares their photos, stories, or reviews of their favorite bakery treats, fostering connections and relationships with followers.
- Organize a themed photo challenge on social media platforms where followers can participate by sharing photos related to a specific theme or prompt, such as their favorite bakery-inspired recipe or dessert creation, encouraging creativity and engagement.
- Create a branded Instagram sticker or filter featuring the bakery's logo or signature products, allowing followers to add a personalized touch to their photos and stories while promoting the bakery's brand.
- Collaborate with local photographers or content creators to organize photo walks or styled photoshoots featuring the bakery's products, encouraging participants to share their photos on social media with the bakery's branded hashtag.
- Host a virtual bake-off competition where followers can participate by baking their own versions of a specific recipe or dessert and sharing photos or videos of their creations on social media, with prizes awarded to the most creative or impressive entries.
- Create a loyalty program or rewards system where customers earn points or discounts for sharing user-generated content, such as photos or reviews of bakery products, on social media platforms, incentivizing engagement and advocacy.

- Partner with complementary businesses or organizations to cross-promote user-generated content, such as sharing photos of bakery treats paired with coffee from a local cafe or wine from a nearby vineyard, expanding reach and visibility for both brands.
- Host a "fan of the month" contest on social media profiles where followers can nominate themselves or others for recognition as the bakery's biggest fan, with winners featured on the bakery's website or social media profiles and receiving special discounts or perks.
- Create a branded community group or forum on social media platforms where customers can connect with each other, share baking tips and recipes, and discuss their favorite bakery treats, fostering a sense of belonging and camaraderie among followers.
- Incorporate user-generated content into email marketing campaigns by featuring photos, reviews, or testimonials from satisfied customers, adding authenticity and social proof to promotional messages and encouraging recipients to visit the bakery.
- Host virtual tasting events or product samplings where followers can join live video sessions to sample and review new bakery products, encouraging participants to share their experiences and photos on social media.
- Create a "best of" compilation video featuring highlights of user-generated content shared by customers, such as photos, videos, or reviews of their favorite bakery treats, to showcase the diversity and enthusiasm of the bakery's fan base.
- Collaborate with local bloggers or influencers to organize meet-ups or tasting events at the bakery's storefront, encouraging attendees to share their experiences and photos on social media and generate user-generated content that promotes the bakery to their followers.
- Incorporate user-generated content into advertising campaigns by featuring photos or testimonials from satisfied customers in digital ads, print materials, or promotional videos, adding authenticity and credibility to marketing messages.
- Host virtual workshops or cooking classes where followers can learn new baking techniques or recipes from the bakery's expert staff, encouraging participants to share their creations on social media and generate user-generated content that promotes the bakery.
- Utilize user-generated content as social proof on the bakery's website or product pages by featuring photos, videos, or reviews from satisfied customers, reassuring visitors and potential customers of the quality and popularity of the bakery's offerings.
- Analyze user-generated content metrics and engagement data regularly to assess the impact and effectiveness of user-generated content strategies, identify top-performing posts and influencers, and optimize future social media marketing efforts for maximum engagement and impact.

Influencer Partnerships for Bakeries

- Collaborate with local food bloggers who have a significant following in your area to showcase your bakery's specialties, such as artisan bread or custom cakes.
- Partner with lifestyle influencers who align with your bakery's brand values to create visually appealing content featuring your baked goods in their daily routines.
- Host an exclusive tasting event for influencers where they can sample your latest creations and share their experiences with their followers in real-time.
- Create custom discount codes or special promotions for influencers to share with their audience, driving traffic to your bakery both online and in-store.
- Organize a baking workshop or masterclass led by your bakery's head pastry chef, inviting influencers to participate and share their newfound skills with their followers.
- Collaborate with micro-influencers, individuals with smaller but highly engaged audiences, to promote your bakery's seasonal offerings or limited-time promotions.
- Partner with fitness or wellness influencers to highlight your bakery's healthier options, such as whole grain bread or sugar-free pastries, catering to health-conscious consumers.
- Engage with local influencers who specialize in home cooking or baking, encouraging them to incorporate your bakery's products into their recipes and share them with their followers.
- Host a social media contest where influencers can create and share their own unique recipes using your bakery's ingredients, encouraging user-generated content and engagement.
- Sponsor a giveaway with influencers where their followers can enter to win a selection of your bakery's treats, increasing brand awareness and engagement.
- Collaborate with travel influencers visiting your city, offering them a taste of your bakery's specialties to feature in their exploration of local cuisine.
- Partner with mommy bloggers or parenting influencers to promote your bakery's children's birthday party packages or custom cake designs for special occasions.
- Organize a blogger meet-up or influencer brunch at your bakery, providing an opportunity for influencers to network while enjoying your delicious offerings.
- Work with fashion influencers to style your bakery's desserts in aesthetically pleasing flat lays or outfit pairings, appealing to a style-conscious audience.
- Partner with influencers who specialize in DIY or home decor to feature your bakery's desserts as part of their entertaining or hosting inspiration content.
- Collaborate with pet influencers to create pet-friendly treats using your bakery's ingredients, tapping into the pet-owner market segment.
- Host a charity event or fundraiser in partnership with influencers, donating a portion of proceeds from select products to a cause aligned with your bakery's values.
- Partner with eco-conscious influencers to promote your bakery's sustainable practices, such as using locally sourced ingredients or reducing food waste.
- Collaborate with beauty influencers to create visually stunning content featuring your bakery's desserts as part of makeup flat lays or skincare routines.

- Sponsor local events or festivals where influencers can sample your bakery's treats and share their experiences with their followers in real-time.
- Partner with influencers who specialize in meal prep or food planning to incorporate your bakery's items into their weekly menus, showcasing versatility and convenience.
- Collaborate with influencers who focus on mental health and wellness to promote the mood-boosting benefits of indulging in your bakery's comfort foods.
- Host a behind-the-scenes tour of your bakery for influencers, offering insights into your baking process and allowing them to create content for their followers.
- Partner with influencers from diverse cultural backgrounds to feature your bakery's international or fusion-inspired offerings, appealing to a broader audience.

Promoting Your Bakery's Events on Social Media

- Create visually appealing event graphics and share them across all your bakery's social media platforms to announce upcoming events, ensuring consistency in branding and messaging.
- Leverage Instagram Stories to provide sneak peeks of event preparations, such as behind-the-scenes footage of baking or decorating, to build anticipation among your followers.
- Utilize Facebook Events to create listings for your bakery's events, allowing users to RSVP, share with friends, and receive notifications about event updates or reminders.
- Partner with local influencers or food bloggers to co-host or promote your bakery's events on their social media channels, tapping into their audience and extending your reach.
- Encourage user-generated content by creating event-specific hashtags and encouraging attendees to share their experiences and photos on social media, fostering community engagement.
- Host live Q&A sessions or virtual tours on platforms like Facebook Live or Instagram Live to provide followers with more information about your bakery's events and offerings in real-time.
- Share countdown posts or daily event reminders leading up to the event date to keep your audience excited and informed about what to expect.
- Collaborate with complementary businesses, such as local coffee shops or florists, to cross-promote each other's events on social media and attract a broader audience.
- Offer exclusive promotions or discounts to followers who RSVP to your bakery's events through social media platforms, incentivizing attendance and engagement.
- Create event-specific Facebook Groups or LinkedIn Events for networking and discussions among attendees before and after the event, fostering a sense of community and connection.
- Utilize targeted social media advertising to reach users who may be interested in attending your bakery's events, based on demographics, interests, or location.
- Showcase testimonials or reviews from past event attendees on your bakery's social media profiles to build credibility and trust among potential attendees.
- Collaborate with local event listing websites or community calendars to promote your bakery's events to a broader audience beyond your social media following.
- Share teaser videos or behind-the-scenes clips of event preparations on platforms like TikTok or Reels to capture the attention of younger audiences and drive engagement.
- Host a social media contest or giveaway where followers can enter to win free tickets or exclusive access to your bakery's events, encouraging participation and excitement.
- Utilize Instagram Guides or Pinterest boards to curate content related to your bakery's events, such as recipe ideas, decorating tips, or inspiration boards, to provide value to your audience.
- Engage with comments, questions, and inquiries about your bakery's events on social media promptly and professionally, fostering a positive customer experience and encouraging

attendance.
- Collaborate with local media outlets or food influencers to cover your bakery's events and share their experiences with their audiences, generating buzz and credibility.
- Create event-specific Instagram Reels or TikTok videos showcasing highlights from past events or sneak peeks of what attendees can expect, capturing attention and driving interest.
- Utilize Instagram's Shopping feature to tag products or menu items featured at your bakery's events in your social media posts, making it easy for followers to learn more and purchase.
- Collaborate with food delivery apps or online platforms to offer virtual event experiences or exclusive discounts to users who order from your bakery during the event period, driving sales and engagement.
- Create shareable event invitations or digital flyers that followers can easily repost or share on their own social media profiles, extending your event's reach to their networks.
- Share behind-the-scenes stories or anecdotes about the inspiration behind your bakery's events on platforms like Twitter or LinkedIn to humanize your brand and connect with your audience on a deeper level.
- Follow up with attendees after your bakery's events by sharing recap posts, thanking them for their participation, and encouraging them to stay connected with your bakery on social media for future updates and events.

Effective Use of Hashtags

- Research popular and relevant hashtags within the bakery industry, such as #BakeryLife or #SweetTreats, to use in your social media posts to increase visibility and reach among your target audience.
- Create branded hashtags unique to your bakery, such as #YourBakeryNameBakes or #DeliciousCreations, to encourage user-generated content and foster community engagement.
- Utilize trending hashtags related to baking or food trends, such as #HomeBaking or #FoodieFaves, to join larger conversations and increase the discoverability of your bakery's social media content.
- Incorporate location-based hashtags, such as #CityBakery or #LocalTreats, to target users within your bakery's geographical area and attract local customers to your store.
- Mix popular hashtags with niche or specific ones, such as #DessertLovers and #VeganBakery, to reach a more targeted audience interested in your bakery's specialty offerings.
- Use seasonal or holiday-themed hashtags, such as #SummerSweets or #HolidayTreats, to capitalize on timely events and trends and stay relevant to your audience throughout the year.
- Monitor trending topics and hashtags on social media platforms like Twitter and Instagram to identify opportunities for your bakery to participate in relevant conversations and gain exposure.
- Research competitor hashtags to see which ones are performing well for similar businesses and incorporate them into your social media strategy to increase visibility and competitiveness.
- Create campaign-specific hashtags for special promotions or events, such as #GrandOpeningSpecials or #BirthdayCakeGiveaway, to track engagement and measure the success of your marketing efforts.
- Experiment with different combinations of hashtags in your posts to see which ones generate the most engagement and reach, and refine your strategy based on the results.
- Analyze the performance of your hashtags using social media analytics tools to understand which ones are driving the most traffic, engagement, and conversions for your bakery.
- Encourage customers to use your branded hashtags when posting about their bakery experiences on social media, such as enjoying a slice of cake or attending a baking class, to amplify your brand's reach.
- Participate in popular hashtag challenges or trends, such as #ThrowbackThursday or #FlashbackFriday, by sharing relevant content from your bakery's archives to increase engagement and visibility.
- Use a mix of broad and niche hashtags in your posts to strike a balance between reaching a wide audience and targeting specific segments interested in your bakery's offerings.

- Create themed hashtag campaigns, such as #CakeOfTheWeek or #CookieCravings, to showcase different products or promotions regularly and keep your social media content fresh and engaging.
- Include industry-related hashtags, such as #ArtisanBakery or #GourmetDesserts, to position your bakery as a leader in quality and craftsmanship within the baking community.
- Research popular hashtags used by influencers or industry experts in your niche and incorporate them into your social media strategy to increase your content's visibility and credibility.
- Monitor and engage with conversations happening around your chosen hashtags by liking, commenting, or sharing relevant posts from other users to build relationships and foster community engagement.
- Use hashtags strategically in your Instagram Stories and TikTok videos to increase discoverability and reach among users browsing content on these platforms.
- Keep an eye on trending topics and news events relevant to your bakery's audience and incorporate trending hashtags into your social media posts to capitalize on current events and increase engagement.
- Create themed hashtag series, such as #MondayMotivationBakes or #WeekendTreats, to provide consistent and regular content for your audience while encouraging engagement and interaction.
- Collaborate with local influencers or partners to create co-branded hashtags for joint promotions or events, leveraging their audience to increase reach and engagement for your bakery.
- Use a mix of long-tail and short-tail hashtags in your posts to capture both broad and specific search queries and increase the likelihood of your content being discovered by potential customers.
- Regularly review and update your list of hashtags based on changing trends, seasons, and customer preferences to ensure your social media strategy remains relevant and effective in reaching your target audience.

Paid Advertising Strategies on Social Platforms

- Utilize Facebook Ads to target specific demographics, such as local residents or dessert enthusiasts, and promote your bakery's latest products, promotions, or events directly to your target audience.
- Experiment with different ad formats on Facebook, including carousel ads showcasing multiple products or video ads featuring behind-the-scenes footage of your bakery, to capture users' attention and drive engagement.
- Leverage Instagram Ads to showcase visually appealing images or videos of your bakery's creations and reach a younger, more visually-oriented audience interested in food and lifestyle content.
- Utilize Instagram Stories Ads to create immersive and interactive ad experiences, such as polls or quizzes related to your bakery's products, to increase engagement and brand awareness.
- Invest in promoted Tweets on Twitter to amplify your bakery's message and reach a broader audience, using targeted keywords or interests to ensure your ads are seen by users interested in baking or food-related content.
- Experiment with Twitter Conversational Ads to encourage users to engage with your bakery's brand by participating in hashtag campaigns or sharing their favorite dessert memories, driving organic reach and engagement.
- Utilize LinkedIn Ads to target business professionals or corporate clients interested in catering services or bulk orders from your bakery, leveraging the platform's professional network for B2B marketing opportunities.
- Experiment with LinkedIn Sponsored Content to promote thought leadership content from your bakery, such as blog posts or industry insights, to establish your brand as an authority in the baking industry and attract potential customers.
- Invest in Pinterest Ads to showcase your bakery's products and recipes to users searching for baking inspiration or planning their next event, leveraging the platform's visual discovery features to drive traffic and sales.
- Utilize Pinterest Promoted Pins to highlight seasonal or holiday-themed offerings from your bakery, such as Valentine's Day desserts or Halloween treats, to capitalize on trending topics and increase engagement.
- Experiment with TikTok Ads to create engaging and entertaining video content featuring your bakery's products or staff, leveraging the platform's viral potential to increase brand awareness and reach a younger audience.
- Collaborate with influencers on TikTok to create sponsored content featuring your bakery's products or participating in viral challenges, tapping into their large and engaged follower base to increase brand visibility.
- Invest in YouTube Ads to showcase recipe tutorials or baking tips from your bakery's chefs, positioning your brand as a helpful resource for home bakers and attracting subscribers to your channel.

- Utilize YouTube TrueView Ads to promote longer-form video content, such as virtual bakery tours or baking classes, to users interested in learning more about your bakery's offerings and expertise.
- Experiment with Google Ads to target users searching for terms related to your bakery, such as "best bakery near me" or "custom birthday cakes," using search ads or display ads to increase visibility and drive website traffic.
- Invest in Google Shopping Ads to showcase your bakery's products, such as specialty cakes or gift baskets, to users actively searching for similar items online, driving qualified leads and sales.
- Leverage Google Display Ads to retarget users who have visited your bakery's website or engaged with your social media content, reminding them of your offerings and encouraging them to return and make a purchase.
- Experiment with geotargeting in your paid advertising campaigns to reach users within a specific radius of your bakery's location, ensuring your ads are seen by potential customers in your area.
- Utilize remarketing strategies in your paid advertising campaigns to re-engage users who have previously interacted with your bakery's website or social media profiles, encouraging them to return and complete a purchase.
- Experiment with A/B testing in your paid advertising campaigns to compare different ad creatives, messaging, or targeting strategies and optimize your campaigns for maximum effectiveness and return on investment.
- Invest in influencer partnerships as part of your paid advertising strategy, collaborating with popular food bloggers or local influencers to promote your bakery's products or events to their engaged audience.
- Utilize affiliate marketing programs to incentivize partners or customers to promote your bakery's products or services on social media, paying them a commission for each sale or referral generated through their unique tracking link.
- Experiment with sponsored content partnerships on social media platforms, such as sponsored posts or sponsored stories, to increase your bakery's visibility and reach a larger audience through trusted and influential channels.
- Monitor and analyze the performance of your paid advertising campaigns using social media analytics tools and advertising platforms' built-in reporting features, adjusting your strategy and allocation of resources based on insights and data-driven decisions.

Analyzing Social Media Analytics

- Utilize social media analytics tools provided by platforms like Facebook Insights, Instagram Insights, and Twitter Analytics to track key metrics such as reach, engagement, and follower growth over time.
- Monitor demographic data available through social media analytics to understand your bakery's audience demographics, including age, gender, location, and interests, and tailor your content and messaging accordingly.
- Analyze engagement metrics such as likes, comments, shares, and retweets to identify which types of content resonate most with your audience and drive the highest levels of interaction and participation.
- Track click-through rates (CTR) on links shared in your social media posts to measure the effectiveness of your call-to-action (CTA) and drive traffic to your bakery's website, online ordering platform, or blog.
- Monitor follower growth and churn rates over time to understand trends in your bakery's social media following and identify opportunities to attract new followers and retain existing ones through targeted content and engagement strategies.
- Analyze post-performance data to identify top-performing content in terms of engagement, reach, and conversions, and use these insights to inform your content strategy and optimize future posts for maximum impact.
- Utilize hashtag analytics to track the performance of branded hashtags, campaign-specific hashtags, and industry-related hashtags used in your social media posts, identifying which ones generate the most visibility and engagement for your bakery.
- Monitor sentiment analysis data to gauge the overall sentiment of your bakery's social media mentions and conversations, identifying areas of opportunity for improving brand perception and addressing customer feedback or concerns.
- Track referral traffic from social media channels to your bakery's website or online ordering platform to measure the impact of your social media marketing efforts on website traffic and conversions.
- Analyze social media ad performance metrics such as click-through rates (CTR), conversion rates, and return on ad spend (ROAS) to assess the effectiveness of your paid advertising campaigns and optimize your ad targeting and creative accordingly.
- Monitor social media customer service metrics such as response time, resolution rate, and customer satisfaction scores to evaluate the effectiveness of your bakery's social media customer service efforts and identify areas for improvement.
- Use social media listening tools to monitor brand mentions, keywords, and industry trends across social media platforms, identifying opportunities to join conversations, address customer inquiries, and stay informed about market developments.
- Analyze audience engagement patterns, such as peak posting times and days of the week with the highest levels of engagement, to optimize your posting schedule and ensure your content reaches your audience when they are most active and receptive.

- Conduct competitive analysis to benchmark your bakery's social media performance against competitors in the industry, identifying areas of strength and opportunities for improvement relative to key competitors.
- Monitor social media sentiment trends over time to track shifts in consumer attitudes and preferences related to your bakery's brand, products, and services, informing strategic decision-making and marketing initiatives.
- Use social media analytics to track the performance of influencer partnerships and sponsored content collaborations, measuring key metrics such as reach, engagement, and ROI to assess the effectiveness of your influencer marketing efforts.
- Analyze customer feedback and sentiment expressed in social media comments, messages, and reviews to identify trends, pain points, and areas for improvement in your bakery's products, services, and customer experience.
- Monitor social media trends and industry insights to stay informed about emerging trends, technologies, and best practices in social media marketing, ensuring your bakery remains competitive and innovative in its approach.
- Use social media analytics to track the effectiveness of promotional campaigns, seasonal promotions, and special offers, measuring key metrics such as reach, engagement, and conversion rates to assess the impact on sales and revenue.
- Analyze audience segmentation data to identify different audience segments within your bakery's social media following, such as loyal customers, casual followers, and potential customers, and tailor your content and messaging to each segment's preferences and interests.
- Monitor social media crisis management metrics such as response time, resolution rate, and sentiment impact to assess your bakery's effectiveness in managing and mitigating crises or negative publicity on social media platforms.
- Utilize social media analytics to track the performance of content partnerships and collaborations with other businesses, influencers, or community organizations, measuring key metrics such as reach, engagement, and ROI to evaluate the success of these partnerships.
- Analyze social media conversion data to track the impact of social media marketing efforts on sales and revenue generation, measuring key metrics such as conversion rates, average order value, and customer lifetime value to assess the ROI of your social media marketing initiatives.
- Use social media analytics to generate regular reports and performance summaries for key stakeholders, such as bakery owners, marketing teams, and executive leadership, providing actionable insights and recommendations for optimizing social media marketing strategies and driving business results.

Managing Negative Feedback Online

- Monitor your bakery's social media channels regularly to promptly identify and address any negative feedback or complaints from customers.
- Respond to negative feedback publicly and promptly, acknowledging the customer's concerns and expressing a sincere apology for any inconvenience or dissatisfaction they may have experienced.
- Take the conversation offline by providing contact information or directing the customer to reach out via direct message or email to discuss their concerns in more detail and resolve the issue privately.
- Avoid deleting negative comments or reviews unless they violate your bakery's community guidelines or contain inappropriate content, as doing so may escalate the situation and damage your bakery's reputation.
- Maintain a professional and empathetic tone in your responses to negative feedback, demonstrating your commitment to customer satisfaction and willingness to address any issues or concerns raised.
- Address the specific concerns or issues raised by the customer in their feedback, providing transparent explanations or solutions to resolve the problem and prevent similar issues from occurring in the future.
- Offer to make amends or provide compensation to the customer, such as offering a refund, replacement product, or discount on their next purchase, as a gesture of goodwill and to restore their trust in your bakery.
- Follow up with the customer after resolving their issue to ensure they are satisfied with the outcome and to thank them for bringing their concerns to your attention, demonstrating your commitment to customer service.
- Encourage satisfied customers to share their positive experiences and feedback on social media, helping to counteract any negative feedback and showcase your bakery's commitment to customer satisfaction.
- Train your bakery staff to handle negative feedback professionally and effectively, providing them with guidelines and resources for addressing customer complaints and resolving issues in a timely manner.
- Monitor online review platforms such as Yelp, Google Reviews, and TripAdvisor for any negative reviews or feedback about your bakery, and respond promptly and professionally to address the customer's concerns.
- Use negative feedback as an opportunity for improvement by identifying any recurring issues or areas for enhancement in your bakery's products, services, or customer experience.
- Implement a proactive approach to managing negative feedback by soliciting feedback from customers through surveys, feedback forms, or comment cards, and addressing any issues or concerns raised in a timely manner.

- Consider implementing a social media listening tool to monitor mentions of your bakery's name, products, or keywords on social media platforms, allowing you to identify and address negative feedback quickly and efficiently.
- Encourage customers to reach out to your bakery directly with any concerns or feedback they may have, rather than airing their grievances publicly on social media, to provide an opportunity for resolution before issues escalate.
- Respond to negative feedback with transparency and honesty, providing factual information and avoiding defensiveness or excuses, to demonstrate your bakery's accountability and commitment to customer satisfaction.
- Empower your bakery's social media team to make decisions and take action to address negative feedback promptly, without the need for extensive approval processes, to ensure timely resolution and customer satisfaction.
- Monitor the tone and sentiment of negative feedback to gauge the severity of the issue and prioritize responses accordingly, focusing on addressing urgent or high-impact issues first.
- Use negative feedback as an opportunity to engage with customers and build relationships by demonstrating your willingness to listen to their concerns and take proactive steps to address them.
- Implement a system for tracking and documenting customer feedback and complaints, including the nature of the issue, the actions taken to resolve it, and any follow-up or feedback received from the customer.
- Communicate openly and transparently with customers about any changes or improvements implemented in response to their feedback, demonstrating your bakery's commitment to continuous improvement and customer satisfaction.
- Monitor the impact of negative feedback on your bakery's reputation and brand perception over time, using social media analytics and online reputation management tools to track sentiment trends and measure the effectiveness of your response efforts.
- Encourage customers to share their positive experiences and feedback on social media platforms, such as leaving reviews or tagging your bakery in their posts, to help offset any negative feedback and maintain a positive online reputation.
- Continuously review and refine your bakery's approach to managing negative feedback online based on feedback from customers, insights from social media analytics, and industry best practices, to ensure your bakery remains responsive, proactive, and customer-focused in addressing customer concerns and maintaining a positive online reputation.

Collaborations with Food Bloggers

- Reach out to local food bloggers who have a significant following in your area and offer to collaborate on a sponsored blog post or social media campaign featuring your bakery's products.
- Invite food bloggers to visit your bakery for a tasting or behind-the-scenes tour, allowing them to sample your offerings and create authentic content about their experience.
- Offer complimentary products or samples to food bloggers for them to feature in their content, such as custom cakes, specialty pastries, or seasonal treats, to showcase your bakery's unique offerings.
- Collaborate with food bloggers on recipe development projects, providing them with your bakery's ingredients or products to create original recipes or dishes to feature on their blog or social media channels.
- Host a blogger meet-up or tasting event at your bakery, inviting local food bloggers to network with each other and sample your bakery's products, encouraging them to share their experiences with their followers.
- Partner with food bloggers on giveaways or contests featuring your bakery's products as prizes, leveraging their audience and engagement to increase brand visibility and attract new customers.
- Collaborate with food bloggers on sponsored content campaigns, such as sponsored posts, sponsored videos, or sponsored social media shoutouts, to promote your bakery's products to their engaged audience.
- Offer exclusive discounts or promotions to food bloggers and their followers, encouraging them to visit your bakery and share their experiences with their audience in exchange for special offers.
- Provide food bloggers with branded merchandise or swag, such as branded aprons, tote bags, or mugs, to thank them for their collaboration and encourage ongoing promotion of your bakery.
- Collaborate with food bloggers on themed content series, such as holiday baking guides, seasonal recipe roundups, or product reviews, to showcase your bakery's products in a variety of contexts.
- Partner with food bloggers on sponsored events or pop-up collaborations, such as bake sales, cooking classes, or tasting events, to introduce your bakery's products to new audiences and foster community engagement.
- Collaborate with food bloggers on cross-promotional campaigns, such as guest blogging, social media takeovers, or joint giveaways, to leverage each other's audiences and increase brand exposure for both parties.
- Invite food bloggers to participate in influencer marketing campaigns or ambassador programs for your bakery, providing them with exclusive perks or benefits in exchange for ongoing promotion and support.

- Collaborate with food bloggers on sponsored content collaborations, such as recipe videos, cooking tutorials, or product reviews, to showcase your bakery's products in an engaging and visually appealing way.
- Offer food bloggers the opportunity to host a meet-and-greet event or cooking demonstration at your bakery, allowing them to connect with their audience in person and showcase your bakery's offerings.
- Collaborate with food bloggers on sponsored content collaborations, such as recipe development, cooking tutorials, or product reviews, to showcase your bakery's products in a creative and informative manner.
- Host a blogger outreach event or workshop at your bakery, providing food bloggers with insights and tips on how to create engaging content featuring your bakery's products and offerings.
- Collaborate with food bloggers on sponsored content campaigns, such as recipe development, cooking tutorials, or product reviews, to showcase your bakery's products in a visually appealing and informative manner.
- Offer food bloggers the opportunity to host a giveaway or contest featuring your bakery's products as prizes, encouraging their followers to engage with their content and visit your bakery.
- Collaborate with food bloggers on sponsored content collaborations, such as recipe videos, cooking tutorials, or product reviews, to showcase your bakery's products in an authentic and relatable way.
- Provide food bloggers with exclusive access to new product launches or menu items at your bakery, allowing them to be among the first to sample and review your offerings.
- Collaborate with food bloggers on sponsored content collaborations, such as recipe development, cooking tutorials, or product reviews, to showcase your bakery's products in a creative and engaging way.
- Offer food bloggers the opportunity to host a giveaway or contest featuring your bakery's products as prizes, encouraging their followers to engage with their content and visit your bakery.
- Collaborate with food bloggers on sponsored content campaigns, such as recipe development, cooking tutorials, or product reviews, to showcase your bakery's products in a visually appealing and informative manner.

Behind-the-Scenes Content Creation

- Give followers a sneak peek into your bakery's daily operations by sharing behind-the-scenes photos or videos of your team baking, decorating, and preparing delicious treats.
- Host live streaming sessions on social media platforms like Instagram Live or Facebook Live, allowing followers to virtually join you in the kitchen and ask questions in real-time as you demonstrate baking techniques or share recipe tips.
- Take followers on a virtual tour of your bakery, showcasing different areas such as the kitchen, storage areas, and display cases, giving them a glimpse into the inner workings of your business.
- Share stories and anecdotes about your bakery's history, traditions, and values, giving followers a deeper understanding of what sets your bakery apart and the passion behind your creations.
- Introduce followers to your bakery's talented team members, such as pastry chefs, bakers, or decorators, highlighting their skills, expertise, and contributions to your bakery's success.
- Document the process of creating a new menu item or specialty product from start to finish, sharing behind-the-scenes insights into recipe development, testing, and final presentation.
- Collaborate with local suppliers or vendors to showcase the ingredients and materials used in your bakery's creations, highlighting the quality and freshness of your ingredients.
- Share tips and tricks for home baking enthusiasts, such as ingredient substitutions, baking hacks, or decorating techniques, demonstrating your bakery's expertise and providing value to your followers.
- Host virtual baking classes or workshops on social media platforms, guiding followers through step-by-step tutorials for making your bakery's signature recipes or specialty treats at home.
- Share stories about the inspiration behind your bakery's creations, such as family recipes, cultural influences, or seasonal ingredients, giving followers insight into the creative process behind your menu.
- Highlight special events or collaborations your bakery is involved in, such as pop-up markets, food festivals, or charity fundraisers, giving followers a behind-the-scenes look at your participation and contributions.
- Showcase the care and attention to detail that goes into every aspect of your bakery's operations, from selecting the finest ingredients to handcrafting each pastry or dessert with love and precision.
- Share behind-the-scenes moments of camaraderie and teamwork among your bakery staff, showcasing the passion and dedication that drives your business and fosters a positive work culture.
- Document the process of creating custom cakes or special orders for customers, from initial consultations and design sketches to the final delivery or pickup, highlighting your bakery's personalized service and attention to detail.

- Share stories about your bakery's commitment to sustainability and environmental responsibility, such as reducing food waste, using eco-friendly packaging, or supporting local farmers and producers.
- Showcase the tools and equipment used in your bakery's kitchen, such as mixers, ovens, and piping bags, giving followers a behind-the-scenes look at the tools of the trade and how they're used to create your bakery's delicious treats.
- Share stories about the challenges and triumphs your bakery faces on a day-to-day basis, from overcoming supply chain disruptions to celebrating milestones and achievements, giving followers a glimpse into the highs and lows of running a small business.
- Highlight your bakery's involvement in community events or initiatives, such as sponsoring local sports teams, volunteering at food banks, or supporting charitable organizations, demonstrating your bakery's commitment to giving back to the community.
- Share stories about the evolution of your bakery's menu and offerings over time, from introducing new flavors and seasonal specials to retiring old favorites, giving followers a sense of the ongoing innovation and creativity that drives your business.
- Showcase the creativity and artistry of your bakery's decorators, sharing behind-the-scenes videos of them piping intricate designs, sculpting fondant decorations, or hand-painting edible masterpieces.
- Share stories about the traditions and rituals that are part of your bakery's culture, such as holiday baking traditions, birthday cake ceremonies, or special rituals for good luck and prosperity, giving followers insight into the rich history and heritage of your bakery.
- Collaborate with local artisans or craftsmen to showcase handmade items or artisanal products that complement your bakery's offerings, such as handcrafted ceramics for serving pastries or artisanal jams and preserves for pairing with bread.
- Share stories about the challenges and triumphs of owning and operating a bakery, from navigating the ups and downs of the business cycle to finding creative solutions to common industry challenges, giving followers a behind-the-scenes look at the realities of entrepreneurship.
- Invite followers to share their own behind-the-scenes moments with your bakery, such as photos of them enjoying your treats at home, baking with their families, or celebrating special occasions with your desserts, fostering a sense of community and connection among your followers.

Seasonal and Holiday Campaigns

- Plan ahead and create a content calendar that aligns with seasonal holidays and events throughout the year, ensuring your bakery's social media marketing efforts are timely and relevant to your audience.
- Tailor your social media content to reflect the changing seasons and holidays, incorporating seasonal themes, colors, and imagery into your posts to capture the attention of your followers.
- Create seasonal promotions or special offers, such as holiday-themed discounts, BOGO deals, or limited-time menu items, to drive traffic to your bakery and encourage repeat purchases from customers.
- Showcase your bakery's seasonal specialties and holiday-themed treats through visually appealing photos and videos on social media platforms like Instagram, Facebook, and Pinterest, enticing followers to visit your bakery or place an order.
- Share behind-the-scenes content of your bakery staff preparing for seasonal holidays, such as baking festive cookies, decorating cakes, or packaging gift baskets, giving followers a glimpse into the magic happening behind the scenes.
- Encourage user-generated content by inviting followers to share photos of their favorite seasonal treats from your bakery using a branded hashtag, such as #HolidayTreats or #SeasonalSpecials, and feature the best submissions on your social media profiles.
- Collaborate with local influencers or food bloggers to create sponsored content featuring your bakery's seasonal offerings, leveraging their audience and credibility to increase exposure and drive sales.
- Host seasonal events or promotions at your bakery, such as holiday-themed tastings, decorating workshops, or charity drives, and promote them on social media to attract customers and generate buzz.
- Create seasonal gift guides or product showcases on social media platforms like Instagram Stories or Facebook Collections, highlighting your bakery's top picks for holiday gifts, party favors, or hostess gifts.
- Leverage Facebook Ads or Instagram Ads to target users interested in seasonal holidays or events, such as Valentine's Day, Easter, Halloween, or Christmas, and promote your bakery's seasonal specials or promotions directly to them.
- Create themed social media contests or giveaways tied to seasonal holidays, such as a Valentine's Day dessert contest or a Halloween costume contest, to engage your audience and generate excitement around your bakery's offerings.
- Partner with local businesses or organizations to cross-promote each other's seasonal campaigns or events on social media, reaching new audiences and driving traffic to both businesses.
- Share seasonal recipes or baking tips on your bakery's social media profiles, providing value to your audience and positioning your bakery as a trusted resource for holiday baking inspiration.

- Collaborate with local hotels, restaurants, or event venues to provide catering or dessert services for their seasonal events or parties, and promote these partnerships on social media to showcase your bakery's capabilities.
- Create themed social media challenges or hashtags, such as #HolidayBakingChallenge or #SeasonalDessertShowdown, and encourage followers to participate by sharing photos or videos of their holiday baking creations.
- Host seasonal photo contests on social media platforms like Instagram or Facebook, encouraging followers to share their holiday-themed photos featuring your bakery's products for a chance to win prizes or discounts.
- Share tips and ideas for holiday entertaining on your bakery's social media profiles, such as dessert pairing suggestions, table decorating tips, or party planning hacks, to position your bakery as a go-to resource for holiday hosting inspiration.
- Offer seasonal packaging or gift wrapping options for your bakery's products, such as festive boxes, ribbons, or tags, and promote them on social media to attract customers looking for convenient and stylish holiday gifts.
- Collaborate with local influencers or micro-influencers to host seasonal events or meet-ups at your bakery, such as a holiday cookie decorating party or a gingerbread house-building workshop, and promote these events on social media to attract attendees.
- Share festive playlists or curated music recommendations on your bakery's social media profiles, setting the mood for seasonal celebrations and creating a memorable experience for your followers.
- Create themed social media polls or surveys to gather feedback from your audience about their favorite seasonal treats or holiday traditions, and use this data to inform your bakery's seasonal menu offerings and marketing strategies.
- Collaborate with local photographers or artists to create custom holiday-themed content for your bakery's social media profiles, such as seasonal photo shoots or digital illustrations, to enhance your brand's visual appeal and storytelling.
- Offer seasonal gift cards or e-gift certificates for your bakery's products, allowing customers to give the gift of delicious treats to their loved ones during the holidays, and promote these gift options on social media as convenient and versatile gift ideas.
- Share stories and anecdotes about your bakery's own holiday traditions and celebrations on social media, giving followers a personal and authentic glimpse into the festive spirit that inspires your bakery's seasonal offerings and promotions.

Leveraging Pinterest for Bakery Inspiration

- Create a Pinterest account for your bakery and optimize your profile with a compelling description, high-quality profile picture, and relevant keywords to attract followers interested in baking and dessert inspiration.
- Create boards on Pinterest dedicated to different categories of bakery inspiration, such as cake decorating ideas, cookie recipes, bread baking tips, and seasonal desserts, to organize your content and make it easy for followers to find what they're looking for.
- Pin high-quality images of your bakery's products, including cakes, pastries, cookies, bread, and other treats, to showcase your offerings and inspire followers to visit your bakery or try your recipes at home.
- Share step-by-step tutorials or recipe cards for your bakery's signature dishes or popular items, providing followers with detailed instructions and visual guidance to recreate your delicious treats in their own kitchens.
- Collaborate with food bloggers or influencers in the baking niche to create guest boards on Pinterest featuring their favorite recipes, baking tips, and product recommendations, expanding your reach and engaging with a wider audience.
- Create seasonal boards on Pinterest featuring holiday-themed desserts, seasonal ingredients, and festive baking ideas, providing followers with inspiration and ideas for celebrating special occasions throughout the year.
- Share behind-the-scenes content on Pinterest, such as photos or videos of your bakery staff preparing and decorating treats, giving followers a glimpse into the creative process behind your bakery's delicious creations.
- Pin user-generated content from your customers, such as photos of them enjoying your bakery's treats or recreating your recipes at home, to showcase the love and loyalty of your fan base and foster a sense of community on Pinterest.
- Create boards on Pinterest dedicated to baking tips and techniques, such as cake decorating tutorials, bread baking basics, or cookie decorating hacks, providing followers with valuable information and guidance to improve their baking skills.
- Curate boards on Pinterest featuring baking trends and innovations, such as new ingredients, techniques, or design styles, to keep followers informed and inspired by the latest developments in the baking world.
- Share infographics or visual guides on Pinterest featuring baking measurements, conversions, and substitutions, providing followers with helpful reference materials to use in their own baking endeavors.
- Create boards on Pinterest dedicated to specific dietary preferences or restrictions, such as gluten-free baking, vegan desserts, or low-sugar recipes, to cater to followers with diverse tastes and dietary needs.
- Pin links to your bakery's blog posts, articles, or other content on Pinterest to drive traffic to your website and increase visibility for your brand, leveraging Pinterest as a valuable traffic-driving tool for your bakery.

- Collaborate with other local businesses or organizations on Pinterest to create group boards featuring recipes, tips, and ideas for enjoying baked goods in your community, fostering partnerships and cross-promotion opportunities.
- Share boards on Pinterest featuring themed collections of your bakery's products, such as birthday cakes, wedding desserts, or baby shower treats, to showcase your bakery's expertise and offerings for special occasions.
- Create boards on Pinterest dedicated to baking inspiration from around the world, featuring recipes, ingredients, and techniques from different cultures and cuisines, to broaden your audience and introduce followers to new flavors and traditions.
- Pin links to your bakery's online ordering platform or delivery service on Pinterest to make it easy for followers to purchase your products directly from your website, streamlining the shopping experience and driving sales.
- Share boards on Pinterest featuring DIY baking projects or crafts, such as homemade gifts, edible decorations, or themed party favors, to inspire followers to get creative in the kitchen and personalize their baked goods.
- Collaborate with local event planners or wedding vendors on Pinterest to create boards featuring inspiration and ideas for weddings, birthdays, and other special events, showcasing your bakery's offerings as part of the celebration.
- Pin links to your bakery's social media profiles and newsletters on Pinterest to encourage followers to connect with your brand across multiple channels and stay updated on the latest news, promotions, and events.
- Create boards on Pinterest featuring seasonal ingredients or flavors, such as pumpkin spice, peppermint, or citrus, and share recipes and ideas for incorporating these ingredients into your baking repertoire throughout the year.
- Pin links to your bakery's press coverage, awards, or accolades on Pinterest to showcase your bakery's achievements and credibility, building trust and confidence in your brand among followers.
- Share boards on Pinterest featuring baking hacks, shortcuts, and time-saving tips, providing followers with practical advice and solutions to common challenges in the kitchen.
- Collaborate with local influencers or micro-influencers on Pinterest to co-create boards featuring their favorite baking recipes, kitchen gadgets, and pantry staples, leveraging their expertise and credibility to engage with a targeted audience of baking enthusiasts.

Utilizing Facebook Groups for Community Building

- Create a Facebook group dedicated to your bakery's community, inviting customers, fans, and local residents to join and connect with each other over their shared love of baking and desserts.
- Set clear guidelines and rules for your Facebook group to ensure a positive and welcoming environment for members, including guidelines for respectful behavior, relevant topics of discussion, and promotional content.
- Encourage members to introduce themselves and share their baking stories, favorite recipes, and photos of their creations in the group, fostering engagement and building a sense of camaraderie among members.
- Share exclusive content and behind-the-scenes updates in your Facebook group, such as sneak peeks of new menu items, special promotions, or upcoming events, to reward members for their participation and loyalty.
- Host regular Q&A sessions or live streaming events in your Facebook group, allowing members to ask questions, share tips, and interact with your bakery staff in real-time, building trust and rapport with your audience.
- Create themed discussion threads or challenges in your Facebook group, such as weekly recipe swaps, baking contests, or ingredient spotlights, to keep members engaged and encourage active participation.
- Feature member spotlight posts in your Facebook group, highlighting the contributions and accomplishments of individual members, such as their baking achievements, creative recipes, or community involvement, to celebrate their talents and build a sense of recognition and appreciation.
- Share educational content and resources in your Facebook group, such as baking tutorials, ingredient guides, or troubleshooting tips, to help members improve their baking skills and expand their knowledge.
- Encourage members to share feedback and suggestions for your bakery's products, services, and events in the group, demonstrating your commitment to listening to your customers and continuously improving your offerings based on their input.
- Collaborate with local businesses or organizations to co-host events or promotions in your Facebook group, such as pop-up markets, cooking classes, or charity fundraisers, to provide value to members and strengthen community ties.
- Use polls and surveys in your Facebook group to gather feedback from members on topics such as their favorite menu items, preferred flavors, or suggestions for future events or promotions, giving them a voice in shaping the direction of your bakery.
- Share user-generated content from group members on your bakery's social media profiles, such as photos of their visits to your bakery or testimonials about their favorite treats, to showcase the vibrant and engaged community that exists within your Facebook group.
- Foster connections and collaboration among group members by facilitating introductions, networking opportunities, and partnerships, such as recipe exchanges, ingredient swaps, or

joint baking projects, to encourage camaraderie and support within the group.
- Highlight community events and initiatives in your Facebook group, such as local food festivals, farmers markets, or charity drives, to keep members informed about opportunities to get involved and support the broader community.
- Create a sense of exclusivity and belonging in your Facebook group by offering special perks or benefits to members, such as discounts on bakery products, early access to new menu items, or invitations to VIP events, to reward their loyalty and encourage continued engagement.
- Share inspirational stories and testimonials from group members who have benefited from their participation in the community, such as connecting with like-minded bakers, discovering new recipes, or making lasting friendships, to showcase the positive impact of your Facebook group on members' lives.
- Collaborate with local influencers or micro-influencers to co-host events or promotions in your Facebook group, leveraging their influence and credibility to attract new members and engage with a wider audience.
- Use your Facebook group to promote community initiatives and causes that are important to your bakery and its customers, such as supporting local farmers, reducing food waste, or addressing food insecurity, to demonstrate your bakery's commitment to social responsibility and community involvement.
- Share updates and announcements about your bakery's operations, such as changes to opening hours, menu updates, or safety protocols, in your Facebook group to keep members informed and engaged with your business.
- Create a sense of excitement and anticipation in your Facebook group by teasing upcoming events, product launches, or special promotions, and encouraging members to stay tuned for more details and announcements.
- Use your Facebook group to crowdsource ideas and feedback from members on potential new menu items, flavor combinations, or event themes, tapping into the collective wisdom and creativity of your community to inspire innovation and experimentation.
- Organize group meet-ups or events for members to connect in person, such as bakery tours, tasting parties, or coffee mornings, to strengthen relationships and foster a sense of belonging among members.
- Partner with local organizations or charities to support community initiatives and projects through your Facebook group, such as fundraising campaigns, volunteer opportunities, or donation drives, to make a positive impact in your local area.
- Regularly engage with members in your Facebook group by responding to comments, questions, and messages in a timely and personalized manner, demonstrating your commitment to building a vibrant and supportive community around your bakery.

SOCIAL MEDIA MARKETING IDEAS

Social Media Tips for Launching New Products

- Build anticipation for your new product launch by teasing it on your bakery's social media profiles in the days or weeks leading up to the release date, sharing sneak peeks, behind-the-scenes photos, or cryptic clues to pique curiosity and generate excitement among your followers.
- Create a dedicated hashtag for your new product launch and encourage followers to use it when discussing or sharing content related to the launch on social media, allowing you to track engagement and amplify the reach of your campaign.
- Share teaser videos or countdown posts on your bakery's social media profiles to build anticipation for your new product launch, using dynamic visuals, catchy music, or suspenseful narration to captivate your audience and keep them engaged.
- Collaborate with local influencers or food bloggers to create sponsored content featuring your new product, leveraging their credibility and reach to generate buzz and excitement among their followers.
- Host a launch event or tasting party at your bakery to introduce your new product to customers and members of the community, inviting local influencers, media outlets, and loyal customers to attend and share their experiences on social media.
- Offer exclusive sneak peeks or early access to your new product for followers who sign up for your bakery's email newsletter or join a VIP mailing list, rewarding their loyalty and creating a sense of exclusivity around the launch.
- Share behind-the-scenes content on social media documenting the process of developing and testing your new product, giving followers insight into the creative process and craftsmanship that went into its creation.
- Create visually appealing product images or graphics to showcase your new product on social media platforms like Instagram, Facebook, and Pinterest, using professional photography, styling, and editing techniques to make your product stand out and entice customers.
- Host a social media giveaway or contest featuring your new product as the prize, encouraging followers to participate by sharing, liking, or commenting on your posts to increase engagement and generate excitement around the launch.
- Leverage Facebook Ads or Instagram Ads to target users who are likely to be interested in your new product, such as followers of similar brands or users who have shown interest in related keywords or topics, and promote your product directly to them.
- Create a series of teaser posts or stories on social media platforms like Instagram and Snapchat, gradually revealing more details about your new product as the launch date approaches, building anticipation and suspense among your audience.
- Partner with other local businesses or organizations to cross-promote your new product launch on social media, such as collaborating on joint events, promotions, or giveaways, to reach new audiences and expand your reach.

- Share user-generated content featuring your new product on your bakery's social media profiles, such as photos or reviews from customers who have already tried it, to showcase its popularity and appeal to potential buyers.
- Create a dedicated landing page on your bakery's website for your new product launch, featuring product photos, descriptions, testimonials, and ordering information, and share the link on your social media profiles to drive traffic and conversions.
- Collaborate with local photographers or influencers to create visually stunning content featuring your new product, such as styled photoshoots or recipe videos, to showcase its versatility and inspire customers to try it for themselves.
- Share stories and anecdotes about the inspiration behind your new product, such as family recipes, culinary traditions, or personal experiences, on your bakery's social media profiles to connect with customers on a deeper level and humanize your brand.
- Create social media ads or sponsored posts featuring testimonials or reviews from satisfied customers who have already tried your new product, using their positive feedback to build credibility and trust with potential buyers.
- Host a virtual launch event or livestream on social media platforms like Facebook Live or Instagram Live, allowing followers to join you in real-time as you unveil your new product, answer questions, and interact with viewers from around the world.
- Partner with local influencers or food bloggers to host a takeover on your bakery's social media profiles, allowing them to share their experiences with your new product and engage with your audience in a genuine and authentic way.
- Create a series of social media posts or stories featuring different ways to enjoy or use your new product, such as recipe ideas, serving suggestions, or pairing recommendations, to inspire followers and showcase its versatility.
- Share behind-the-scenes content on social media platforms like Instagram Stories or Snapchat, giving followers a sneak peek into the production process of your new product and the dedication and passion that went into creating it.
- Collaborate with local media outlets or influencers to secure press coverage or feature articles about your new product launch, leveraging their reach and credibility to increase visibility and generate buzz around the release.
- Offer special promotions or discounts for customers who purchase your new product during the launch period, such as limited-time offers, bundle deals, or exclusive perks, to incentivize sales and reward early adopters.
- Monitor social media conversations and feedback related to your new product launch, actively engaging with customers, addressing questions or concerns, and expressing gratitude for their support and enthusiasm.

500+ Brand Marketing Ideas for Bakeries

SECTIONS IN THIS CHAPTER:

1. Defining Your Bakery's Brand Identity – Page 96
2. Crafting a Memorable Bakery Logo – Page 98
3. Creating a Consistent Visual Theme – Page 100
4. Storytelling Through Your Brand – Page 102
5. Building a Strong Brand Voice – Page 104
6. Designing Engaging Packaging – Page 106
7. Effective Signage and Storefront Design – Page 108
8. The Art of Menu Design and Branding – Page 110
9. Hosting Brand-Building Events – Page 112
10. Collaborations and Co-Branding Opportunities – Page 114
11. Leveraging Local Ingredients in Branding – Page 116
12. Implementing Sustainable Practices in Brand Messaging – Page 118
13. Employee Advocacy and Uniform Branding – Page 120
14. Customer Service as a Brand Pillar – Page 122
15. Building an Online Community – Page 124
16. Influencer and Brand Ambassador Programs – Page 126
17. Brand Presence on Social Media – Page 128
18. Email Marketing with a Personal Touch – Page 130
19. Crafting Press Releases for Your Bakery – Page 132
20. Utilizing Content Marketing – Page 134
21. Managing Brand Reputation – Page 136
22. Measuring Brand Impact and Adjusting Strategies – Page 138

Defining Your Bakery's Brand Identity

- Begin by delving into the rich history of your bakery. Uncover stories of its founding, family traditions, and unique recipes that have been passed down through generations. These narratives can form the foundation of your brand identity, connecting customers to the heart and soul of your business.
- Conduct a thorough analysis of your target audience to understand their preferences, lifestyles, and values. This insight will enable you to tailor your brand identity to resonate with their needs and desires.
- Craft a compelling brand story that encapsulates the essence of your bakery. Highlight what sets you apart from competitors and the values that drive your business forward. This narrative should evoke emotions and create a memorable impression in the minds of consumers.
- Develop a distinctive visual identity that reflects the personality of your bakery. This includes designing a logo, selecting color schemes, and choosing fonts that convey your brand's character and style.
- Emphasize the quality and authenticity of your ingredients. Whether it's locally sourced produce, organic flour, or homemade preserves, showcase the freshness and integrity of your culinary offerings.
- Showcase the craftsmanship and expertise of your bakers. Highlight their dedication to perfection and the artistry behind each creation. This human element adds a personal touch to your brand identity and fosters trust with customers.
- Create an inviting ambiance in your bakery that reflects your brand's values and aesthetic. Consider elements such as decor, music, and lighting to enhance the overall customer experience.
- Incorporate storytelling into your product packaging and marketing materials. Use descriptive language and imagery to convey the heritage and passion behind your baked goods.
- Foster a sense of community by hosting events, workshops, or tasting sessions in your bakery. This allows customers to connect with your brand on a deeper level and fosters loyalty.
- Partner with local artisans, farmers, or suppliers to reinforce your commitment to sustainability and support for the community. Collaborations can also introduce new flavors and products to your bakery's offerings.
- Engage with customers on social media platforms to build relationships and cultivate brand advocates. Share behind-the-scenes glimpses, customer testimonials, and user-generated content to humanize your brand.
- Offer personalized experiences, such as custom cake designs or special-order options, to cater to individual preferences and occasions.
- Leverage nostalgia by tapping into childhood memories and comfort foods that evoke feelings of warmth and familiarity.

- Embrace innovation by experimenting with unique flavor combinations, trendy ingredients, or unconventional baking techniques. This demonstrates your bakery's creativity and willingness to push boundaries.
- Collaborate with influencers or local celebrities to amplify your brand's reach and credibility within the community.
- Support charitable causes or participate in philanthropic initiatives to showcase your bakery's commitment to social responsibility.
- Create a loyalty program to reward repeat customers and incentivize future visits. This could include discounts, exclusive offers, or members-only events.
- Invest in professional photography to showcase your baked goods in their best light. High-quality imagery enhances the visual appeal of your brand and entices customers to indulge in your offerings.
- Utilize email marketing campaigns to stay connected with customers and promote upcoming promotions, new products, or seasonal offerings.
- Develop strategic partnerships with local businesses or event organizers to expand your brand's visibility and attract new customers.
- Establish your bakery as a culinary authority by sharing recipes, baking tips, and educational content on your website or blog.
- Create a signature scent for your bakery that evokes the aroma of freshly baked goods. This sensory experience leaves a lasting impression on customers and reinforces your brand identity.
- Encourage user-generated content by hosting contests or challenges that invite customers to share their experiences with your bakery on social media.
- Solicit feedback from customers through surveys or comment cards to continuously refine and strengthen your brand identity based on their preferences and insights.

Crafting a Memorable Bakery Logo

- Begin by researching your bakery's history, values, and unique selling points to derive inspiration for your logo design. This ensures that your logo accurately represents the essence of your brand and resonates with your target audience.
- Consider incorporating elements of baking, such as rolling pins, mixing bowls, or wheat sheaves, into your logo to instantly convey the nature of your business to customers.
- Explore typography options that complement your bakery's aesthetic and personality. Whether it's classic and elegant script fonts or modern and playful sans-serifs, the right typography sets the tone for your brand identity.
- Experiment with different color palettes to evoke the desired emotions and associations. Warm tones like reds and oranges can convey a sense of comfort and indulgence, while pastel hues evoke freshness and sophistication.
- Aim for simplicity and versatility in your logo design to ensure it remains memorable and effective across various platforms and applications, from storefront signage to digital marketing materials.
- Incorporate subtle visual cues that nod to your bakery's heritage or location, such as local landmarks or cultural symbols, to establish a sense of authenticity and connection with customers.
- Pay attention to negative space and optical balance to create a harmonious and visually pleasing logo that commands attention and leaves a lasting impression.
- Conduct market research and competitor analysis to ensure your logo stands out from the crowd and avoids similarities with existing brands in the industry.
- Test different logo variations and gather feedback from stakeholders, employees, and target customers to refine your design and ensure it resonates with the intended audience.
- Explore unique design elements, such as illustrations, patterns, or textures, to add visual interest and personality to your bakery logo.
- Consider the scalability of your logo design to ensure it remains legible and recognizable whether it's displayed on a billboard or printed on a business card.
- Think about how your logo will translate across different mediums and formats, including print, digital, and merchandise, to maintain consistency and coherence in your brand identity.
- Aim for timelessness in your logo design to ensure it remains relevant and impactful for years to come, avoiding trendy elements that may quickly become outdated.
- Experiment with different logo layouts and compositions to find the most effective arrangement that balances visual appeal with brand recognition.
- Incorporate symbolism and storytelling into your logo design to create intrigue and captivate the imagination of customers, sparking curiosity about your bakery's story and offerings.
- Hire a professional graphic designer or design agency with experience in branding and logo design to bring your vision to life and ensure the highest quality outcome.

- Seek inspiration from a variety of sources, including nature, art, and architecture, to infuse creativity and originality into your bakery logo.
- Test your logo design across various backgrounds and color combinations to ensure it remains legible and impactful in different contexts.
- Explore different logo formats, such as wordmarks, lettermarks, or combination marks, to find the most suitable option that aligns with your bakery's brand identity and objectives.
- Consider incorporating hidden meanings or Easter eggs into your logo design that add layers of depth and intrigue for observant customers to discover over time.
- Collaborate with stakeholders, employees, and customers throughout the design process to foster a sense of ownership and alignment with your bakery's brand identity.
- Conduct focus groups or surveys to gather feedback on your logo design from target customers and use this insight to make informed decisions and revisions.
- Ensure your logo design is legally protected by trademarking it to prevent unauthorized use or infringement by competitors.
- Launch your bakery logo with a cohesive branding strategy that integrates it across all touchpoints, from packaging and signage to online presence and advertising campaigns, to maximize its impact and recognition.

Creating a Consistent Visual Theme

- Start by defining the key visual elements that will form the foundation of your bakery's brand identity, including color palette, typography, imagery style, and graphic motifs.
- Choose a color palette that reflects the personality and values of your bakery, whether it's warm and inviting earth tones, fresh and vibrant pastels, or sophisticated and modern neutrals.
- Select typography that complements your bakery's aesthetic and conveys the desired tone, whether it's classic and elegant serif fonts, playful and whimsical script fonts, or clean and modern sans-serifs.
- Develop a cohesive imagery style that aligns with your brand's visual identity, whether it's bright and colorful photography, minimalist and monochromatic images, or whimsical illustrations.
- Create graphic motifs or patterns that can be used consistently across various branding materials, such as packaging, signage, and marketing collateral, to reinforce your bakery's visual theme and create a cohesive look.
- Establish guidelines for the use of your visual elements, including logo placement, sizing, spacing, and usage on different backgrounds, to ensure consistency and coherence in your branding materials.
- Consider the sensory experience of visiting your bakery and how it can be translated into your visual theme, whether it's through the use of texture, pattern, or imagery that evokes the aroma and taste of your baked goods.
- Incorporate elements of your bakery's heritage, location, or specialty offerings into your visual theme to create a unique and memorable brand identity that resonates with customers.
- Utilize photography to showcase your baked goods in their best light, capturing their texture, color, and mouthwatering appeal to entice customers and evoke cravings.
- Experiment with different compositions, angles, and lighting techniques to create visually stunning images that convey the quality and craftsmanship of your baked goods.
- Invest in professional photography equipment or hire a professional photographer to ensure high-quality images that meet the standards of your bakery's brand identity.
- Develop a consistent aesthetic for your social media presence, including Instagram, Facebook, and Pinterest, by applying your visual theme to profile images, cover photos, and post layouts.
- Create branded templates for social media posts, stories, and promotions that feature your bakery's logo, colors, typography, and imagery style to maintain consistency and recognition across platforms.
- Engage with your audience on social media by sharing behind-the-scenes glimpses, customer testimonials, and user-generated content that aligns with your bakery's visual theme and brand identity.

- Use your visual theme to enhance the packaging of your baked goods, whether it's through custom labels, tags, or boxes that feature your logo, colors, typography, and graphic motifs.
- Consider eco-friendly packaging options that align with your bakery's values and sustainability efforts, such as biodegradable materials, recyclable packaging, or reusable containers.
- Extend your visual theme to your bakery's physical space, including interior decor, signage, menus, and displays, to create a cohesive and immersive brand experience for customers.
- Incorporate elements of texture, color, and branding into your bakery's interior design, such as custom wallpaper, wall decals, or branded merchandise displays, to reinforce your visual theme.
- Create signage that reflects your bakery's visual theme and brand identity, whether it's through hand-painted murals, neon signs, or dimensional lettering that showcases your logo and typography.
- Implement digital signage solutions, such as menu boards or promotional displays, that feature your bakery's branding elements and visual theme to attract attention and drive sales.
- Use your visual theme to design marketing materials, such as flyers, posters, brochures, and business cards, that effectively communicate your bakery's offerings, promotions, and brand message.
- Ensure consistency in your branding materials by using templates, style guides, and design systems that outline the proper usage of your visual elements across different channels and mediums.
- Train your staff on your bakery's visual theme and brand identity to ensure they understand the importance of consistency in maintaining a cohesive and professional image for your business.
- Regularly review and update your visual theme to keep it fresh, relevant, and aligned with evolving trends, customer preferences, and business goals, while still maintaining the core elements that define your bakery's brand identity.

Storytelling Through Your Brand

- Begin by uncovering the unique story behind your bakery, whether it's a family tradition, a passion for baking, or a journey of culinary discovery. This narrative will serve as the foundation for your brand's storytelling efforts.
- Share the personal anecdotes and experiences that inspired the creation of your bakery, from the first batch of cookies baked in your grandmother's kitchen to the moment you decided to pursue your dream of opening a bakery.
- Highlight the craftsmanship and dedication that goes into each baked good, showcasing the skill and expertise of your bakers and the attention to detail that sets your bakery apart.
- Celebrate the local community and culture that influences your bakery's offerings, whether it's sourcing ingredients from nearby farms and artisans or drawing inspiration from regional culinary traditions.
- Introduce the people behind your bakery, from the founder and head baker to the friendly staff members who greet customers with a smile and share their passion for baking.
- Use storytelling to convey the values and principles that guide your bakery's operations, whether it's a commitment to quality ingredients, sustainable practices, or exceptional customer service.
- Share behind-the-scenes glimpses of your bakery's daily operations, from early morning dough prep to the bustling activity of the kitchen during peak hours.
- Highlight the seasonal flavors and ingredients that inspire your bakery's menu, from fresh strawberries in the spring to pumpkin spice in the fall, creating anticipation and excitement among customers.
- Invite customers to be part of your bakery's story by sharing their own experiences, memories, and favorite treats on social media or through testimonials and reviews.
- Incorporate storytelling into your marketing materials, including website content, social media posts, and promotional campaigns, to create an emotional connection with customers and build brand loyalty.
- Create themed events or promotions that tie into your bakery's story, whether it's a heritage baking workshop, a holiday cookie decorating contest, or a fundraiser for a local charity.
- Collaborate with other businesses or organizations in your community to co-create storytelling initiatives, such as a food tour highlighting the culinary heritage of your city or a cookbook featuring recipes from local chefs and bakers.
- Host storytelling sessions or workshops in your bakery, where customers can learn about the history of baking, discover new recipes, or share their own baking tips and traditions.
- Incorporate storytelling into your product packaging and branding materials, using descriptive language, imagery, and design elements to evoke the emotions and memories associated with your baked goods.
- Create a blog or newsletter where you can share longer-form stories, recipes, and interviews with customers, employees, and suppliers, allowing readers to delve deeper into your bakery's narrative.

- Capture the essence of your bakery's story through visual storytelling, whether it's through photography, videography, or illustration, that brings to life the sights, sounds, and aromas of your bakery.
- Organize storytelling contests or challenges on social media, where customers can share their own baking stories, photos, and recipes for a chance to win prizes or recognition.
- Partner with local media outlets or influencers to amplify your bakery's story and reach a wider audience through feature articles, interviews, or guest appearances.
- Create branded merchandise that allows customers to take a piece of your bakery's story home with them, whether it's a cookbook filled with signature recipes, a tote bag featuring your logo, or a coffee mug adorned with illustrations of your baked goods.
- Use storytelling to differentiate your bakery from competitors, emphasizing the unique aspects of your story, menu, and customer experience that set you apart in the crowded marketplace.
- Incorporate storytelling into your customer interactions, whether it's through friendly conversations at the counter, handwritten notes on orders, or personalized recommendations based on each customer's preferences and tastes.
- Leverage storytelling to create emotional connections with customers, tapping into universal themes of nostalgia, comfort, and celebration that resonate across cultures and generations.
- Seek out opportunities to share your bakery's story beyond the confines of your physical location, whether it's through participation in community events, collaboration with other businesses, or outreach to media outlets and influencers.
- Continuously evolve and adapt your bakery's storytelling efforts to keep them fresh, engaging, and relevant to your audience, while staying true to the core values and principles that define your brand.

Building a Strong Brand Voice

- Define your bakery's unique personality and tone of voice, whether it's friendly and approachable, sophisticated and elegant, or quirky and playful. This sets the foundation for your brand's communication style and helps differentiate your bakery in the marketplace.
- Consider the preferences and characteristics of your target audience when developing your brand voice, ensuring it resonates with their interests, values, and communication preferences.
- Infuse your brand voice with authenticity and sincerity, reflecting the genuine passion and enthusiasm that drives your bakery's operations and customer interactions.
- Incorporate elements of storytelling into your brand voice, sharing anecdotes, traditions, and experiences that convey the heritage and personality of your bakery.
- Use language that reflects the sensory experience of visiting your bakery, evoking the aroma, taste, and texture of your baked goods to create a mouthwatering appeal for customers.
- Develop a set of brand guidelines or style rules that outline the key characteristics and parameters of your bakery's brand voice, including vocabulary, tone, grammar, and punctuation usage.
- Consistently apply your brand voice across all communication channels and touchpoints, including website content, social media posts, marketing materials, and customer interactions, to maintain coherence and recognition.
- Tailor your brand voice to suit the specific context and platform of each communication channel, adapting your tone and messaging to align with the expectations and norms of each audience.
- Humanize your brand voice by engaging in authentic conversations with customers, responding to comments, messages, and reviews in a timely and personalized manner.
- Inject humor and personality into your brand voice, using wit, puns, and lighthearted language to entertain and engage customers while staying true to your bakery's identity.
- Showcase your expertise and passion for baking through informative and educational content that shares tips, recipes, and insights with your audience, positioning your bakery as a trusted authority in the industry.
- Foster a sense of community and belonging through inclusive and welcoming language that invites customers to be part of your bakery's story and journey.
- Incorporate seasonal themes and timely references into your brand voice, keeping your messaging fresh, relevant, and aligned with current events, holidays, and trends.
- Collaborate with influencers or brand ambassadors who embody your bakery's brand voice and values, amplifying your message and reach through their authentic endorsement and advocacy.
- Create branded hashtags and user-generated content campaigns that encourage customers to share their experiences, photos, and stories using your bakery's brand voice and messaging.

- Showcase customer testimonials and success stories that illustrate the impact and value of your bakery's products and services, lending credibility and authenticity to your brand voice.
- Experiment with different formats and styles of content, including blog posts, videos, podcasts, and live streams, to diversify your brand voice and appeal to a wider audience.
- Incorporate emotive language and storytelling techniques into your marketing campaigns and promotions, tapping into the emotions and aspirations of your audience to create resonance and connection.
- Use your brand voice to convey your bakery's values and commitments to sustainability, community engagement, and social responsibility, inspiring customers to support your mission and initiatives.
- Monitor and analyze customer feedback, engagement metrics, and sentiment analysis to evaluate the effectiveness of your brand voice and make informed adjustments and refinements as needed.
- Stay true to your brand's core identity and values while remaining adaptable and responsive to evolving trends, customer preferences, and market dynamics in order to maintain relevance and resonance.
- Train your staff on your bakery's brand voice and communication guidelines to ensure consistency and coherence in customer interactions, both online and offline.
- Seek feedback and input from customers, employees, and stakeholders on your bakery's brand voice, fostering a culture of collaboration and continuous improvement.
- Continuously evolve and refine your bakery's brand voice over time, staying attuned to changes in the competitive landscape, emerging trends, and shifting consumer preferences to maintain a strong and relevant presence in the market.

BRAND MARKETING IDEAS

Designing Engaging Packaging

- Begin by understanding the role packaging plays in your bakery's brand identity and customer experience, recognizing that it serves as a tangible representation of your products and brand values.
- Consider the practical aspects of packaging, such as protecting your baked goods during transport and storage, while also focusing on its aesthetic appeal and ability to engage customers.
- Incorporate elements of your bakery's visual identity, including logo, colors, typography, and graphic motifs, into your packaging design to create a cohesive and recognizable brand image.
- Choose packaging materials that align with your bakery's values and sustainability efforts, such as recyclable or compostable materials, to demonstrate your commitment to environmental responsibility.
- Experiment with different shapes, sizes, and formats of packaging to suit the specific needs and preferences of your bakery's products, whether it's individual portions, gift boxes, or bulk packaging options.
- Personalize your packaging with custom labels, tags, or stickers that feature your bakery's branding elements and messaging, creating a memorable and distinctive impression for customers.
- Use descriptive language and imagery on your packaging to highlight the unique qualities and flavors of your baked goods, enticing customers and sparking their curiosity.
- Incorporate storytelling into your packaging design, sharing anecdotes, recipes, or testimonials that convey the heritage and personality of your bakery and create an emotional connection with customers.
- Create themed packaging designs for seasonal holidays, special occasions, or limited-edition product releases that capture the spirit and excitement of each event and encourage impulse purchases.
- Design packaging that appeals to all the senses, from the visual appeal of vibrant colors and appetizing imagery to the tactile experience of textured materials and embossed finishes.
- Consider the convenience and functionality of your packaging, including features such as resealable closures, easy-open tabs, or ergonomic handles, to enhance the user experience for customers.
- Collaborate with local artists, illustrators, or designers to create custom artwork or patterns for your packaging that reflect the unique culture and character of your bakery's community.
- Offer customizable packaging options that allow customers to personalize their orders with special messages, custom designs, or branded ribbons, adding a personal touch to their purchase.
- Use packaging as a marketing tool by incorporating QR codes, NFC tags, or scannable links that direct customers to your website, social media profiles, or promotional offers.

- Create interactive packaging designs that engage customers and encourage them to interact with your brand, whether it's through games, puzzles, or hidden surprises.
- Incorporate sustainability messaging and educational content on your packaging to inform customers about your bakery's environmental initiatives and encourage eco-friendly behaviors.
- Design packaging that tells a story about the origins and journey of your ingredients, from farm to table, highlighting the quality, freshness, and traceability of your baked goods.
- Offer reusable or collectible packaging options that incentivize customers to return to your bakery for refills or additional purchases, creating a sense of loyalty and repeat business.
- Implement seasonal packaging refreshes or limited-edition collaborations with local artists, designers, or brands to keep your packaging designs fresh, relevant, and exciting for customers.
- Conduct market research and gather feedback from customers on your packaging designs to identify areas for improvement and ensure they resonate with your target audience.
- Utilize social media and digital platforms to showcase your packaging designs and engage with customers, inviting them to share photos, feedback, and experiences using branded hashtags or user-generated content campaigns.
- Partner with complementary businesses or events to distribute your packaged goods as promotional giveaways, gifts, or souvenirs, expanding your brand's reach and visibility.
- Consider the entire customer journey when designing your packaging, from the moment it catches their eye on the shelf to the unboxing experience at home, ensuring each touchpoint reinforces your bakery's brand identity and values.
- Continuously innovate and iterate on your packaging designs, staying attuned to evolving trends, customer preferences, and industry best practices to maintain a competitive edge and keep customers excited about your bakery's products.

Effective Signage and Storefront Design

- Begin by assessing your bakery's physical location and surroundings to identify opportunities for effective signage and storefront design that maximize visibility, accessibility, and curb appeal.
- Invest in high-quality signage that prominently displays your bakery's name, logo, and branding elements, ensuring they are easily recognizable and legible from a distance.
- Consider the architectural style and layout of your building when designing your storefront signage, opting for designs that complement and enhance its aesthetic appeal while standing out from neighboring businesses.
- Use signage to communicate key information to passersby, such as operating hours, special promotions, or featured products, to attract attention and encourage foot traffic into your bakery.
- Incorporate eye-catching visuals, such as mouthwatering images of your baked goods or creative illustrations that reflect your bakery's brand personality, to capture the interest and curiosity of potential customers.
- Implement signage solutions that are durable and weather-resistant, capable of withstanding outdoor elements such as rain, wind, and sunlight to maintain their visibility and effectiveness over time.
- Utilize lighting techniques to illuminate your signage and storefront design, enhancing visibility during evening hours and creating a welcoming ambiance that draws customers in.
- Design cohesive storefront displays that showcase your bakery's products, specials, and seasonal offerings, using creative arrangements, props, and signage to capture attention and entice customers.
- Incorporate interactive elements into your storefront design, such as digital displays, touch screens, or interactive kiosks, that engage customers and provide valuable information about your bakery's menu, history, or promotions.
- Create branded merchandise or promotional items that double as storefront decor, such as branded umbrellas, chalkboard signs, or window decals, to reinforce your bakery's brand identity and messaging.
- Optimize your storefront layout and design to facilitate smooth traffic flow and easy navigation for customers, ensuring clear pathways and unobstructed views of your bakery's interior and products.
- Design signage and storefront displays that cater to the preferences and needs of your target audience, whether it's families with children, health-conscious consumers, or foodies seeking artisanal treats.
- Incorporate elements of seasonal decor into your storefront design, such as themed window displays, festive banners, or holiday wreaths, to create excitement and anticipation among customers.

- Collaborate with local artists, designers, or craftsmen to create custom signage and storefront installations that reflect the unique character and culture of your bakery's community.
- Implement sustainability-focused signage and messaging to communicate your bakery's commitment to eco-friendly practices, such as using compostable packaging, reducing food waste, or supporting local farmers.
- Leverage signage to highlight your bakery's unique selling points and competitive advantages, whether it's specialty ingredients, artisanal techniques, or award-winning recipes, to differentiate your brand in the market.
- Incorporate social media integration into your signage and storefront design, such as QR codes or hashtags, that encourage customers to engage with your bakery online and share their experiences with their networks.
- Experiment with dynamic signage solutions, such as LED displays, digital billboards, or projection mapping, that allow for real-time updates and interactive content to capture attention and drive foot traffic.
- Conduct regular maintenance and upkeep of your signage and storefront design to ensure they remain in pristine condition, repairing any damage, updating outdated information, and refreshing displays as needed.
- Consider the customer journey from the street to the entrance of your bakery when designing your storefront signage and displays, strategically guiding and enticing customers along the way.
- Offer branded merchandise or promotional giveaways at your storefront to incentivize visits and purchases, such as branded tote bags, coffee mugs, or pastry samples, that serve as souvenirs and reminders of your bakery.
- Engage with the local community through signage and storefront design initiatives, such as hosting sidewalk sales, pop-up events, or outdoor seating areas, that foster a sense of belonging and connection.
- Monitor the effectiveness of your signage and storefront design through customer feedback, foot traffic analysis, and sales data, making adjustments and refinements as needed to optimize performance and results.
- Continuously innovate and refresh your signage and storefront design to stay relevant, memorable, and engaging in the eyes of customers, keeping them excited and intrigued about your bakery's offerings and experiences.

The Art of Menu Design and Branding

- Begin by understanding the role of your bakery's menu as a key touchpoint for communicating your brand identity, showcasing your offerings, and influencing customer perceptions and decisions.
- Consider the layout and organization of your menu design, ensuring it is intuitive, visually appealing, and easy to navigate for customers of all ages and preferences.
- Incorporate elements of your bakery's visual identity, including logo, colors, typography, and imagery, into your menu design to create a cohesive and recognizable brand image.
- Use descriptive language and enticing imagery to showcase your bakery's products and specialties, capturing the attention and appetite of customers and sparking their curiosity.
- Highlight the unique qualities and flavors of your baked goods, whether it's through creative names, mouthwatering descriptions, or tempting visuals that convey their freshness, quality, and indulgence.
- Create a consistent theme or narrative for your menu design that aligns with your bakery's brand personality and values, whether it's whimsical and playful, elegant and refined, or rustic and homely.
- Tailor your menu design to suit the preferences and expectations of your target audience, whether it's families seeking comfort food classics, health-conscious consumers looking for gluten-free or vegan options, or foodies craving artisanal delights.
- Incorporate storytelling into your menu design, sharing anecdotes, recipes, or insights that convey the heritage, craftsmanship, and passion behind your bakery's offerings and create an emotional connection with customers.
- Use visual hierarchy and formatting techniques to guide customers' attention to key menu items, specials, or promotions, ensuring they stand out and capture interest without overwhelming or distracting from the overall experience.
- Implement seasonal or thematic menu updates that reflect changes in ingredients, flavors, or holidays, creating excitement and anticipation among customers and encouraging repeat visits.
- Offer customization options or build-your-own menus that empower customers to personalize their orders according to their preferences, dietary restrictions, or special occasions, enhancing their sense of ownership and satisfaction.
- Incorporate pricing strategies and menu layout techniques to maximize profitability and encourage upselling or cross-selling of complementary items, such as beverage pairings or add-on toppings.
- Showcase your bakery's commitment to quality and craftsmanship through menu design elements that convey freshness, authenticity, and attention to detail, such as hand-drawn illustrations, artisanal fonts, or vintage-inspired accents.
- Highlight customer favorites, bestsellers, or signature dishes on your menu to create social proof and guide customers' decision-making process, reassuring them of the popularity and satisfaction of your offerings.

- Use menu design as a branding opportunity to communicate your bakery's values, sustainability efforts, or community involvement initiatives, fostering goodwill and loyalty among customers who share similar beliefs.
- Incorporate interactive elements into your menu design, such as QR codes, augmented reality features, or digital ordering platforms, that engage customers and enhance their overall dining experience.
- Collaborate with local artists, illustrators, or designers to create custom artwork or graphics for your menu design that reflect the unique character and culture of your bakery's community.
- Offer a variety of menu formats and sizes to accommodate different preferences and contexts, whether it's a concise one-page menu for quick service or a comprehensive booklet for leisurely browsing and exploration.
- Use menu design to tell a story about your bakery's sourcing practices, ingredient origins, or culinary inspirations, educating and inspiring customers while enhancing their appreciation for your offerings.
- Incorporate sustainability messaging and eco-friendly practices into your menu design, such as using recycled paper, vegetable-based inks, or digital menus to minimize environmental impact and align with customer values.
- Leverage menu design as a marketing tool to promote special events, seasonal promotions, or loyalty programs, encouraging repeat visits and engagement from customers.
- Conduct usability testing and gather feedback from customers on your menu design to identify areas for improvement and ensure it meets their needs, preferences, and expectations.
- Train your staff on your menu offerings, descriptions, and branding messages to ensure they can effectively communicate and upsell to customers, enhancing the overall customer experience and satisfaction.
- Continuously monitor and evaluate the performance of your menu design through sales data, customer feedback, and competitive analysis, making adjustments and refinements as needed to optimize results and stay ahead of the competition.

BRAND MARKETING IDEAS

Hosting Brand-Building Events

- Start by identifying the goals and objectives of your brand-building events, whether it's increasing brand awareness, driving foot traffic, promoting new products, or fostering community engagement.
- Consider the preferences and interests of your target audience when planning event concepts and activities, ensuring they align with their tastes, lifestyles, and values to maximize attendance and participation.
- Host themed events that reflect the unique personality and offerings of your bakery, whether it's a cupcake decorating workshop, a bread baking class, or a pastry tasting extravaganza, to create memorable and immersive experiences for attendees.
- Collaborate with complementary businesses, organizations, or influencers to co-host events that expand your reach and appeal to new audiences, leveraging their networks and expertise to enhance the event's success and impact.
- Utilize your bakery's physical space for hosting events, whether it's a cozy cafe setting, a spacious kitchen area, or an outdoor patio, that provides a welcoming and comfortable environment for attendees to gather and interact.
- Offer exclusive perks or incentives to event attendees, such as discounts on future purchases, complimentary samples, or branded merchandise, to reward their participation and encourage ongoing engagement with your bakery.
- Incorporate interactive elements into your events, such as live demonstrations, hands-on activities, or product tastings, that engage attendees and allow them to experience your bakery's offerings firsthand.
- Create social media-worthy moments and photo opportunities at your events, whether it's a stunning dessert display, a selfie station with branded props, or a backdrop featuring your bakery's logo and hashtag, that encourage attendees to share their experiences online and amplify your brand's reach.
- Provide educational content or expert insights at your events, such as cooking demonstrations, ingredient sourcing talks, or nutrition workshops, that showcase your bakery's expertise and commitment to quality and craftsmanship.
- Host community-focused events that give back to local charities, schools, or nonprofits, whether it's a bake sale fundraiser, a donation drive, or a volunteer day, that demonstrate your bakery's commitment to social responsibility and community engagement.
- Invite local media outlets, bloggers, and influencers to attend and cover your events, whether it's through event previews, live coverage on social media, or post-event reviews and recaps, that generate buzz and exposure for your bakery.
- Incorporate elements of surprise and excitement into your events, such as raffles, giveaways, or special guest appearances, that keep attendees engaged and eager to participate until the very end.
- Create a sense of exclusivity and anticipation around your events by offering limited ticket quantities, VIP packages, or early access for loyal customers, creating a sense of urgency

and desirability among attendees.
- Leverage technology to enhance the event experience, whether it's through event registration and ticketing platforms, live streaming or virtual attendance options, or interactive event apps that facilitate networking and engagement among attendees.
- Partner with local vendors, suppliers, or sponsors to provide additional amenities or services at your events, such as refreshments, entertainment, or product demonstrations, that enhance the overall attendee experience and add value to your brand.
- Host recurring event series or themed nights at your bakery, whether it's a weekly open mic night, a monthly pastry pop-up, or a seasonal holiday celebration, that create a sense of anticipation and loyalty among attendees.
- Offer personalized experiences or customization options at your events, such as custom cake decorating, personalized cookie orders, or bespoke tasting menus, that cater to individual preferences and create memorable moments for attendees.
- Collect feedback and insights from event attendees through surveys, comment cards, or social media polls, that inform future event planning and help refine your approach to hosting brand-building events.
- Partner with local schools, community centers, or youth organizations to host educational workshops or youth-focused events, such as baking classes, career days, or summer camps, that inspire and empower the next generation of bakers and food enthusiasts.
- Leverage holidays, seasons, or cultural celebrations as opportunities to host themed events and promotions at your bakery, whether it's a Valentine's Day dessert tasting, a summer picnic social, or a Diwali sweets showcase, that resonate with your target audience and create memorable experiences.
- Offer behind-the-scenes tours or kitchen experiences at your bakery as part of your event programming, giving attendees a glimpse into the inner workings of your bakery and the craftsmanship that goes into your products.
- Host networking events or industry mixers at your bakery that bring together local businesses, entrepreneurs, and professionals, creating opportunities for collaboration, partnership, and community-building within your industry.
- Collaborate with local artists, musicians, or performers to provide entertainment or live performances at your events, whether it's a live music showcase, an art exhibit, or a theatrical performance, that enhance the ambiance and atmosphere for attendees.
- Continuously evaluate the success and impact of your brand-building events through metrics such as attendance, engagement, and sales data, that inform future event planning and help refine your approach to hosting memorable and effective events.

BRAND MARKETING IDEAS

Collaborations and Co-Branding Opportunities

- Partner with a local coffee shop to create a unique coffee blend exclusively available at your bakery. This collaboration can attract coffee lovers to your bakery and introduce your pastries to a new audience.
- Collaborate with a nearby florist to offer special packages combining freshly baked goods with beautiful floral arrangements, perfect for special occasions like birthdays or anniversaries.
- Join forces with a local brewery to host beer and pastry pairing events, showcasing how your bakery treats complement different types of beer.
- Team up with a gourmet ice cream shop to create decadent dessert sandwiches, featuring your bakery's signature cookies paired with artisanal ice cream flavors.
- Partner with a nearby winery to host wine tasting events paired with dessert samplings, highlighting how your pastries complement different wines.
- Collaborate with a popular food truck to offer joint promotions where customers can purchase your bakery items along with the food truck's specialties.
- Create limited edition co-branded merchandise in collaboration with a local artist, such as branded tote bags or mugs featuring both your bakery's logo and the artist's designs.
- Team up with a yoga studio to offer wellness-themed pastry workshops, where participants can learn about mindful eating while indulging in your bakery's treats.
- Partner with a local cheese shop to create savory pastry options featuring high-quality cheeses, appealing to customers looking for unique flavor combinations.
- Collaborate with a fitness studio to offer post-workout snack packs, featuring your bakery's healthier options tailored to active lifestyles.
- Join forces with a nearby bed and breakfast to offer exclusive breakfast packages, showcasing your bakery's pastries as part of the morning spread for guests.
- Team up with a popular food blogger or influencer to co-create a series of recipe videos featuring your bakery's products, reaching a wider online audience.
- Partner with a culinary school to offer baking classes taught by your bakery's chefs, providing an interactive way for customers to learn new skills while promoting your brand.
- Collaborate with a local charity or nonprofit organization to host fundraising events at your bakery, showcasing your commitment to giving back to the community.
- Join forces with a children's bookstore to host themed storytelling events paired with special treats designed to appeal to young readers and their families.
- Team up with a local farm to create seasonal pastry specials featuring fresh fruits or vegetables sourced directly from the farm, highlighting your bakery's commitment to using local ingredients.
- Partner with a popular food delivery service to offer exclusive discounts or promotions on your bakery items for online orders, reaching customers who prefer the convenience of delivery.

- Collaborate with a nearby hotel to offer customized dessert platters for their room service menu, providing guests with a taste of your bakery's offerings during their stay.
- Join forces with a cooking school to offer joint baking workshops where participants can learn advanced techniques while using your bakery's ingredients.
- Partner with a nearby pet store to create dog-friendly pastry options, allowing customers to treat their furry companions while shopping for themselves.
- Collaborate with a local brewery or distillery to create pastry-infused alcoholic beverages, such as beer-flavored cupcakes or whiskey-infused brownies, adding a unique twist to your bakery's offerings.
- Team up with a popular food podcast to sponsor episodes featuring interviews with your bakery's chefs or behind-the-scenes glimpses into your baking process, reaching a dedicated audience of food enthusiasts.
- Partner with a nearby theater to offer themed pastry packages for patrons attending specific shows or performances, creating a memorable dining experience to complement their entertainment.
- Collaborate with a lifestyle magazine to feature your bakery's products in editorial spreads or recipe columns, increasing brand visibility among readers interested in food and culinary trends.

Leveraging Local Ingredients in Branding

- Highlight the use of locally sourced ingredients in your bakery's branding materials, such as website content, social media posts, and in-store signage, to emphasize your commitment to supporting local farmers and producers.
- Partner with nearby farms or farmer's markets to feature seasonal produce prominently in your bakery's menu offerings, showcasing the freshness and quality of local ingredients.
- Create special limited-time menu items that spotlight a particular local ingredient, such as a blueberry lemon scone made with locally grown blueberries, to generate excitement and interest among customers.
- Host tasting events or workshops where customers can sample and learn about the local ingredients used in your bakery's products, providing educational opportunities while reinforcing your brand's connection to the community.
- Collaborate with local artisans or food producers to create exclusive ingredient blends or toppings for your bakery's products, offering unique flavor combinations that set your brand apart.
- Feature profiles or interviews with the farmers and producers behind your bakery's local ingredients on your website or social media channels, helping customers connect with the people and stories behind their food.
- Offer behind-the-scenes tours or field trips to local farms or suppliers for customers interested in learning more about where your bakery's ingredients come from, strengthening transparency and trust in your brand.
- Incorporate storytelling into your marketing efforts by sharing anecdotes or anecdotes about the origins of your bakery's local ingredients, engaging customers on an emotional level and deepening their loyalty to your brand.
- Host farm-to-table dinners or pop-up events in collaboration with local restaurants or chefs, showcasing how your bakery's products can be incorporated into gourmet dining experiences using locally sourced ingredients.
- Create partnerships with local food cooperatives or community-supported agriculture (CSA) programs to offer discounts or promotions to their members, expanding your reach within the local food community.
- Sponsor or participate in community events such as farmers' markets, food festivals, or agricultural fairs to raise awareness of your bakery's commitment to using local ingredients and connect with potential customers face-to-face.
- Develop relationships with local food bloggers, influencers, or media outlets to generate buzz and coverage around your bakery's use of local ingredients, leveraging their platforms to reach a wider audience.
- Incorporate educational elements into your bakery's marketing materials, such as blog posts, recipe videos, or workshops, to teach customers about the nutritional benefits and sustainability of locally sourced ingredients.

- Collaborate with local breweries, wineries, or distilleries to create specialty baked goods infused with their products, highlighting the versatility and creativity of using local ingredients in your bakery's offerings.
- Participate in farm-to-school programs or initiatives that promote healthy eating and local food sourcing in schools, demonstrating your bakery's commitment to supporting the community and fostering positive relationships with future customers.
- Engage with local food advocacy groups or initiatives focused on sustainability, food justice, or supporting small-scale producers to align your bakery's branding with broader social and environmental values shared by your target audience.
- Create branded merchandise featuring images or illustrations of local farms, landmarks, or landscapes to further emphasize your bakery's connection to the community and celebrate the beauty of the region.
- Offer customizable options or build-your-own products that allow customers to choose their preferred local ingredients, empowering them to create personalized experiences while showcasing the diversity of local flavors available.
- Partner with local schools or community organizations to develop educational programs or workshops focused on topics such as gardening, cooking, or food preservation, reinforcing your bakery's role as a resource for culinary education and empowerment.
- Incorporate interactive elements into your bakery's website or mobile app, such as interactive maps or virtual tours highlighting the locations where your local ingredients are sourced, to provide customers with a deeper understanding of your supply chain and production process.
- Collaborate with local artists, designers, or photographers to create visually stunning marketing materials that showcase the beauty and diversity of the local ingredients used in your bakery's products, capturing the attention and imagination of your audience.
- Highlight the environmental benefits of using local ingredients in your bakery's branding, such as reduced carbon emissions from transportation and support for sustainable farming practices, to appeal to environmentally conscious consumers and differentiate your brand from competitors.
- Partner with local chefs or culinary experts to develop recipes or cooking demonstrations featuring your bakery's products and locally sourced ingredients, providing customers with inspiration and ideas for incorporating local flavors into their own cooking and baking endeavors.
- Engage with your community through philanthropic initiatives or donations that support local food banks, agricultural education programs, or other organizations working to address food insecurity and promote access to healthy, locally sourced food options for all residents.

Implementing Sustainable Practices in Brand Messaging

- Incorporate messaging about your bakery's commitment to sustainability into your brand's mission statement, website, and social media profiles to communicate your values to customers from the outset.
- Highlight specific sustainable practices implemented in your bakery, such as reducing food waste, conserving energy, or using eco-friendly packaging, in marketing materials such as flyers, posters, or digital ads.
- Create a dedicated section on your bakery's website or blog to educate customers about the importance of sustainability in the food industry and share tips for reducing environmental impact in their own lives.
- Develop partnerships with suppliers and vendors who share your commitment to sustainability, and feature these partnerships prominently in your brand messaging to demonstrate your dedication to supporting ethical practices throughout your supply chain.
- Offer discounts or incentives for customers who bring their own reusable containers or bags when purchasing bakery items, encouraging sustainable consumer behavior while reinforcing your brand's eco-friendly values.
- Host workshops or events focused on sustainable living or eco-friendly baking practices, inviting customers to learn new skills while promoting your bakery as a hub for sustainability education and advocacy.
- Participate in local environmental initiatives or clean-up efforts, and document your involvement on social media platforms to showcase your bakery's active role in supporting environmental stewardship within the community.
- Create a loyalty program that rewards customers for making sustainable choices, such as earning points for bringing reusable cups or utensils, to incentivize ongoing engagement with your bakery's sustainability initiatives.
- Partner with environmental organizations or nonprofits to co-host fundraising events or donation drives at your bakery, leveraging your brand's platform to raise awareness and support for important environmental causes.
- Develop eco-friendly packaging options for your bakery's products, such as compostable or biodegradable materials, and prominently feature these options in your marketing materials to attract environmentally conscious consumers.
- Share behind-the-scenes glimpses into your bakery's sustainability practices on social media platforms, such as videos or photos showcasing recycling efforts or energy-saving measures, to humanize your brand and build trust with customers.
- Incorporate sustainability-focused storytelling into your bakery's marketing content, such as blog posts or email newsletters highlighting the journey of locally sourced ingredients from farm to table, to engage customers on an emotional level and reinforce your brand's values.
- Offer educational resources or guides on sustainable baking techniques or ingredient sourcing, positioning your bakery as a trusted authority on environmentally friendly practices within the baking industry.

- Participate in industry events or conferences focused on sustainability in food production, and share insights or best practices from these events with your customers through blog posts, social media updates, or in-store signage.
- Implement initiatives to reduce single-use plastics and other non-recyclable materials in your bakery operations, and communicate these efforts to customers through signage or packaging labels to demonstrate your commitment to minimizing environmental impact.
- Collaborate with local environmental experts or organizations to conduct sustainability audits or assessments of your bakery's operations, and use the findings to identify areas for improvement and set goals for future sustainability initiatives.
- Engage with your community through educational outreach programs focused on environmental stewardship, such as hosting school field trips or partnering with youth organizations to teach children about sustainable living practices and the importance of protecting the planet.
- Source ingredients locally whenever possible to reduce carbon emissions associated with transportation and support local farmers and producers, and highlight these partnerships in your brand messaging to showcase your bakery's commitment to sustainability and community support.
- Offer plant-based or vegan options on your bakery's menu to cater to customers seeking environmentally friendly food choices, and promote these options prominently in your marketing materials to attract environmentally conscious consumers.
- Invest in energy-efficient equipment and technologies for your bakery's operations, such as LED lighting or energy-saving appliances, and share updates on these investments with customers through social media posts or website updates to demonstrate your commitment to sustainability.
- Host zero-waste events or promotions at your bakery, such as "bring your own container" days or waste-free baking workshops, to raise awareness about the importance of reducing waste and encourage sustainable consumer behavior among your customer base.
- Implement a composting program for organic waste generated in your bakery's operations, and share updates on the program's progress with customers through social media updates or in-store signage to demonstrate your commitment to closing the loop on food waste.
- Partner with local sustainability-focused businesses or organizations to co-create branded merchandise or promotional materials, such as reusable shopping bags or water bottles, to further promote your bakery's commitment to sustainability and encourage eco-friendly consumer behavior.
- Encourage employee engagement with your bakery's sustainability initiatives by providing training and resources on environmentally friendly practices, and recognize and reward staff members who contribute innovative ideas or suggestions for improving sustainability in the workplace.

Employee Advocacy and Uniform Branding

- Develop a comprehensive training program for bakery staff that emphasizes brand values, product knowledge, and customer service, empowering employees to become knowledgeable advocates for the bakery brand.
- Implement a rewards system to incentivize staff members who actively promote the bakery brand both in-store and on social media platforms.
- Create branded uniforms for bakery employees that not only reflect the bakery's aesthetic but also serve as a walking advertisement for the brand.
- Encourage employees to engage with customers authentically, sharing personal stories about their experiences with the bakery and its products, fostering a deeper connection between the brand and its clientele.
- Host internal workshops or seminars to educate staff on the importance of their role in brand representation and how their actions contribute to the overall success of the bakery.
- Provide employees with branded merchandise such as hats, aprons, or shirts to wear outside of work, extending the bakery's reach beyond the confines of the store.
- Create a dedicated hashtag for employees to use when posting about the bakery on social media, allowing their personal networks to discover and engage with the brand.
- Feature employee spotlights on the bakery's website or social media channels, showcasing the individuals behind the scenes and highlighting their passion for the brand.
- Foster a sense of ownership among staff members by involving them in decision-making processes related to branding initiatives and encouraging their feedback and ideas.
- Offer exclusive discounts or perks to employees as a way to thank them for their advocacy efforts and encourage continued brand loyalty.
- Develop a brand ambassador program within the bakery staff, selecting enthusiastic employees to represent the brand at community events, tastings, or media opportunities.
- Provide ongoing support and resources to employees interested in improving their social media presence, offering tips and guidelines for creating engaging content that aligns with the bakery's brand image.
- Host regular team-building activities or outings to strengthen employee camaraderie and reinforce their connection to the bakery brand.
- Incorporate brand messaging and imagery into the physical environment of the bakery, including signage, packaging, and décor, to ensure a consistent brand experience for customers.
- Recognize and celebrate employee achievements and milestones related to their advocacy efforts, whether through formal awards or informal acknowledgments.
- Partner with local influencers or community leaders who are also bakery customers, leveraging their platforms to amplify the bakery's message and reach new audiences.
- Offer training sessions on effective communication and storytelling techniques to help employees articulate the bakery's unique selling points and connect with customers on a deeper level.

- Encourage employees to share behind-the-scenes glimpses of bakery life on social media, offering a transparent and authentic look at the brand's operations.
- Provide opportunities for employees to participate in community service or volunteer initiatives on behalf of the bakery, further integrating the brand into the fabric of the local community.
- Establish clear guidelines and protocols for employee advocacy, ensuring that all communications and interactions align with the bakery's brand identity and values.
- Create a dedicated section on the bakery's website or app where customers can learn more about the staff members serving them and their personal connections to the brand.
- Invite employees to contribute ideas for new products, promotions, or marketing campaigns, fostering a sense of ownership and investment in the bakery's success.
- Organize regular feedback sessions or surveys to gather input from employees on their experiences representing the brand and identify areas for improvement or innovation.
- Cultivate a culture of pride and enthusiasm among bakery staff, celebrating their role as ambassadors for the brand and empowering them to share their passion with others both inside and outside the workplace.

Customer Service as a Brand Pillar

- Develop a comprehensive customer service training program that emphasizes the bakery's brand values, ensuring all staff members understand the importance of exceptional service in reinforcing the brand identity.
- Implement a customer feedback system to gather insights and identify areas for improvement in the bakery's service delivery, demonstrating a commitment to listening to and valuing customer opinions.
- Create branded customer service guidelines and protocols to ensure consistency across all customer interactions, from greeting to follow-up, reflecting the bakery's unique personality and values.
- Empower frontline staff with the authority and resources to resolve customer issues promptly and effectively, fostering trust and loyalty among patrons.
- Offer personalized experiences for customers, such as customized orders or recommendations based on their preferences and past purchases, demonstrating a commitment to meeting individual needs.
- Provide ongoing training and support to staff members to equip them with the skills and knowledge necessary to deliver exceptional service in various situations, including handling difficult customers or resolving complaints.
- Showcase customer testimonials and positive reviews prominently on the bakery's website and social media channels to build credibility and trust with potential customers.
- Implement a loyalty program that rewards repeat customers for their patronage and encourages them to engage with the bakery on a regular basis, fostering long-term relationships.
- Regularly evaluate and refine customer service processes and procedures based on feedback and performance metrics, ensuring continuous improvement and alignment with evolving customer expectations.
- Leverage technology to enhance the customer service experience, such as offering online ordering and delivery options, implementing chatbots for instant support, or using customer relationship management (CRM) software to track interactions and preferences.
- Train staff members to anticipate and proactively address customer needs, such as replenishing popular items before they run out or offering samples to enhance the shopping experience.
- Create a welcoming and inviting atmosphere in the bakery environment, with friendly greetings, pleasant music, and comfortable seating areas, to enhance the overall customer experience.
- Encourage staff members to go above and beyond in exceeding customer expectations, whether through small gestures of kindness or personalized touches that make patrons feel valued and appreciated.
- Foster a culture of empathy and compassion among staff members, empowering them to connect with customers on a human level and address their needs with sincerity and

understanding.
- Solicit feedback from customers through surveys, focus groups, or comment cards to gain insights into their preferences, perceptions, and pain points, informing future customer service initiatives and marketing strategies.
- Develop partnerships with other local businesses or organizations to offer joint promotions or discounts to customers, providing added value and enhancing the overall customer experience.
- Train staff members to be knowledgeable about the bakery's products, ingredients, and production processes, enabling them to answer questions confidently and provide helpful recommendations to customers.
- Implement a system for recognizing and rewarding outstanding customer service efforts by staff members, whether through formal awards or informal praise and recognition.
- Invest in employee training and development programs that emphasize the importance of empathy, communication, and problem-solving skills in delivering exceptional customer service, empowering staff to excel in their roles.
- Regularly communicate with customers through email newsletters, social media updates, or in-store signage to keep them informed about new products, promotions, or events, demonstrating a commitment to staying connected and engaged.
- Establish clear expectations and standards for customer service excellence, with measurable goals and benchmarks to track performance and hold staff members accountable for delivering on the bakery's brand promise.
- Encourage staff members to take ownership of the customer experience and proactively seek out opportunities to delight and surprise patrons, whether through special promotions, personalized recommendations, or unexpected gestures of kindness.
- Monitor online review platforms and social media channels for customer feedback and respond promptly and professionally to comments, questions, and concerns, demonstrating a commitment to transparency and accountability.
- Celebrate customer appreciation events or milestones, such as anniversaries or holidays, to show gratitude to patrons and reinforce the bakery's commitment to building lasting relationships with its community.

BRAND MARKETING IDEAS

Building an Online Community

- Create a dedicated online platform, such as a website forum or social media group, where bakery enthusiasts can connect, share baking tips, exchange recipes, and engage with the brand and each other.
- Host virtual baking classes or workshops led by expert bakers, offering participants the opportunity to learn new skills, ask questions, and connect with fellow baking enthusiasts in a supportive online environment.
- Develop a branded mobile app that offers users exclusive content, such as behind-the-scenes glimpses of bakery operations, special promotions, and interactive challenges to encourage engagement and loyalty.
- Launch a weekly or monthly newsletter featuring curated content, including recipes, baking tips, customer spotlights, and upcoming events, to keep subscribers informed and engaged with the bakery brand.
- Partner with influencers or bloggers in the baking and foodie community to co-create content, such as recipe videos, product reviews, or collaborative challenges, reaching new audiences and driving traffic to the bakery's online platforms.
- Host live Q&A sessions or "ask me anything" (AMA) events with the bakery's head baker or other key team members, allowing customers to interact directly with the people behind the brand and learn more about their craft.
- Encourage user-generated content by hosting photo contests, recipe challenges, or themed baking competitions on social media, inviting followers to share their creations using a branded hashtag and offering prizes or recognition for the best submissions.
- Create a series of interactive quizzes or polls related to baking trends, flavor preferences, or favorite bakery products, encouraging followers to participate and share their opinions while gathering valuable insights for future marketing campaigns.
- Establish a loyalty program that rewards members for engaging with the bakery brand online, such as earning points for participating in community activities, sharing content on social media, or referring friends to join the community.
- Collaborate with other businesses or organizations in the baking industry to co-host virtual events, such as panel discussions, product launches, or networking mixers, providing added value and exposure for all parties involved.
- Share behind-the-scenes content on social media, such as photos and videos of the baking process, staff profiles, or sneak peeks of upcoming products, to give followers a glimpse into the inner workings of the bakery and foster a sense of connection.
- Create interactive challenges or games on social media, such as recipe scavenger hunts, trivia quizzes, or baking bingo, to encourage engagement and interaction among followers while promoting the bakery brand in a fun and creative way.
- Offer exclusive perks or discounts to members of the online community, such as early access to new products, special promotions, or invitations to VIP events, as a way to reward their loyalty and foster a sense of belonging.

- Host virtual tasting events or product demos, where customers can sample new bakery offerings from the comfort of their own homes and provide feedback in real-time, creating a sense of excitement and anticipation around the brand.
- Leverage user-generated content by reposting and sharing customer photos, reviews, and testimonials on the bakery's social media channels, showcasing the community's enthusiasm and loyalty for the brand.
- Create a dedicated hashtag for the bakery's online community and encourage followers to use it when sharing content related to the brand, making it easy to discover and engage with user-generated posts.
- Collaborate with local influencers or community leaders to host offline events, such as bake sales, pop-up shops, or charity fundraisers, bringing the online community together in person and strengthening connections with the brand.
- Offer virtual consultations or personalized baking advice sessions with the bakery's expert staff, allowing customers to receive tailored guidance and support for their baking projects while deepening their relationship with the brand.
- Host themed online challenges or contests, such as holiday baking competitions or seasonal recipe swaps, to spark creativity and excitement among community members while generating buzz and engagement for the bakery brand.
- Create a loyalty program that rewards members for engaging with the bakery brand online, such as earning points for participating in community activities, sharing content on social media, or referring friends to join the community.
- Collaborate with other businesses or organizations in the baking industry to co-host virtual events, such as panel discussions, product launches, or networking mixers, providing added value and exposure for all parties involved.
- Share behind-the-scenes content on social media, such as photos and videos of the baking process, staff profiles, or sneak peeks of upcoming products, to give followers a glimpse into the inner workings of the bakery and foster a sense of connection.
- Create interactive challenges or games on social media, such as recipe scavenger hunts, trivia quizzes, or baking bingo, to encourage engagement and interaction among followers while promoting the bakery brand in a fun and creative way.
- Offer exclusive perks or discounts to members of the online community, such as early access to new products, special promotions, or invitations to VIP events, as a way to reward their loyalty and foster a sense of belonging.

Influencer and Brand Ambassador Programs

- Identify influencers in the food and baking niche whose values and aesthetic align with those of the bakery brand, and reach out to them with personalized pitches highlighting potential collaboration opportunities.
- Develop a tiered ambassador program that offers different levels of perks and incentives based on the influencer's reach, engagement, and alignment with the bakery's target audience and brand values.
- Create branded content kits for influencers, including high-quality images, key messaging points, and product samples, to streamline the collaboration process and ensure consistency in brand representation across different platforms.
- Host influencer events or exclusive tasting experiences at the bakery's location, inviting influencers to sample new products, meet the bakery team, and create content in a unique and immersive setting.
- Offer affiliate or commission-based partnerships to influencers, where they receive a percentage of sales generated through their unique tracking links or discount codes, incentivizing them to promote the bakery brand to their audience.
- Collaborate with micro-influencers or local food bloggers who have a smaller but highly engaged audience, leveraging their authenticity and trustworthiness to reach niche markets and drive targeted traffic to the bakery's online and offline channels.
- Establish clear expectations and guidelines for influencer partnerships, including content requirements, posting schedules, and disclosure policies, to ensure that collaborations align with the bakery's brand values and messaging.
- Leverage user-generated content from influencers by reposting and sharing their photos, reviews, and testimonials on the bakery's social media channels, extending the reach of their content and amplifying the impact of the partnership.
- Provide influencers with exclusive access to behind-the-scenes content, product launches, or special events, giving them unique insights and experiences to share with their audience and fostering a sense of exclusivity and privilege.
- Collaborate with influencers on co-branded product launches or limited-edition collaborations, leveraging their creativity and influence to create buzz and excitement around new offerings from the bakery brand.
- Offer influencers opportunities for long-term partnerships or brand ambassadorships, where they become ongoing advocates for the bakery brand and its products, building deeper relationships and fostering loyalty over time.
- Monitor and track the performance of influencer partnerships using metrics such as reach, engagement, and conversion rates, to evaluate the effectiveness of different collaborations and inform future marketing strategies.
- Provide influencers with opportunities for cross-promotion, such as guest blogging, social media takeovers, or joint giveaways, to expose their audience to the bakery brand and vice versa, expanding reach and driving mutual growth.

- Offer influencers access to exclusive discounts, promotions, or product previews, incentivizing them to share their experiences with their audience and drive traffic to the bakery's website or physical locations.
- Collaborate with influencers on sponsored content campaigns, such as recipe tutorials, product reviews, or sponsored posts, that showcase the bakery's products in an authentic and engaging way while reaching new audiences.
- Invite influencers to participate in product development or menu ideation sessions, soliciting their feedback and ideas to create offerings that resonate with their audience and align with current food and baking trends.
- Partner with influencers on philanthropic or community initiatives, such as charity bake sales or fundraising events, leveraging their platform and influence to support causes that align with the bakery's values and mission.
- Provide influencers with opportunities for co-creation, such as designing custom packaging or creating signature products, allowing them to put their own unique spin on the bakery brand and engage their audience in the creative process.
- Offer influencers exclusive access to VIP events or experiences, such as private tastings or chef-led workshops, as a way to show appreciation for their partnership and build stronger relationships with key advocates of the brand.
- Collaborate with influencers on themed content series or challenges, such as "bake-along" videos or recipe exchanges, encouraging their audience to participate and engage with the bakery brand in a fun and interactive way.
- Establish a referral program for influencers, where they earn incentives or rewards for referring other influencers or brand ambassadors to collaborate with the bakery, creating a network effect and driving organic growth of the partnership program.
- Provide influencers with access to exclusive resources or tools, such as recipe development support or photography assistance, to help them create high-quality content that aligns with the bakery's brand standards and aesthetic.
- Offer influencers opportunities for sponsored travel or experiences, such as culinary tours or food festivals, where they can explore different culinary cultures and share their adventures with their audience, incorporating the bakery brand into their storytelling.
- Develop long-term relationships with influencers based on trust, transparency, and mutual respect, fostering open communication and collaboration to create meaningful and impactful partnerships that drive tangible results for the bakery brand.

Brand Presence on Social Media

- Develop a content calendar outlining themed posts, promotions, and engagement strategies to maintain a consistent and engaging presence on social media platforms.
- Create visually appealing and shareable content, such as high-quality photos, recipe videos, and mouth-watering food shots, to showcase the bakery's products and attract attention on social media.
- Utilize storytelling techniques to humanize the brand and connect with followers on a deeper level, sharing behind-the-scenes glimpses of bakery life, staff profiles, and customer testimonials.
- Engage with followers in real-time by responding promptly to comments, messages, and mentions, fostering a sense of community and building stronger relationships with customers on social media.
- Leverage user-generated content by reposting and sharing customer photos, reviews, and testimonials on the bakery's social media channels, showcasing the community's enthusiasm and loyalty for the brand.
- Utilize social media advertising to reach new audiences and promote special offers, events, or product launches, targeting specific demographics and interests to maximize effectiveness and ROI.
- Collaborate with influencers or brand ambassadors in the food and baking niche to reach new audiences and amplify the bakery's message on social media, leveraging their credibility and influence to drive engagement and awareness.
- Host live streaming events or Q&A sessions on social media platforms, allowing followers to interact with the bakery team in real-time, ask questions, and learn more about the brand and its products.
- Incorporate interactive features such as polls, quizzes, and contests into social media posts to encourage engagement and participation from followers, driving excitement and interaction around the bakery brand.
- Use hashtags strategically to increase visibility and reach on social media platforms, researching trending topics and relevant keywords to optimize the bakery's content for discovery and engagement.
- Collaborate with other local businesses or organizations on social media cross-promotions, sharing content, and promoting each other's products or services to reach new audiences and build mutually beneficial relationships.
- Monitor social media analytics and insights to track performance, identify trends, and measure the effectiveness of different content types and strategies, optimizing future marketing efforts based on data-driven insights.
- Create interactive experiences for followers, such as virtual tastings, recipe challenges, or DIY tutorials, to encourage participation and engagement with the bakery brand on social media.

- Develop partnerships with food delivery platforms or online marketplaces to showcase the bakery's products and drive online sales through social media advertising and promotions.
- Share educational and informative content related to baking tips, ingredient sourcing, and cooking techniques to provide value to followers and establish the bakery as a trusted authority in the food and baking niche.
- Collaborate with local influencers or community leaders to host offline events, such as bake sales, pop-up shops, or charity fundraisers, bringing the online community together in person and strengthening connections with the brand.
- Experiment with different content formats and platforms, such as Instagram Reels, TikTok videos, or Facebook Live, to diversify the bakery's social media presence and reach new audiences with engaging and shareable content.
- Encourage customer reviews and feedback on social media platforms, responding thoughtfully to both positive and negative comments to demonstrate the bakery's commitment to customer satisfaction and continuous improvement.
- Share seasonal or holiday-themed content on social media, such as festive recipes, decorating ideas, or special promotions, to capitalize on seasonal trends and generate excitement and engagement among followers.
- Partner with local influencers or food bloggers to host sponsored content campaigns, such as recipe tutorials, product reviews, or sponsored posts, that showcase the bakery's products in an authentic and engaging way while reaching new audiences.
- Collaborate with local photographers or content creators to produce high-quality visual content for social media, showcasing the bakery's products in an appealing and aspirational light to attract attention and drive engagement.
- Offer exclusive promotions or discounts to followers who engage with the bakery's social media posts, such as limited-time offers or flash sales, rewarding loyalty and encouraging repeat engagement with the brand.
- Share customer testimonials and success stories on social media, highlighting positive experiences and feedback from satisfied customers to build credibility and trust with potential new followers and customers.
- Foster a sense of community and connection among followers by sharing relatable and authentic content that reflects the bakery's values, personality, and commitment to excellence in every aspect of the business.

Email Marketing with a Personal Touch

- Segment the bakery's email list based on customer preferences, behaviors, and purchase history to deliver personalized content and offers tailored to each subscriber's interests and needs.
- Use dynamic content blocks in email campaigns to customize messaging, product recommendations, and calls to action based on individual subscriber data, creating a more relevant and engaging experience for recipients.
- Incorporate personalization tokens, such as the subscriber's name or location, in email subject lines and greetings to grab attention and create a sense of familiarity and connection with the recipient.
- Send personalized birthday or anniversary emails to subscribers with special offers or discounts as a way to celebrate milestones and show appreciation for their loyalty to the bakery brand.
- Leverage triggered email campaigns based on specific customer actions or events, such as abandoned cart reminders, post-purchase follow-ups, or re-engagement campaigns, to deliver timely and relevant messages that drive conversion and retention.
- Use storytelling techniques in email content to humanize the brand and connect with subscribers on an emotional level, sharing personal anecdotes, behind-the-scenes stories, and customer testimonials to build rapport and trust.
- Invite subscribers to share their feedback, ideas, and suggestions through surveys, polls, or feedback forms in email campaigns, demonstrating a commitment to listening to and valuing their input and opinions.
- Offer exclusive content or sneak peeks of upcoming products or promotions to email subscribers as a way to reward their loyalty and make them feel like valued insiders and members of the bakery's community.
- Personalize product recommendations and upsell/cross-sell offers based on each subscriber's purchase history and browsing behavior, using data-driven insights to suggest relevant products and increase average order value.
- Send personalized thank-you emails to customers after they make a purchase, expressing gratitude for their support and including a special offer or incentive to encourage repeat business and foster long-term loyalty.
- Use email segmentation and targeting to deliver location-specific promotions or events to subscribers based on their geographic location, ensuring that campaigns are relevant and timely for each recipient.
- Implement a preference center or subscription management options in email communications, allowing subscribers to customize their email preferences and choose the types of content they want to receive from the bakery brand.
- Send personalized recommendations or tips based on each subscriber's dietary preferences, allergies, or restrictions, demonstrating a commitment to meeting individual needs and providing value beyond just promotional offers.

- Use dynamic countdown timers in email campaigns to create a sense of urgency and drive action, such as limited-time offers or flash sales, prompting subscribers to act quickly to take advantage of the opportunity.
- Incorporate user-generated content from customers, such as photos, reviews, or testimonials, into email campaigns to showcase social proof and build credibility for the bakery brand among subscribers.
- Send personalized anniversary emails to long-term subscribers or VIP customers, thanking them for their continued support and loyalty and offering exclusive perks or rewards as a token of appreciation.
- Use A/B testing to experiment with different email subject lines, content formats, and calls to action to identify what resonates best with subscribers and optimize future campaigns for maximum engagement and conversion.
- Share exclusive behind-the-scenes content or insider updates with email subscribers, such as sneak peeks of new products in development, staff profiles, or upcoming events, to make them feel like valued members of the bakery's inner circle.
- Implement a referral program or incentivized sharing mechanism in email campaigns, encouraging subscribers to refer friends and family to join the bakery's email list and rewarding them for their advocacy and support.
- Send personalized re-engagement emails to inactive subscribers, offering special incentives or reminders to encourage them to re-engage with the bakery brand and become active members of the email community once again.
- Use storytelling techniques in email content to humanize the brand and connect with subscribers on an emotional level, sharing personal anecdotes, behind-the-scenes stories, and customer testimonials to build rapport and trust.
- Provide subscribers with exclusive access to pre-sale events, product launches, or limited-edition offerings as a way to reward their loyalty and make them feel like valued insiders and VIPs.
- Use email automation workflows to nurture leads and guide subscribers through the customer journey, delivering personalized content and offers at each stage of the buying process to drive engagement and conversion.
- Monitor email performance metrics such as open rates, click-through rates, and conversion rates to track the effectiveness of personalization strategies and optimize future campaigns for better results and ROI.

Crafting Press Releases for Your Bakery

- Highlight the bakery's unique selling points, such as its commitment to using locally sourced ingredients, artisanal baking techniques, or innovative flavor combinations, to differentiate the brand and attract the interest of journalists and media outlets.
- Announce new product launches or menu additions with press releases that emphasize the creativity, quality, and craftsmanship behind each offering, generating excitement and anticipation among customers and the media.
- Share stories of community involvement and philanthropic initiatives, such as charity bake sales, donations to local organizations, or partnerships with food banks, to showcase the bakery's commitment to giving back and making a positive impact in the community.
- Showcase awards, accolades, or certifications received by the bakery, such as recognition for excellence in baking, food safety compliance, or sustainability practices, to build credibility and reinforce the bakery's reputation as a trusted industry leader.
- Highlight partnerships or collaborations with other local businesses, organizations, or influencers in the food and hospitality industry, demonstrating the bakery's commitment to supporting the local economy and fostering mutually beneficial relationships.
- Share success stories or milestones achieved by the bakery, such as anniversary celebrations, expansion into new markets, or record-breaking sales figures, to celebrate accomplishments and generate positive publicity for the brand.
- Announce special events or promotions happening at the bakery, such as holiday-themed menus, seasonal discounts, or limited-time offers, to drive foot traffic and sales while creating buzz and excitement in the media.
- Provide expert insights or commentary on baking trends, industry developments, or consumer preferences in press releases, positioning the bakery's leadership team as thought leaders and subject matter experts in the field.
- Showcase the bakery's commitment to sustainability and environmental stewardship through initiatives such as zero-waste packaging, energy-efficient operations, or partnerships with local farmers and suppliers, to appeal to environmentally conscious consumers and media outlets.
- Share stories of employee achievements, such as promotions, certifications, or milestones, to recognize and celebrate the contributions of staff members and foster a sense of pride and camaraderie within the bakery team.
- Announce renovations, upgrades, or improvements made to the bakery's facilities, equipment, or infrastructure, highlighting investments in quality and innovation that enhance the customer experience and support business growth.
- Provide insights into the bakery's creative process and product development efforts, sharing stories of inspiration, experimentation, and collaboration that showcase the passion and dedication of the bakery team.
- Highlight customer testimonials and success stories in press releases, sharing real-life experiences and feedback from satisfied patrons to build credibility and trust in the bakery's

products and services.

- Announce partnerships with local schools, community centers, or educational institutions to provide opportunities for hands-on baking workshops, mentorship programs, or internship opportunities, demonstrating the bakery's commitment to nurturing future talent and giving back to the community.
- Share stories of innovation and experimentation in press releases, such as the development of new recipes, techniques, or product lines, to showcase the bakery's creative spirit and commitment to continuous improvement and growth.
- Provide updates on industry-related news or developments that may impact the bakery, such as changes in regulations, consumer trends, or competitive landscape, to demonstrate awareness and adaptability in the face of evolving market conditions.
- Announce partnerships or sponsorships with local events, festivals, or cultural celebrations to increase visibility and brand exposure in the community while supporting causes and activities that align with the bakery's values and mission.
- Provide insights into the bakery's commitment to food safety and quality assurance practices, sharing stories of rigorous testing, inspections, and compliance measures that ensure the highest standards of product integrity and safety.
- Highlight the bakery's commitment to inclusivity and diversity through initiatives such as workforce diversity, accessibility accommodations, or partnerships with minority-owned businesses or organizations, to promote a culture of equity and inclusion within the community.
- Share stories of customer engagement and interaction, such as contests, giveaways, or customer appreciation events, to showcase the bakery's dedication to building meaningful relationships with patrons and fostering a sense of belonging and loyalty.
- Announce new hires or additions to the bakery team, highlighting the skills, expertise, and contributions of each individual and reinforcing the bakery's commitment to attracting and retaining top talent in the industry.
- Provide updates on corporate social responsibility initiatives undertaken by the bakery, such as sustainability commitments, charitable donations, or volunteer efforts, to demonstrate a broader commitment to social and environmental stewardship beyond business success.
- Share stories of resilience and adaptation in response to challenges or setbacks, such as economic downturns, natural disasters, or public health crises, showcasing the bakery's ability to overcome adversity and emerge stronger and more resilient than before.
- Provide insights into the bakery's long-term vision, goals, and strategies for future growth and expansion, sharing stories of innovation, ambition, and determination that inspire confidence and excitement in the bakery's prospects and potential.

BRAND MARKETING IDEAS

Utilizing Content Marketing

- Create a blog on the bakery's website featuring articles, recipes, baking tips, and behind-the-scenes stories to engage and educate customers while showcasing the bakery's expertise and personality.
- Develop a content calendar outlining topics, themes, and publication schedules for blog posts, social media updates, and other content marketing initiatives to maintain consistency and relevance.
- Share recipe tutorials, how-to guides, and cooking tips on social media platforms such as Instagram, Facebook, and YouTube to provide value to followers and showcase the bakery's products and expertise.
- Produce high-quality photos and videos showcasing the bakery's products, facilities, and staff to create visually appealing and shareable content that captures the attention of customers and drives engagement on social media.
- Collaborate with food bloggers, influencers, and content creators in the baking and foodie community to co-create content, such as recipe videos, product reviews, or sponsored posts, that reaches new audiences and drives traffic to the bakery's website and social media channels.
- Develop a series of educational workshops or seminars on topics such as baking techniques, flavor pairings, or cake decorating to provide value to customers while showcasing the bakery's expertise and creating opportunities for engagement and interaction.
- Host live streaming events or Q&A sessions on social media platforms, such as Instagram Live or Facebook Live, where customers can interact with the bakery team in real-time, ask questions, and learn more about baking and pastry techniques.
- Create downloadable resources such as e-books, infographics, or printable recipe cards featuring the bakery's signature recipes, baking tips, and product information to provide value to customers and encourage engagement with the brand.
- Develop a series of email newsletters featuring curated content, special offers, and insider updates to keep subscribers informed and engaged while driving traffic to the bakery's website and encouraging repeat visits and purchases.
- Share user-generated content from customers, such as photos, reviews, and testimonials, on social media platforms and the bakery's website to showcase social proof and build credibility and trust with potential new customers.
- Produce branded podcasts or audio content featuring interviews with industry experts, baking enthusiasts, and members of the bakery team to provide value to listeners and create opportunities for engagement and interaction.
- Create interactive quizzes, polls, or surveys on social media platforms to engage customers, gather feedback, and generate insights into their preferences, interests, and buying behavior.
- Develop a series of themed content campaigns around seasonal holidays, special occasions, or trending topics to create buzz and excitement around the bakery brand while driving

traffic and sales both online and offline.
- Share stories of the bakery's history, heritage, and values on social media platforms and the bakery's website to create a sense of connection and nostalgia with customers while reinforcing the brand's identity and authenticity.
- Leverage influencer marketing strategies to amplify the reach and impact of content marketing initiatives, collaborating with influencers in the food and baking niche to co-create content and reach new audiences with authentic and engaging messaging.
- Develop a series of video tutorials or cooking demonstrations featuring the bakery's products and recipes to provide value to customers and showcase the versatility and quality of the bakery's offerings.
- Create interactive online experiences such as virtual tastings, recipe challenges, or DIY workshops to engage customers and create opportunities for interaction and community building around the bakery brand.
- Share customer testimonials, success stories, and case studies on social media platforms and the bakery's website to showcase real-life experiences and build credibility and trust with potential new customers.
- Develop a series of guest blog posts or contributed articles featuring insights, tips, and expertise from industry experts, baking enthusiasts, and members of the bakery team to provide value to readers and drive traffic to the bakery's website.
- Partner with local businesses, organizations, and influencers to co-host events, workshops, or collaborations that provide value to customers while increasing visibility and reach for the bakery brand.
- Develop a series of educational resources such as online courses, webinars, or downloadable guides on topics such as baking basics, cake decorating, or pastry techniques to provide value to customers and position the bakery as a trusted resource and authority in the industry.
- Share stories of innovation, creativity, and experimentation on social media platforms and the bakery's website to showcase the bakery's commitment to continuous improvement and excellence in every aspect of the business.
- Create branded hashtags and encourage customers to share their experiences, photos, and recipes using the hashtags on social media platforms to create user-generated content and build a sense of community and belonging around the bakery brand.
- Monitor and analyze performance metrics such as website traffic, social media engagement, and email open rates to track the effectiveness of content marketing initiatives and optimize future campaigns for better results and ROI.

Managing Brand Reputation

- Monitor online reviews, mentions, and conversations about the bakery brand on social media platforms, review websites, and forums to stay informed about customer feedback and perceptions.
- Respond promptly and professionally to customer complaints, concerns, and negative reviews, demonstrating a commitment to customer satisfaction and resolving issues in a transparent and empathetic manner.
- Implement a proactive approach to managing brand reputation by regularly engaging with customers on social media platforms, responding to comments, messages, and mentions, and actively participating in conversations about the bakery brand.
- Develop and maintain relationships with local media outlets, journalists, and influencers to proactively share positive news, stories, and updates about the bakery brand and its products and services.
- Monitor industry trends, news, and developments that may impact the bakery brand's reputation, such as food safety recalls, competitor actions, or emerging consumer preferences, and adapt strategies accordingly.
- Create and distribute press releases, blog posts, or social media updates to address and clarify any misinformation, rumors, or negative publicity surrounding the bakery brand, ensuring accuracy and transparency in communication.
- Monitor and manage online listings and directories for accuracy and consistency of information, such as business hours, contact details, and location addresses, to ensure a positive and seamless customer experience.
- Establish clear brand guidelines and communication protocols for staff members and representatives to follow when interacting with customers and addressing inquiries, complaints, or issues related to the bakery brand.
- Conduct regular audits and assessments of customer sentiment and brand perception through surveys, focus groups, or social media listening tools to identify areas for improvement and address potential reputational risks.
- Implement proactive measures to prevent and mitigate potential crises or reputation-damaging events, such as developing contingency plans, crisis communication strategies, and media response protocols.
- Monitor and address customer feedback and complaints received through customer service channels, such as phone calls, emails, and in-person interactions, to identify recurring issues and implement corrective actions.
- Establish and enforce quality control measures and standards for product consistency, freshness, and presentation to maintain customer trust and confidence in the bakery brand's offerings.
- Foster a culture of transparency, accountability, and ethical conduct within the bakery team by providing ongoing training, support, and guidance on customer service best practices and brand representation.

- Leverage positive customer testimonials, reviews, and feedback to showcase the bakery brand's strengths, quality, and reputation for excellence in marketing materials, website content, and social media posts.
- Monitor and manage online reputation platforms and review websites, such as Yelp, Google My Business, and TripAdvisor, to respond to customer reviews, address concerns, and maintain a positive online presence.
- Monitor and address any instances of brand infringement, unauthorized use of intellectual property, or misrepresentation of the bakery brand by competitors, counterfeiters, or unauthorized sellers.
- Collaborate with industry organizations, trade associations, and regulatory agencies to stay informed about industry standards, best practices, and compliance requirements related to food safety, labeling, and marketing.
- Implement measures to protect customer data and privacy, such as secure online payment processing, data encryption, and compliance with data protection regulations, to build trust and confidence in the bakery brand's commitment to privacy and security.
- Monitor and address any instances of negative publicity, rumors, or misinformation circulating online about the bakery brand, taking swift and decisive action to correct inaccuracies and prevent reputational harm.
- Establish and enforce social media moderation policies and guidelines to maintain a respectful and positive online community, addressing any instances of hate speech, harassment, or inappropriate content promptly and effectively.
- Invest in online reputation management tools and services to monitor, track, and analyze mentions, reviews, and sentiment about the bakery brand across digital channels and platforms.
- Conduct regular reviews and assessments of the bakery brand's online presence, including website content, social media profiles, and search engine results, to ensure consistency, accuracy, and relevance in messaging and branding.
- Collaborate with brand ambassadors, influencers, and satisfied customers to generate positive word-of-mouth and endorsements for the bakery brand, leveraging their credibility and influence to enhance brand reputation and visibility.
- Continuously evaluate and refine brand reputation management strategies and tactics based on feedback, insights, and performance metrics to adapt to evolving customer expectations, market dynamics, and competitive pressures.

Measuring Brand Impact and Adjusting Strategies

- Conduct regular surveys or feedback polls to measure brand awareness, perception, and sentiment among target audiences, gathering insights into customer attitudes, preferences, and behaviors related to the bakery brand.
- Monitor key performance indicators (KPIs) such as website traffic, social media engagement, email open rates, and conversion rates to track the effectiveness of brand marketing initiatives and identify areas for improvement.
- Analyze sales data and revenue metrics to assess the impact of brand marketing campaigns on business growth, identifying trends, patterns, and correlations between marketing efforts and sales performance.
- Utilize web analytics tools such as Google Analytics or Adobe Analytics to track user behavior, traffic sources, and conversion paths on the bakery's website, gaining insights into the effectiveness of digital marketing strategies and content.
- Measure brand reach and exposure through social media analytics, tracking metrics such as follower growth, impressions, reach, and engagement to evaluate the impact of social media marketing efforts and adjust strategies accordingly.
- Conduct brand audits and competitive analysis to benchmark the bakery brand against competitors and assess its positioning, differentiation, and market share within the industry.
- Monitor online reputation and sentiment using social listening tools and sentiment analysis algorithms to track mentions, reviews, and conversations about the bakery brand across digital channels and platforms.
- Implement customer lifetime value (CLV) analysis to assess the long-term impact of brand marketing initiatives on customer acquisition, retention, and lifetime value, identifying opportunities to optimize marketing strategies and investments.
- Conduct focus groups or qualitative research studies to gather in-depth insights into customer perceptions, attitudes, and preferences related to the bakery brand, gaining a deeper understanding of consumer motivations and decision-making processes.
- Measure brand equity and brand loyalty through metrics such as Net Promoter Score (NPS), customer satisfaction scores (CSAT), and repeat purchase rates to gauge the strength of customer relationships and brand affinity over time.
- Analyze customer feedback and reviews from multiple touchpoints, such as social media, review websites, and customer service interactions, to identify areas for improvement and inform strategic decisions and adjustments.
- Implement A/B testing or multivariate testing to experiment with different messaging, creative elements, and campaign variables to identify the most effective strategies and tactics for driving brand awareness, engagement, and conversion.
- Track brand sentiment and sentiment shifts over time using sentiment analysis tools and algorithms to identify emerging trends, issues, or opportunities that may impact the bakery brand's reputation and perception.

- Measure brand recall and recognition through surveys, recall tests, or brand association studies to assess the effectiveness of brand marketing efforts in creating memorable and distinctive brand experiences for customers.
- Implement brand tracking studies or brand health surveys to monitor changes in brand perception, attitudes, and preferences among target audiences over time, identifying strengths, weaknesses, and areas for improvement in brand positioning and messaging.
- Analyze customer demographics and segmentation data to identify target audience segments with the highest brand affinity, engagement, and conversion rates, tailoring marketing strategies and messaging to resonate with specific customer segments.
- Monitor social media sentiment and engagement during brand events, promotions, or campaigns to assess audience reactions, feedback, and sentiment in real-time, adjusting strategies and tactics based on audience response and feedback.
- Utilize marketing attribution models such as first-touch attribution, last-touch attribution, or multi-touch attribution to evaluate the contribution of different marketing channels and touchpoints to overall brand impact and business outcomes.
- Implement brand tracking dashboards or scorecards to visualize and communicate key brand performance metrics, trends, and insights to stakeholders, facilitating data-driven decision-making and alignment around brand objectives and strategies.
- Measure brand salience and brand recall through surveys, recall tests, or brand recognition studies to assess the effectiveness of brand marketing efforts in establishing and maintaining top-of-mind awareness among target audiences.
- Conduct brand health assessments or brand perception surveys among internal stakeholders, such as employees, partners, and investors, to gain insights into perceptions of the bakery brand and alignment with brand values and mission.
- Monitor brand mentions, sentiment, and share of voice in media coverage and press mentions to assess the bakery brand's visibility, reputation, and influence within the industry and among key stakeholders.
- Evaluate the effectiveness of brand partnerships, sponsorships, and collaborations through metrics such as reach, engagement, and brand association, identifying opportunities to optimize partnerships and maximize brand impact.
- Continuously iterate and refine brand measurement and monitoring processes based on feedback, insights, and changing business objectives, ensuring that brand impact is effectively measured and strategies are adjusted to drive continuous improvement and growth.

500+ Content Marketing Ideas for Bakeries

SECTIONS IN THIS CHAPTER:

1. Identifying Key Content Themes for Bakeries – Page 142
2. Blogging Basics for Bakery Websites – Page 144
3. Creating Engaging Social Media Posts – Page 146
4. Developing a Recipe Sharing Strategy – Page 148
5. Crafting Email Newsletters Customers Love – Page 150
6. Video Content Creation for Bakeries – Page 152
7. Hosting Live Baking Demonstrations Online – Page 154
8. Utilizing User-Generated Content – Page 156
9. Behind-the-Scenes Looks at Bakery Operations – Page 158
10. Highlighting Customer Stories and Testimonials – Page 160
11. Seasonal and Holiday Content Planning – Page 162
12. Photography Tips for Mouth-Watering Visuals – Page 164
13. Collaborating with Food Bloggers and Influencers – Page 166
14. Building a Content Calendar – Page 168
15. Writing Press Releases for Bakery Events – Page 170
16. Engaging with Q&A Sessions on Social Media – Page 172
17. Creating Downloadable Baking Guides and Ebooks – Page 174
18. Podcasting for Bakeries – Page 176
19. Implementing SEO Best Practices in Content – Page 178
20. Analyzing Content Performance and Engagement – Page 180
21. Refreshing Old Content for New Engagement – Page 182
22. Storytelling Through Your Bakery's Brand – Page 184

CONTENT MARKETING IDEAS

Identifying Key Content Themes for Bakeries

- Showcase the Art of Baking: Offer behind-the-scenes glimpses into the bakery kitchen, featuring skilled bakers crafting delicious treats from scratch.
- Seasonal Specials: Create content around seasonal ingredients and flavors, highlighting how the bakery incorporates them into their products to celebrate holidays and seasons.
- Customer Stories and Testimonials: Share heartwarming stories and testimonials from satisfied customers who have had memorable experiences at the bakery.
- Health and Wellness: Develop content that emphasizes the use of wholesome ingredients and the health benefits of certain bakery items, catering to health-conscious consumers.
- DIY Baking Tips and Recipes: Provide easy-to-follow recipes and baking tips that customers can try at home, showcasing the expertise of the bakery's chefs.
- Local Sourcing and Sustainability: Highlight the bakery's commitment to sourcing ingredients locally and practicing sustainable baking methods, resonating with eco-conscious consumers.
- Historical Insights: Explore the rich history and traditions behind popular baked goods, educating customers while fostering a deeper appreciation for the bakery's heritage.
- Community Involvement: Showcase the bakery's involvement in local events, fundraisers, and charity initiatives, emphasizing its role as a valued community member.
- Culinary Trends: Stay ahead of the curve by creating content that taps into current culinary trends and how the bakery incorporates them into their offerings.
- Staff Spotlights: Introduce the talented individuals behind the scenes, from passionate bakers to creative pastry chefs, giving customers a glimpse into the faces behind their favorite treats.
- Interactive Contests and Challenges: Engage customers with fun contests and challenges related to baking, encouraging them to interact with the bakery's brand on social media.
- Celebrating Milestones: Commemorate significant milestones, such as the bakery's anniversary or the launch of a new product line, with special content and promotions.
- Baking for Special Occasions: Provide inspiration and ideas for baking customized treats for birthdays, weddings, holidays, and other special occasions.
- Flavor Pairing Guides: Educate customers on the art of flavor pairing, suggesting delicious combinations for pastries, bread, and other baked goods.
- Baking Techniques Demystified: Break down complex baking techniques into easy-to-understand steps, empowering customers to explore their own baking skills.
- Virtual Bakery Tours: Take customers on virtual tours of the bakery, offering a behind-the-scenes look at the equipment, processes, and people that make it all possible.
- Holiday Traditions Around the World: Explore different holiday traditions and the baked goods associated with them, celebrating cultural diversity and culinary heritage.
- Baking for Dietary Restrictions: Develop content focused on accommodating various dietary restrictions, such as gluten-free, vegan, or allergen-friendly options, to cater to a

diverse customer base.
- Seasonal Decorating Ideas: Inspire customers with creative decorating ideas for cakes, cookies, and pastries, tying into seasonal themes and festivities.
- Baking with Kids: Share family-friendly baking activities and recipes that parents can enjoy with their children, fostering bonding experiences and creating lasting memories.
- Baking as Therapy: Highlight the therapeutic benefits of baking, from stress relief to creative expression, encouraging customers to indulge in the joy of baking.
- Q&A Sessions with Bakers: Host live or pre-recorded Q&A sessions where customers can ask questions and learn from the bakery's experienced bakers.
- Baking for Beginners: Offer beginner-friendly baking tutorials and resources, catering to aspiring home bakers who are eager to learn the basics.
- Secret Recipes Revealed: Generate excitement by occasionally revealing the recipes for some of the bakery's most beloved creations, allowing customers to recreate them at home.

CONTENT MARKETING IDEAS

Blogging Basics for Bakery Websites

- Introduction to Baking: Craft informative blog posts introducing readers to the art and science of baking, covering topics such as ingredient selection, baking techniques, and essential equipment.
- Recipe Features: Share step-by-step recipes for signature bakery items, accompanied by mouthwatering photos and detailed instructions to inspire readers to recreate them at home.
- Seasonal Flavors and Trends: Keep readers engaged by regularly updating the blog with content that showcases seasonal flavors, trends, and themed recipes tailored to holidays and special occasions.
- Meet the Team: Humanize the bakery brand by spotlighting staff members through blog interviews or profiles, allowing readers to get to know the passionate individuals behind the scenes.
- Behind-the-Scenes Insights: Offer exclusive behind-the-scenes glimpses into the bakery's daily operations, from the baking process to product development and quality control.
- Ingredient Spotlights: Educate readers about different baking ingredients, their unique properties, and how they contribute to the flavor and texture of various baked goods.
- Baking Tips and Tricks: Share expert tips and tricks to help readers improve their baking skills, covering topics such as troubleshooting common baking issues, achieving perfect texture, and enhancing flavor.
- Health and Wellness: Address health-conscious readers by providing blog content that explores topics such as alternative ingredients, nutritious baking swaps, and mindful indulgence.
- Baking for Special Diets: Cater to readers with dietary restrictions by featuring recipes and resources for gluten-free, vegan, or allergen-friendly baking options.
- Local Partnerships and Collaborations: Showcase collaborations with local farmers, suppliers, or artisans through blog features that highlight the bakery's commitment to supporting the community and sourcing high-quality ingredients.
- Baking Inspiration from Around the World: Broaden readers' culinary horizons by sharing recipes and stories inspired by international baking traditions and flavors.
- Customer Stories and Testimonials: Use the blog as a platform to share heartwarming stories and testimonials from satisfied customers, highlighting memorable experiences and favorite bakery treats.
- Baking History and Heritage: Explore the rich history and cultural significance of beloved baked goods through informative blog posts that delve into their origins, evolution, and traditional preparation methods.
- Interactive Polls and Surveys: Engage readers by incorporating interactive elements such as polls and surveys into blog posts, inviting them to share their preferences, opinions, and feedback.
- DIY Baking Projects: Encourage reader participation with fun and creative DIY baking projects, such as decorating tutorials, edible crafts, and holiday-themed treats.

- Baking with Kids: Provide family-friendly baking ideas and activities that parents can enjoy with their children, fostering bonding experiences and nurturing a love for baking from an early age.
- Baking for Celebrations: Inspire readers with ideas and recipes for baking customized treats for birthdays, weddings, anniversaries, and other special occasions.
- Baking Competitions and Challenges: Organize baking competitions or challenges for readers, encouraging them to showcase their skills and creativity while generating buzz and excitement around the bakery brand.
- Baking Book Club: Create a virtual baking book club where readers can explore and discuss baking-related books, cookbooks, and culinary memoirs, fostering a sense of community and shared enthusiasm for baking.
- Baking Science Explained: Break down the science behind baking with informative blog posts that explore topics such as fermentation, gluten development, and the role of leavening agents in baking.
- Sustainability Initiatives: Share the bakery's sustainability initiatives and eco-friendly practices through blog updates that highlight efforts to reduce waste, conserve resources, and minimize environmental impact.
- Baking for a Cause: Use the blog to raise awareness and support for charitable causes and community outreach programs, sharing stories of how the bakery is making a positive difference in the lives of others.
- Baking Events and Workshops: Promote upcoming baking events, workshops, or classes hosted by the bakery through blog announcements, encouraging readers to participate and expand their baking skills.
- Interactive Recipe Contests: Host recipe contests where readers can submit their original recipes using specific ingredients or themes, with the chance to win prizes and have their recipes featured on the blog.

CONTENT MARKETING IDEAS

Creating Engaging Social Media Posts

- Visual Feast: Capture attention with visually stunning photos and videos showcasing the bakery's delectable treats, enticing followers with irresistible images of freshly baked goods.
- Behind-the-Scenes Sneak Peeks: Offer exclusive behind-the-scenes glimpses into the bakery's kitchen and production process, giving followers a sense of insider access and appreciation for the craftsmanship behind each creation.
- Interactive Polls and Quizzes: Encourage engagement by posting polls and quizzes related to baking preferences, flavor preferences, or bakery trivia, inviting followers to share their opinions and knowledge.
- Fan Favorites: Highlight customer favorites and best-selling items through social media posts, leveraging user-generated content and testimonials to showcase the bakery's most beloved treats.
- Mouthwatering Recipe Videos: Share captivating recipe videos featuring step-by-step demonstrations of how to prepare signature bakery items, providing followers with inspiration and guidance for their own baking adventures.
- Time-Limited Offers and Promotions: Create a sense of urgency and excitement with time-limited offers and promotions, such as flash sales, BOGO deals, or exclusive discounts for social media followers.
- Interactive Storytelling: Craft compelling narratives around the bakery's history, traditions, and values, using storytelling techniques to connect with followers on a deeper level and foster emotional engagement.
- User-Generated Content Contests: Encourage followers to share photos of their bakery purchases or homemade creations using a branded hashtag, and reward the best submissions with prizes or recognition.
- Seasonal Celebrations: Celebrate holidays and seasons with themed social media content, incorporating festive elements and seasonal flavors into posts to align with the current cultural and culinary zeitgeist.
- Recipe Roundups: Curate collections of recipes featuring a specific ingredient, flavor, or theme, providing followers with inspiration and ideas for their own baking projects.
- Interactive Live Streams: Host live baking demonstrations, Q&A sessions, or virtual tastings on social media platforms, allowing followers to interact with the bakery in real-time and ask questions directly to the bakers.
- Community Spotlights: Showcase the bakery's impact on the local community by featuring stories and testimonials from loyal customers, community partners, or charitable initiatives supported by the bakery.
- Trendy TikTok Challenges: Participate in popular TikTok challenges or trends related to baking, putting a creative spin on viral challenges to showcase the bakery's personality and expertise.

- Instagram Story Takeovers: Collaborate with influencers, staff members, or loyal customers to take over the bakery's Instagram Stories for a day, sharing behind-the-scenes content and personal insights.
- Interactive Giveaways: Drive engagement and follower growth with interactive giveaways and contests, encouraging followers to like, comment, and share posts for a chance to win prizes or exclusive experiences.
- Baking Tips and Tricks: Share helpful baking tips, hacks, and troubleshooting advice with followers, positioning the bakery as a trusted source of expertise and guidance in the world of baking.
- Local Foodie Partnerships: Partner with local food bloggers, influencers, or businesses to co-create content and cross-promote each other's brands, tapping into new audiences and expanding the bakery's reach.
- Testimonials and Reviews: Share glowing testimonials and reviews from satisfied customers on social media, reinforcing the bakery's reputation for quality and customer satisfaction.
- Interactive Challenges: Challenge followers to recreate a specific bakery item or baking technique at home and share their results, fostering a sense of community and friendly competition among followers.
- Interactive Story Polls: Use Instagram Stories' interactive features such as polls, sliders, and quizzes to gather feedback from followers on new product ideas, flavor preferences, or menu changes.
- DIY Decorating Tutorials: Create bite-sized DIY decorating tutorials for Instagram Reels or TikTok, demonstrating fun and easy ways to decorate cakes, cookies, and pastries at home.
- Caption Contests: Spark creativity and engagement with caption contests, posting humorous or visually intriguing images and inviting followers to come up with clever captions in the comments.
- Baking Challenges: Launch baking challenges where followers are tasked with recreating a specific recipe or design, with the opportunity to be featured on the bakery's social media channels.
- Virtual Taste Tests: Host virtual taste tests or blind tastings on social media, inviting followers to participate by voting on their favorite bakery items or flavor combinations in real-time.

CONTENT MARKETING IDEAS

Developing a Recipe Sharing Strategy

- Recipe of the Week: Implement a weekly series where the bakery shares a new recipe on its website and social media platforms, enticing followers with fresh culinary inspiration.
- Guest Chef Collaborations: Partner with local chefs or food influencers to create collaborative recipes featuring the bakery's products, leveraging their expertise and audience reach for increased exposure.
- Seasonal Recipe Collections: Curate collections of seasonal recipes that highlight ingredients and flavors relevant to each time of year, providing followers with ideas for festive baking projects.
- Recipe Contests: Host recipe contests where customers can submit their original recipes using the bakery's products, with the chance to win prizes or have their recipe featured on the bakery's website or menu.
- Interactive Recipe Polls: Engage followers by polling them on social media platforms to determine which recipes they would like to see featured next, allowing them to have a say in the bakery's content.
- Recipe Videos and Tutorials: Create engaging recipe videos and tutorials that walk viewers through the steps of preparing bakery favorites, catering to different learning styles and preferences.
- Community Cookbook: Compile a community cookbook featuring recipes submitted by customers, staff members, and community partners, celebrating the diversity and creativity of the bakery's community.
- Recipe Cards with Purchases: Include recipe cards featuring bakery-inspired recipes with customer purchases, encouraging them to try new baking projects at home using the bakery's products.
- Baking Classes and Workshops: Offer baking classes and workshops where customers can learn how to recreate bakery recipes under the guidance of experienced bakers, fostering a sense of community and skill-building.
- Recipe eBooks: Create downloadable recipe eBooks that customers can access in exchange for subscribing to the bakery's email list, providing them with valuable content while growing the bakery's email database.
- Virtual Cooking Demos: Host virtual cooking demonstrations on social media platforms or through live streaming services, allowing followers to interact with the bakery's chefs in real-time and ask questions.
- Recipe Pairings: Suggest creative recipe pairings that combine bakery items with complementary flavors or beverages, inspiring customers to experiment with new flavor combinations.
- Ingredient Spotlights: Highlight featured ingredients used in bakery recipes through blog posts, social media content, and in-store displays, educating customers about the quality and versatility of the bakery's products.

- Test Kitchen Trials: Share behind-the-scenes glimpses of the bakery's test kitchen where new recipes are developed and refined, giving followers a sneak peek into the creative process.
- Subscriber-Exclusive Recipes: Reward email subscribers with access to exclusive recipes or sneak peeks of upcoming recipe releases, incentivizing them to stay connected with the bakery's brand.
- Recipe Rating and Reviews: Encourage customers to rate and review bakery recipes on the website or social media platforms, providing valuable feedback and social proof for other customers.
- Interactive Recipe Challenges: Challenge followers to recreate bakery recipes at home and share their results on social media using a designated hashtag, fostering a sense of community and friendly competition.
- Seasonal Ingredient Foraging Guides: Provide guides on foraging for seasonal ingredients that can be used in bakery recipes, connecting followers with local resources and encouraging sustainability.
- Recipe Modification Suggestions: Offer suggestions for modifying bakery recipes to accommodate dietary restrictions or personal preferences, ensuring inclusivity and accessibility for all customers.
- Recipe Testing Panels: Recruit loyal customers or brand ambassadors to participate in recipe testing panels, providing feedback on new recipe concepts and helping to refine them before release.
- Baking Tips and Tricks Blog Series: Create a blog series dedicated to sharing insider baking tips and tricks, covering topics such as ingredient substitutions, troubleshooting common baking issues, and mastering baking techniques.
- Recipe Revamp Challenges: Challenge followers to put their own twist on bakery recipes by adding unique ingredients or incorporating different flavor combinations, sparking creativity and innovation.
- Virtual Recipe Exchanges: Host virtual recipe exchange events where followers can share their favorite recipes and baking tips with each other, fostering a sense of community and connection.
- Recipe Preservation Initiatives: Preserve and share traditional family recipes or cultural baking traditions through blog posts, interviews, and recipe features, celebrating the diversity of baking heritage within the bakery's community.

CONTENT MARKETING IDEAS

Crafting Email Newsletters Customers Love

- Weekly Specials and Promotions: Keep customers informed about weekly specials, discounts, and promotions through email newsletters, providing them with exclusive offers and incentives to visit the bakery.
- New Product Launches: Announce the launch of new bakery products or seasonal offerings to subscribers first, building anticipation and excitement around the latest additions to the menu.
- Recipe Features: Share featured recipes with subscribers, providing step-by-step instructions and tips for recreating bakery favorites at home, and encouraging them to visit the bakery for ingredients or pre-made options.
- Customer Stories and Testimonials: Share heartwarming stories and testimonials from satisfied customers who have had memorable experiences at the bakery, showcasing the bakery's commitment to customer satisfaction and community.
- Behind-the-Scenes Insights: Offer exclusive behind-the-scenes glimpses into the bakery's kitchen, production process, and events, giving subscribers a deeper understanding and appreciation of the bakery's operations.
- Baking Tips and Tricks: Provide subscribers with valuable baking tips, tricks, and hacks to help them improve their baking skills and achieve better results in their own kitchens.
- Seasonal Inspiration: Curate seasonal content that reflects current trends, holidays, and occasions, offering subscribers inspiration and ideas for seasonal baking projects and celebrations.
- Local Foodie Spotlights: Highlight local foodie partners, suppliers, or artisans in email newsletters, showcasing collaborations and partnerships that align with the bakery's values and support the local community.
- Interactive Polls and Surveys: Engage subscribers by including interactive polls and surveys in email newsletters, inviting them to share their opinions, preferences, and feedback on bakery-related topics.
- Exclusive Events and Workshops: Invite subscribers to exclusive events, workshops, or tastings hosted by the bakery, providing them with unique experiences and opportunities to interact with the bakery's team and products.
- Seasonal Menu Previews: Offer subscribers sneak peeks of upcoming seasonal menus and offerings before they are officially launched, giving them early access to limited-time treats and menu items.
- Staff Spotlights: Introduce subscribers to the talented individuals behind the bakery's success through staff spotlights and interviews, allowing them to connect on a personal level with the people who make their favorite treats.
- Interactive Recipe Contests: Host recipe contests or challenges exclusively for subscribers, encouraging them to submit their own recipes or baking creations for a chance to win prizes or recognition.

- Customer Appreciation Events: Show appreciation for loyal subscribers with special events or discounts reserved exclusively for them, fostering a sense of loyalty and gratitude within the bakery's customer base.
- Sustainability Initiatives: Share updates and information about the bakery's sustainability initiatives and eco-friendly practices, demonstrating its commitment to environmental responsibility and transparency.
- Exclusive Discounts and Offers: Provide subscribers with exclusive discounts, offers, or early access to sales events, rewarding them for their loyalty and encouraging repeat visits to the bakery.
- Seasonal Gifting Ideas: Offer subscribers curated lists of seasonal gifting ideas and gift packages available for purchase at the bakery, making it easy for them to find the perfect gift for any occasion.
- Interactive DIY Projects: Include interactive DIY projects or activities in email newsletters, such as decorating tutorials or baking challenges, to inspire subscribers to get creative in their own kitchens.
- Customer Feedback and Surveys: Solicit feedback from subscribers through email surveys or feedback forms, giving them a voice in shaping the bakery's products, services, and customer experience.
- Local Community News and Events: Keep subscribers informed about local community news, events, and happenings that may be of interest, fostering a sense of connection and belonging within the community.
- Seasonal Ingredient Spotlight: Highlight seasonal ingredients used in bakery recipes and products, providing subscribers with information about their availability, benefits, and suggested uses.
- Interactive Games and Quizzes: Include interactive games, quizzes, or puzzles in email newsletters to entertain and engage subscribers, while also reinforcing key messaging or branding elements.
- Exclusive Content Sneak Peeks: Offer subscribers exclusive sneak peeks of upcoming content, such as blog posts, videos, or social media campaigns, giving them insider access to behind-the-scenes developments.
- Birthday and Anniversary Rewards: Recognize and celebrate subscribers' birthdays and anniversaries with special discounts, offers, or personalized messages, showing appreciation for their continued support and loyalty.

Video Content Creation for Bakeries

- Recipe Tutorials: Create step-by-step recipe tutorials showcasing the bakery's signature treats, providing viewers with visual guidance on how to recreate these delicious creations at home.
- Behind-the-Scenes Vlogs: Produce behind-the-scenes vlogs that offer viewers an insider's look into the bakery's daily operations, from the baking process to customer interactions and special events.
- Meet the Baker Series: Introduce viewers to the talented bakers and chefs behind the bakery's creations through a "Meet the Baker" video series, allowing them to connect on a personal level with the faces behind their favorite treats.
- Product Showcases: Showcase the bakery's product lineup in visually appealing product showcase videos, highlighting the craftsmanship, quality ingredients, and mouthwatering flavors of each item.
- Baking Tips and Techniques: Share valuable baking tips, tricks, and techniques in instructional videos, empowering viewers to improve their baking skills and achieve better results in their own kitchens.
- Seasonal Specials Highlights: Create video highlights of seasonal specials and limited-time offerings, enticing viewers with tantalizing visuals and enticing descriptions of the bakery's seasonal creations.
- Customer Testimonials: Capture customer testimonials on video, allowing satisfied customers to share their experiences and rave reviews of the bakery's products and services.
- DIY Decorating Demos: Produce DIY decorating demos that teach viewers how to decorate cakes, cookies, and pastries like a pro, inspiring them to get creative in their own kitchen.
- Local Ingredient Sourcing Stories: Tell the story of the bakery's commitment to sourcing local ingredients in video format, showcasing local farmers, producers, and artisans who contribute to the bakery's products.
- Holiday Baking Series: Launch a holiday baking video series featuring festive recipes and baking ideas for various holidays and occasions throughout the year, catering to seasonal baking trends and traditions.
- Culinary Collaborations: Collaborate with local chefs, food bloggers, or influencers on video content that combines their expertise with the bakery's offerings, showcasing unique culinary creations and collaborations.
- Baking Challenges: Host baking challenges on video platforms where viewers are encouraged to recreate bakery recipes or participate in themed baking challenges, fostering engagement and interaction.
- Virtual Cooking Classes: Offer virtual cooking classes and workshops led by the bakery's chefs, providing viewers with interactive learning experiences and hands-on instruction in the art of baking.
- Taste Test Videos: Produce taste test videos where customers sample and react to the bakery's products, capturing their genuine reactions and feedback for an authentic and

engaging viewing experience.
- Q&A Sessions: Host live Q&A sessions on video platforms where viewers can ask questions and interact with the bakery's team in real-time, building rapport and fostering a sense of community.
- Baking Science Explained: Create educational videos that delve into the science behind baking, explaining concepts such as fermentation, gluten development, and leavening agents in an accessible and engaging manner.
- Employee Spotlights: Spotlight different employees in video interviews, allowing viewers to learn more about their roles, backgrounds, and contributions to the bakery's success.
- DIY Gift Ideas: Share DIY gift ideas and packaging inspiration in video format, showcasing creative ways to present bakery products as gifts for special occasions or holidays.
- Baking for Special Diets: Produce videos featuring recipes and baking tips tailored to special dietary needs, such as gluten-free, vegan, or allergen-friendly baking, catering to a diverse audience.
- Baking with Kids: Create family-friendly baking videos that feature kid-friendly recipes and baking projects, encouraging families to bond over baking and create lasting memories together.
- Bakery Tours: Take viewers on virtual bakery tours that highlight different areas of the bakery, from the kitchen to the storefront, providing an immersive and interactive experience.
- Baking Challenges: Host baking challenges on video platforms where viewers are encouraged to recreate bakery recipes or participate in themed baking challenges, fostering engagement and interaction.
- Culinary Travel Series: Produce a culinary travel series that explores different baking traditions and flavors from around the world, inspiring viewers with global culinary adventures and cultural insights.
- Baking for a Cause: Document the bakery's involvement in charitable initiatives and community outreach programs in video format, showcasing the impact of their efforts and encouraging viewers to support worthy causes.

Hosting Live Baking Demonstrations Online

- Weekly Baking Classes: Host weekly live baking classes online, where viewers can join in real-time to learn how to recreate bakery favorites from the comfort of their own kitchens.
- Interactive Q&A Sessions: Incorporate interactive Q&A sessions into live baking demonstrations, allowing viewers to ask questions and interact with the baker in real-time for personalized guidance and feedback.
- Seasonal Baking Workshops: Offer seasonal baking workshops that focus on holiday-themed treats and seasonal flavors, providing viewers with inspiration and ideas for festive baking projects.
- Guest Chef Collaborations: Collaborate with guest chefs or culinary influencers to co-host live baking demonstrations online, bringing fresh perspectives and expertise to the virtual baking experience.
- Specialty Baking Techniques: Explore specialty baking techniques and skills in live demonstrations, such as cake decorating, bread making, pastry shaping, and chocolate tempering, catering to viewers with diverse interests and skill levels.
- Baking for Special Diets: Dedicate live baking demonstrations to recipes and techniques tailored to special dietary needs, such as gluten-free, vegan, or allergen-friendly baking, providing inclusive content for a diverse audience.
- Recipe Challenges: Engage viewers with live recipe challenges where the baker improvises and creates new recipes using surprise ingredients or limited pantry staples, showcasing creativity and problem-solving skills in real-time.
- Culinary Cultural Explorations: Take viewers on a culinary journey around the world with live demonstrations that explore different baking traditions, flavors, and techniques from various cultures and cuisines.
- Baking Science Demystified: Offer educational live demonstrations that delve into the science behind baking, explaining concepts such as fermentation, gluten development, and leavening agents in an accessible and engaging manner.
- Baking with Kids: Host family-friendly live baking demonstrations that cater to young aspiring bakers, featuring kid-friendly recipes and interactive activities that encourage children to get involved in the kitchen.
- Seasonal Ingredient Showcases: Highlight seasonal ingredients and flavors in live demonstrations, showcasing creative ways to incorporate them into bakery recipes and celebrating the abundance of each season's harvest.
- Baking for Celebrations: Provide live demonstrations focused on baking customized treats for special occasions and celebrations, such as birthdays, weddings, anniversaries, and holidays, offering viewers inspiration and ideas for memorable events.
- Baking Basics Bootcamp: Offer a series of live demonstrations that cover the fundamentals of baking, from measuring ingredients and mixing techniques to baking temperatures and troubleshooting common issues, catering to beginners and novice bakers.

- Baking Challenges: Invite viewers to participate in live baking challenges where they attempt to recreate bakery recipes alongside the baker, fostering a sense of community and friendly competition among participants.
- DIY Baking Kits: Pair live baking demonstrations with DIY baking kits that contain pre-measured ingredients and tools needed to follow along with the recipe, providing convenience and ease for viewers who want to bake along at home.
- Interactive Tastings: Incorporate live tastings into baking demonstrations where viewers can sample bakery treats and provide feedback on flavor, texture, and presentation, creating an interactive and sensory experience.
- Baking for Wellness: Focus on baking recipes that promote health and wellness in live demonstrations, featuring ingredients known for their nutritional benefits and emphasizing mindful baking practices.
- Baking for a Cause: Dedicate live baking demonstrations to raising awareness and support for charitable causes and community initiatives, encouraging viewers to donate and get involved in worthy causes.
- Local Ingredient Sourcing: Showcase the bakery's commitment to sourcing local ingredients in live demonstrations, highlighting partnerships with local farmers, producers, and artisans who contribute to the bakery's products.
- Baking with Seasonal Produce: Highlight the versatility of seasonal produce in live demonstrations, demonstrating how to incorporate fruits, vegetables, and herbs into bakery recipes for fresh and flavorful results.
- Bakery Signature Creations: Feature the bakery's signature creations in live demonstrations, giving viewers an insider's look into the secrets behind these beloved treats and fostering brand loyalty and recognition.
- Virtual Baking Parties: Host virtual baking parties where viewers can bake alongside friends and family members in separate locations, fostering connections and creating shared baking experiences online.
- Baking Hacks and Shortcuts: Share time-saving baking hacks and shortcuts in live demonstrations, providing viewers with practical tips and tricks for streamlining their baking process and achieving better results with less effort.
- Seasonal Baking Challenges: Launch seasonal baking challenges that coincide with holidays and special occasions, encouraging viewers to showcase their baking skills and creativity by sharing their creations on social media.

CONTENT MARKETING IDEAS

Utilizing User-Generated Content

- Encourage customers to share their homemade recipes featuring your bakery's products on social media platforms, showcasing the versatility and creativity of your offerings.
- Host a photo contest where participants submit pictures of their favorite bakery treats, with the winning entries receiving a gift card or free baked goods.
- Create a branded hashtag for customers to use when posting about their bakery experiences, making it easier to track and share user-generated content.
- Feature customer testimonials and reviews prominently on your website and social media channels, highlighting the positive experiences others have had with your bakery.
- Invite loyal customers to take part in a behind-the-scenes tour of your bakery, giving them exclusive access to your production process and encouraging them to share their experience online.
- Run a "Fan of the Week" campaign, selecting one customer each week to spotlight on your social media pages and thanking them for their support.
- Partner with local influencers or bloggers who have a strong following in your area to create content featuring your bakery's products and sharing it with their audience.
- Create a dedicated space in your bakery for customers to leave notes or drawings expressing their love for your baked goods, then share photos of these messages on social media.
- Host a live baking demonstration on social media, inviting customers to tune in and ask questions as you showcase how to make one of your signature treats.
- Launch a loyalty program where customers earn rewards or discounts for sharing their bakery experiences on social media or referring friends.
- Collaborate with customers to co-create new menu items, soliciting suggestions and feedback through social media polls or surveys.
- Showcase customer-generated content on digital signage within your bakery, displaying photos or reviews from social media in real-time.
- Create a community cookbook featuring recipes submitted by customers, with proceeds from sales going to a local charity or organization.
- Host a themed photo challenge, encouraging customers to share pictures of your bakery's treats in unique settings or situations.
- Sponsor a local event or charity fundraiser and encourage attendees to share their experiences at the event, mentioning your bakery in their posts.
- Offer incentives for customers to leave reviews on popular review platforms such as Yelp or Google, helping to boost your bakery's online reputation.
- Collaborate with other local businesses to host joint promotions or giveaways, encouraging customers to engage with both brands and share their experiences.
- Create a dedicated space in your bakery for customers to take Instagram-worthy photos of their purchases, complete with props and backdrops.

- Host a "Customer Appreciation Day" event where customers can enjoy free samples, discounts, and giveaways in exchange for sharing their experience on social media.
- Encourage customers to share their favorite bakery-related memories or traditions on your website or social media channels, fostering a sense of community among your audience.
- Create a "Baker's Spotlight" series where you interview and feature a different customer each month, sharing their story and favorite bakery items with your audience.
- Launch a referral program where customers receive rewards for referring friends or family members to your bakery, incentivizing word-of-mouth marketing.
- Host a baking contest where customers can submit their own recipes using your bakery's products, with the winning recipe featured on your menu.
- Collaborate with local photographers to offer professional photo sessions featuring your bakery's products, providing customers with high-quality images to share on their social media accounts.

CONTENT MARKETING IDEAS

Behind-the-Scenes Looks at Bakery Operations

- Create a video series showcasing the step-by-step process of making your bakery's signature items, providing customers with an insider's view of your operations.
- Host live-streamed baking sessions where viewers can watch your bakers in action, ask questions, and learn tips and tricks for recreating your recipes at home.
- Share behind-the-scenes photos and videos on social media, highlighting the craftsmanship and attention to detail that goes into each batch of baked goods.
- Offer virtual tours of your bakery facilities, giving customers a glimpse into your kitchen, storage areas, and equipment.
- Interview your bakers and staff members to share their stories and expertise with your audience, humanizing your brand and building trust with customers.
- Collaborate with local food bloggers or influencers to create content featuring behind-the-scenes looks at your bakery operations, reaching new audiences and driving engagement.
- Highlight the sourcing of your ingredients and the relationships you have with local farmers and suppliers, emphasizing the quality and freshness of your products.
- Showcase the technology and equipment used in your bakery, explaining how they contribute to the consistency and excellence of your baked goods.
- Share insights into your sustainability practices, such as recycling initiatives or energy-saving measures, demonstrating your commitment to environmental responsibility.
- Offer online workshops or masterclasses where customers can learn advanced baking techniques from your experienced pastry chefs.
- Create an interactive online quiz or game that challenges customers to guess the ingredients or techniques used in your bakery's most popular items.
- Host a "Day in the Life" series on social media, following a staff member as they go about their daily tasks in the bakery, from early morning dough prep to closing time.
- Provide sneak peeks of upcoming menu items or seasonal specials, generating excitement and anticipation among your customer base.
- Share fun facts and trivia about the history of baking or the origins of different types of pastries, educating and entertaining your audience.
- Collaborate with other local businesses to offer exclusive behind-the-scenes tours or experiences, providing added value to your customers.
- Create downloadable resources such as recipe cards or baking guides that customers can access on your website, further establishing your bakery as a trusted source of expertise.
- Host Q&A sessions with your bakers or management team, allowing customers to ask questions about your products, processes, or industry trends.
- Showcase the creativity and innovation behind your bakery's custom cake designs, sharing stories of how each masterpiece comes to life.

- Offer limited-time opportunities for customers to participate in hands-on baking classes or workshops at your bakery location.
- Partner with local schools or community organizations to offer educational tours or field trips to your bakery, fostering connections with future generations of customers.
- Highlight any special certifications or awards your bakery has received, reinforcing your reputation for excellence and quality.
- Share testimonials or reviews from satisfied customers who have had memorable experiences visiting your bakery and witnessing your operations firsthand.
- Collaborate with a videographer to create a professionally produced documentary or mini-series exploring the history and legacy of your bakery.
- Host open house events where customers can mingle with your staff, sample your products, and gain a deeper understanding of what sets your bakery apart from the competition.

CONTENT MARKETING IDEAS

Highlighting Customer Stories and Testimonials

- Create a series of video testimonials featuring satisfied customers sharing their favorite bakery memories, experiences, and the reasons they keep coming back.
- Host a monthly "Customer Spotlight" campaign on your blog or social media platforms, showcasing stories of loyal patrons and their connections to your bakery.
- Encourage customers to share their bakery experiences on social media using a designated hashtag, then curate and share these posts on your own channels.
- Conduct interviews with long-time customers or those with interesting stories related to your bakery, sharing their narratives through blog posts or podcast episodes.
- Create a dedicated webpage on your website where customers can submit their testimonials and stories, providing a platform for their voices to be heard.
- Offer incentives such as discounts or freebies for customers who share their stories and testimonials, encouraging participation and engagement.
- Collaborate with local photographers to capture professional portraits of your customers enjoying your bakery's products, accompanied by their testimonials.
- Share success stories of customers who have achieved milestones or celebrated special occasions with your bakery's treats, illustrating the role your bakery plays in their lives.
- Create a "Wall of Fame" in your bakery featuring photos and testimonials from loyal customers, recognizing and honoring their support.
- Host customer appreciation events where you invite loyal patrons to share their stories in person, fostering a sense of community and connection.
- Create a series of blog posts or articles highlighting different customer personas and their unique preferences and experiences with your bakery.
- Produce mini-documentaries or video profiles showcasing the journeys of customers who have overcome challenges or achieved goals with the support of your bakery.
- Incorporate customer testimonials into your email marketing campaigns, sharing authentic stories that resonate with your subscribers.
- Partner with local media outlets to feature stories about your bakery's impact on the community, leveraging their reach to amplify customer testimonials.
- Offer a platform for customers to leave video testimonials on your website, providing a dynamic and engaging way for others to hear about their experiences.
- Create a loyalty program where customers earn points or rewards for sharing their testimonials or referring new customers to your bakery.
- Share stories of customers who have discovered your bakery through word-of-mouth recommendations, illustrating the power of positive experiences.
- Host "Storytelling Nights" at your bakery where customers can gather to share their memories and anecdotes over coffee and pastries.
- Create a monthly newsletter featuring customer testimonials, stories, and highlights, keeping your audience engaged and connected.

- Partner with local bloggers or influencers to create sponsored content featuring their experiences with your bakery, reaching new audiences with authentic testimonials.
- Create a video series featuring interviews with customers from diverse backgrounds, showcasing the inclusive and welcoming atmosphere of your bakery.
- Collaborate with local charities or organizations to share stories of how your bakery has made a positive impact on the community, aligning your brand with social responsibility.
- Use customer testimonials as social proof in your advertising campaigns, demonstrating the trust and satisfaction others have experienced with your bakery.
- Host contests or giveaways where customers can win prizes for sharing their stories or testimonials, incentivizing engagement and participation.

CONTENT MARKETING IDEAS

Seasonal and Holiday Content Planning

- Create a content calendar outlining seasonal and holiday-themed promotions, events, and campaigns to ensure timely and relevant marketing efforts.
- Develop special menus or limited-edition products specifically for holidays and seasons, leveraging the excitement and anticipation surrounding these occasions.
- Host themed events or workshops at your bakery, such as gingerbread decorating parties for Christmas or pumpkin carving contests for Halloween, to attract customers and drive foot traffic.
- Design festive packaging for your bakery items during holidays and seasons, making them visually appealing and gift-ready for customers looking for presents or party favors.
- Share behind-the-scenes glimpses of your bakery's preparations for seasonal offerings, from recipe development to decoration planning, to build anticipation and generate excitement.
- Collaborate with local businesses or organizations to cross-promote seasonal events or initiatives, expanding your reach and tapping into complementary customer bases.
- Create holiday-themed blog posts or articles offering baking tips, recipe ideas, and entertaining inspiration to engage and inspire your audience.
- Launch a social media campaign inviting customers to share their favorite holiday baking traditions or recipes, fostering community engagement and generating user-generated content.
- Partner with influencers or food bloggers to create sponsored content featuring your bakery's seasonal offerings, reaching new audiences and driving sales.
- Offer seasonal promotions or discounts, such as buy-one-get-one deals or limited-time coupons, to incentivize purchases during peak holiday shopping periods.
- Host a holiday-themed photo contest on social media, encouraging customers to share pictures of themselves enjoying your seasonal treats for a chance to win prizes.
- Organize charitable initiatives tied to seasonal giving, such as donating a portion of proceeds from holiday sales to local food banks or shelters, aligning your brand with goodwill and generosity.
- Create themed gift baskets or bundles featuring a selection of your bakery's seasonal treats, offering convenience and value for customers looking for holiday gifts.
- Launch a countdown campaign leading up to major holidays, unveiling new products, promotions, or exclusive offers each day to build anticipation and drive sales.
- Partner with local hotels or event venues to provide catering services for holiday parties and gatherings, expanding your reach and positioning your bakery as a go-to choice for festive occasions.
- Create seasonal email newsletters featuring exclusive discounts, holiday recipes, and insider updates to keep subscribers engaged and informed.
- Host tasting events or sampling stations in your bakery, allowing customers to try seasonal offerings before making a purchase and enticing them with the flavors of the season.

- Develop holiday-themed social media content, such as festive recipe videos or DIY decorating tutorials, to capture the attention of your audience and drive engagement.
- Offer pre-order options for holiday items to accommodate customers' busy schedules and ensure they can enjoy your bakery's treats during their seasonal celebrations.
- Collaborate with local artisans or craftsmen to create co-branded holiday gift sets or packages, providing customers with unique and curated offerings.
- Host a holiday bake-off competition where customers can submit their own recipes or creations for a chance to be featured on your bakery's menu or social media channels.
- Create a seasonal loyalty program where customers earn rewards or discounts for repeat purchases during peak holiday periods, incentivizing repeat business and customer retention.
- Design interactive online quizzes or polls related to seasonal baking traditions or holiday-themed trivia, engaging your audience and driving traffic to your website or social media channels.
- Collaborate with local media outlets to feature your bakery's seasonal offerings in holiday gift guides or roundups, leveraging their reach to attract new customers and boost sales.

CONTENT MARKETING IDEAS

Photography Tips for Mouth-Watering Visuals

- Create a guide or ebook featuring professional photography tips specifically tailored to capturing the irresistible appeal of bakery products.
- Host a photography workshop or webinar for customers or aspiring food photographers, sharing techniques for styling and shooting bakery items for maximum visual impact.
- Develop a series of blog posts or articles highlighting different photography techniques such as lighting, composition, and editing, with practical tips and examples for bakery-specific imagery.
- Collaborate with local photographers to create sponsored content featuring stunning visuals of your bakery's products, showcasing their expertise while promoting your brand.
- Offer downloadable resources such as photography presets or editing tutorials to help customers enhance their bakery-related images and create eye-catching visuals.
- Create before-and-after photography tutorials demonstrating the difference lighting and styling can make in capturing mouth-watering images of bakery items.
- Host a photo contest on social media where participants submit their best bakery-themed photos, with prizes awarded for the most visually appealing and creative entries.
- Share behind-the-scenes glimpses of your bakery's photography process, including set-up, styling, and editing, to provide insights and inspiration for aspiring photographers.
- Collaborate with food stylists to create visually stunning tableaus featuring your bakery's products, showcasing different presentation ideas and styling techniques.
- Develop a branded hashtag for customers to use when sharing photos of your bakery's treats on social media, making it easier to track user-generated content and engage with your audience.
- Create a dedicated section on your website or social media profiles featuring customer-submitted photos of your bakery's products, celebrating their creativity and loyalty.
- Offer photography tips and advice in your bakery's email newsletters, along with mouth-watering images of your latest creations to inspire customers and drive sales.
- Host Instagram Live sessions where you demonstrate photography techniques for capturing bakery items, interacting with viewers and answering their questions in real-time.
- Partner with local influencers or food bloggers who have a strong following on social media to create sponsored content featuring your bakery's products in visually appealing settings.
- Create a series of video tutorials demonstrating how to style and photograph bakery items using everyday household items and simple techniques.
- Collaborate with local businesses or organizations to host photography meet-ups or photo walks focused on capturing the beauty of bakery items in different environments.
- Offer photography-themed promotions or discounts for customers who share their bakery-related images on social media using your branded hashtag.

- Create a Pinterest board featuring photography inspiration and tips for capturing mouth-watering images of bakery products, attracting followers and driving traffic to your website.
- Host a photography challenge where customers are tasked with recreating a specific bakery item and sharing their photos on social media for a chance to win prizes.
- Create a gallery wall in your bakery showcasing customer-submitted photos of your products, rotating the display regularly to feature new images and encourage ongoing engagement.
- Collaborate with local photography schools or clubs to offer workshops or classes at your bakery, providing hands-on experience and expert guidance for aspiring photographers.
- Highlight the versatility of your bakery's products by featuring them in a variety of settings and compositions in your photography, from elegant dessert tables to casual picnics.
- Share before-and-after examples of edited bakery photos to demonstrate the impact of post-processing techniques such as color correction and retouching on the final image.
- Create a series of Instagram Stories or Reels offering quick photography tips and tricks for capturing mouth-watering images of bakery items, engaging your audience with snackable content.

CONTENT MARKETING IDEAS

Collaborating with Food Bloggers and Influencers

- Identify influential food bloggers and social media influencers whose audience aligns with your bakery's target demographic, focusing on those with a strong following and engaged audience.
- Reach out to potential collaborators with personalized pitches highlighting the unique aspects of your bakery and the mutual benefits of working together.
- Offer complimentary bakery items or exclusive tasting experiences to influencers in exchange for coverage on their platforms, leveraging their reach to increase visibility for your brand.
- Host influencer events or VIP tastings at your bakery, providing influencers with an opportunity to sample your products and create content for their followers.
- Collaborate with influencers to develop co-branded content such as recipe videos, sponsored blog posts, or Instagram takeovers featuring your bakery's products.
- Organize influencer meet-ups or networking events to foster relationships and partnerships with local bloggers and content creators, building rapport and trust within the community.
- Provide influencers with high-quality images and product information to facilitate their content creation process and ensure consistency in branding and messaging.
- Offer affiliate or referral programs for influencers to earn commissions or incentives for driving traffic and sales to your bakery through their unique tracking links or discount codes.
- Host influencer-driven giveaways or contests on social media, leveraging the excitement and engagement generated by their followers to increase brand awareness and customer acquisition.
- Collaborate with influencers to create themed content series or campaigns centered around seasonal promotions, holidays, or special events, capitalizing on timely and relevant topics to drive engagement.
- Invite influencers to participate in live-streamed baking demonstrations or Q&A sessions on social media, allowing them to showcase your products while interacting with their audience in real-time.
- Feature influencer-generated content on your bakery's website or social media channels, crediting the creators and amplifying their reach while showcasing authentic endorsements of your brand.
- Offer influencers exclusive discounts or perks for their followers, incentivizing engagement and driving traffic to your bakery both online and in-store.
- Collaborate with influencers to host sponsored events or pop-ups featuring your bakery's products, providing a platform for them to connect with their audience while showcasing your offerings.
- Leverage influencer-generated content for paid advertising campaigns across various channels, including social media, email, and display ads, to reach new audiences and drive conversions.

- Create influencer ambassador programs to establish long-term partnerships with select content creators, fostering loyalty and advocacy for your bakery's brand.
- Host influencer-led workshops or classes at your bakery, providing educational opportunities for their followers while promoting your products and services.
- Collaborate with influencers to create curated gift guides or product roundups featuring your bakery's offerings, positioning them as must-have items for their audience.
- Offer influencers access to exclusive behind-the-scenes experiences or product launches, allowing them to create unique and compelling content for their followers.
- Collaborate with micro-influencers or nano-influencers who have smaller but highly engaged audiences, maximizing the impact of your collaborations within niche communities.
- Host influencer-driven charity or fundraising events at your bakery, partnering with influencers to raise awareness and support for causes aligned with your brand values.
- Provide influencers with sneak peeks of upcoming menu items or special promotions, allowing them to create anticipation and excitement among their followers.
- Collaborate with influencers to create branded merchandise or limited-edition products featuring their unique designs or input, tapping into their creativity and fan base.
- Measure and track the performance of influencer collaborations using key metrics such as engagement, reach, and conversion rates, adjusting your strategy as needed to optimize results and maximize ROI.

Building a Content Calendar

- Develop a monthly content calendar outlining key themes, topics, and campaigns aligned with your bakery's marketing objectives and seasonal trends.
- Incorporate holidays, special events, and seasonal promotions into your content calendar to ensure timely and relevant messaging that resonates with your audience.
- Create a mix of content types including blog posts, social media posts, videos, email newsletters, and downloadable resources to engage with customers across different channels.
- Research trending topics and popular hashtags related to baking, food, and lifestyle to inform your content calendar and capitalize on opportunities for increased visibility and engagement.
- Collaborate with your bakery team to brainstorm content ideas and identify unique stories, recipes, and behind-the-scenes insights to share with your audience.
- Plan ahead for major holidays and seasonal shifts by scheduling content in advance, allowing time for production, review, and optimization before launch.
- Tailor your content to different audience segments, such as home bakers, foodies, families, or health-conscious consumers, to ensure relevance and resonance with diverse demographics.
- Leverage user-generated content and customer testimonials to supplement your content calendar, showcasing authentic experiences and building community engagement.
- Incorporate storytelling elements into your content calendar to humanize your brand and create emotional connections with your audience, sharing anecdotes, memories, and personal insights.
- Create themed content series or campaigns around specific topics or initiatives, such as baking tips, recipe spotlights, or employee highlights, to maintain consistency and coherence in your messaging.
- Allocate dedicated time slots in your content calendar for engaging with your audience, responding to comments, questions, and feedback across your social media channels.
- Monitor industry trends, competitor activities, and customer feedback to identify opportunities for real-time content creation and agile adjustments to your content calendar.
- Experiment with different content formats and platforms to optimize performance and reach, testing new ideas and strategies to keep your audience engaged and entertained.
- Collaborate with local influencers, bloggers, and community partners to co-create content and amplify your reach, leveraging their audience and expertise to enhance your content calendar.
- Schedule regular content audits and reviews to assess the effectiveness of your content calendar, analyzing key metrics such as engagement, traffic, and conversions to inform future planning and optimization efforts.
- Incorporate evergreen content into your calendar, such as timeless recipes, baking tips, and educational resources, to provide ongoing value to your audience and attract new visitors

over time.
- Integrate calls-to-action (CTAs) strategically throughout your content calendar to drive desired actions such as website visits, newsletter sign-ups, or product purchases.
- Plan themed promotions or sales events to coincide with key dates in your content calendar, incentivizing customer engagement and driving revenue growth.
- Leverage seasonal ingredients, flavors, and trends to inspire content ideas and product offerings that resonate with your audience's preferences and preferences.
- Collaborate with your marketing team to align your content calendar with broader marketing initiatives and campaigns, ensuring consistency and synergy across all touchpoints.
- Use analytics tools and metrics to track the performance of your content calendar over time, identifying areas for improvement and optimization to maximize ROI.
- Engage with your audience proactively by soliciting feedback, conducting surveys, and hosting interactive events to inform your content calendar and strengthen customer relationships.
- Incorporate storytelling elements into your content calendar to humanize your brand and create emotional connections with your audience, sharing anecdotes, memories, and personal insights.
- Stay flexible and adaptable in your content planning process, allowing room for spontaneity, creativity, and responsiveness to emerging trends and opportunities in the ever-evolving digital landscape.

Writing Press Releases for Bakery Events

- Craft a press release announcing the grand opening of your bakery, highlighting key details such as location, offerings, and unique selling points to attract media attention and generate buzz.
- Write a press release to announce the launch of a new product line or menu expansion, emphasizing the innovation, quality, and craftsmanship behind your bakery's offerings.
- Issue a press release to promote special events or promotions at your bakery, such as holiday sales, themed parties, or charity fundraisers, inviting media coverage and community participation.
- Announce collaborations or partnerships with local businesses or organizations in a press release, showcasing the synergy and mutual benefits of the partnership while enhancing your bakery's visibility.
- Write a press release to highlight milestones and achievements for your bakery, such as anniversaries, awards, or certifications, positioning your brand as a leader in the industry.
- Issue a press release to announce the launch of a new website or online ordering platform for your bakery, emphasizing the convenience and accessibility for customers.
- Craft a press release to introduce new leadership or notable hires at your bakery, showcasing the expertise and talent behind your operations while attracting media interest.
- Write a press release to announce participation in local food festivals, markets, or industry events, positioning your bakery as an active and engaged member of the community.
- Issue a press release to announce renovations or expansions at your bakery, highlighting the improvements and enhancements to the customer experience.
- Craft a press release to share charitable initiatives or community involvement efforts by your bakery, demonstrating your commitment to social responsibility and giving back.
- Write a press release to announce special promotions or discounts for loyal customers, encouraging media coverage and driving traffic to your bakery.
- Issue a press release to announce the launch of a customer loyalty program or rewards system at your bakery, incentivizing repeat business and customer retention.
- Craft a press release to announce participation in industry trends or movements, such as offering gluten-free or vegan options, demonstrating your responsiveness to consumer preferences.
- Write a press release to announce seasonal offerings or limited-time menu items at your bakery, leveraging the excitement and anticipation surrounding seasonal trends.
- Issue a press release to announce partnerships with local farmers or suppliers for sourcing ingredients, emphasizing the freshness, quality, and sustainability of your bakery's products.
- Craft a press release to announce the introduction of eco-friendly packaging or sustainable practices at your bakery, highlighting your commitment to environmental stewardship.
- Write a press release to announce participation in food competitions or challenges, showcasing your bakery's creativity, skill, and dedication to excellence.

- Issue a press release to announce sponsorship or involvement in community events or initiatives, reinforcing your bakery's presence and support within the local area.
- Craft a press release to announce the availability of custom catering services or special event packages at your bakery, targeting corporate clients, weddings, and other special occasions.
- Write a press release to announce the launch of a new marketing campaign or branding initiative for your bakery, highlighting the strategic vision and direction of your brand.
- Issue a press release to announce partnerships with local media outlets or influencers for collaborative content creation or promotional campaigns, expanding your reach and audience engagement.
- Craft a press release to announce the release of a cookbook or recipe collection featuring signature recipes from your bakery, positioning your brand as an authority in baking.
- Write a press release to announce participation in charitable events or fundraisers, such as donating proceeds from sales to local causes or sponsoring community initiatives.
- Issue a press release to announce the launch of a customer feedback program or survey at your bakery, demonstrating your commitment to continuous improvement and customer satisfaction.

CONTENT MARKETING IDEAS

Engaging with Q&A Sessions on Social Media

- Host regular Q&A sessions on social media platforms such as Instagram, Facebook, or Twitter, inviting followers to submit their baking-related questions in advance or during the live session.
- Choose a specific theme or topic for each Q&A session, such as cake decorating tips, bread baking basics, or gluten-free baking alternatives, to provide focused and valuable information to your audience.
- Promote your Q&A sessions in advance through posts, stories, and email newsletters to build anticipation and encourage participation from your followers.
- Use interactive features such as polls, quizzes, or live chat functions during your Q&A sessions to engage with your audience in real-time and gather feedback on their preferences and interests.
- Encourage participation by offering incentives or prizes for attendees who ask insightful questions or actively engage in the discussion during your Q&A sessions.
- Invite guest experts or industry professionals to join your Q&A sessions as special guests, providing additional expertise and perspectives to enrich the conversation and attract new followers.
- Record and repurpose your Q&A sessions as on-demand content for viewers who may have missed the live event, making it accessible on your social media profiles or website.
- Solicit feedback and suggestions from your audience on topics they would like to see covered in future Q&A sessions, tailoring your content to address their interests and needs.
- Showcase customer testimonials and success stories during your Q&A sessions to provide social proof and inspire confidence in your bakery's products and services.
- Address common misconceptions or FAQs related to baking, ingredients, or dietary restrictions during your Q&A sessions to educate and inform your audience while dispelling myths.
- Share practical tips, tricks, and hacks for baking success during your Q&A sessions, drawing on your expertise and experience as a professional baker to provide valuable insights to your audience.
- Encourage viewers to share their own baking experiences, recipes, and photos during your Q&A sessions, fostering a sense of community and camaraderie among your followers.
- Monitor comments and questions in real-time during your Q&A sessions, responding promptly and thoughtfully to engage with your audience and provide helpful guidance.
- Collaborate with other businesses or influencers in the food and baking industry to co-host joint Q&A sessions, expanding your reach and attracting new followers from their respective audiences.
- Share behind-the-scenes glimpses of your bakery's operations and production process during your Q&A sessions, offering viewers a behind-the-scenes look at your craft and expertise.

- Provide demonstrations or tutorials during your Q&A sessions to showcase specific techniques or recipes, making it interactive and educational for your audience.
- Incorporate humor and personality into your Q&A sessions to make them entertaining and engaging for viewers, injecting some fun and levity into the conversation.
- Invite customers to share their feedback and suggestions for improvement during your Q&A sessions, demonstrating your commitment to listening to their needs and preferences.
- Highlight special promotions, discounts, or upcoming events during your Q&A sessions to incentivize participation and drive sales for your bakery.
- Collaborate with local media outlets or influencers to promote your Q&A sessions and reach a wider audience, leveraging their platforms and networks to attract new followers and engagement.
- Share resources and recommendations for baking tools, ingredients, and equipment during your Q&A sessions, helping your audience make informed decisions and elevate their baking skills.
- Encourage viewers to tag friends and family members who may be interested in your Q&A sessions, leveraging the power of social sharing to expand your reach and grow your audience.
- Invite viewers to submit their own baking-related challenges or dilemmas for you to address during your Q&A sessions, providing personalized advice and solutions to their specific needs.
- Express gratitude and appreciation to your audience for their participation and engagement during your Q&A sessions, fostering a sense of loyalty and connection with your brand.

CONTENT MARKETING IDEAS

Creating Downloadable Baking Guides and Ebooks

- Develop a comprehensive beginner's guide to baking, covering essential techniques, equipment, and ingredients for novice bakers looking to improve their skills and confidence in the kitchen.
- Create a series of themed recipe ebooks, such as "Decadent Desserts," "Savory Breads," or "Healthy Baking," featuring a curated collection of your bakery's most popular and beloved recipes.
- Produce a holiday baking guide showcasing seasonal favorites and festive treats, providing inspiration and ideas for special occasions throughout the year.
- Design a gluten-free baking guide for individuals with dietary restrictions, offering tips, recipes, and ingredient substitutes to help them enjoy delicious baked goods without gluten.
- Develop a vegan baking ebook featuring plant-based recipes for cakes, cookies, and pastries, catering to the growing demand for cruelty-free and environmentally friendly alternatives.
- Create a kids' baking cookbook filled with fun and easy recipes that children can make with adult supervision, encouraging family bonding and culinary exploration.
- Produce a bread-making guide focusing on artisanal breads and traditional techniques, offering step-by-step instructions and troubleshooting tips for achieving bakery-quality results at home.
- Design a cake decorating ebook showcasing different frosting techniques, piping designs, and decorative accents, empowering home bakers to create stunning custom cakes for any occasion.
- Develop a brunch baking guide featuring recipes for muffins, scones, quiches, and other brunch favorites, perfect for hosting weekend gatherings or leisurely mornings at home.
- Create a healthy baking ebook highlighting recipes made with wholesome ingredients and natural sweeteners, catering to health-conscious consumers seeking guilt-free indulgences.
- Produce a pastry-making guide focusing on classic French pastries and techniques, including croissants, eclairs, and tarts, for bakers looking to master the art of patisserie.
- Design a cookie decorating ebook featuring creative designs, tips, and tricks for decorating cookies with royal icing, fondant, and other decorative elements.
- Develop a seasonal produce baking guide showcasing recipes that incorporate fresh fruits and vegetables, celebrating the flavors of each season and promoting local and seasonal eating.
- Create a high-altitude baking guide for individuals living in mountainous regions, offering adjustments and tips for successful baking at higher elevations where atmospheric conditions differ.
- Produce a breakfast baking ebook featuring recipes for homemade granola, breakfast bars, and baked oatmeal, providing nutritious and convenient options for busy mornings.
- Design a special occasion baking guide for milestone events such as weddings, birthdays, and anniversaries, offering inspiration and ideas for creating memorable and personalized

desserts.
- Develop a sourdough baking guide for enthusiasts interested in mastering the art of naturally leavened bread, covering starter maintenance, fermentation techniques, and sourdough recipes.
- Create a quick and easy baking guide for busy individuals looking to whip up delicious treats in minimal time, featuring recipes that require few ingredients and simple preparation methods.
- Produce a baking with kids ebook featuring family-friendly recipes and activities for children to enjoy, fostering a love of baking and creativity from a young age.
- Design a dessert pairing guide offering recommendations for pairing baked goods with coffee, tea, wine, or spirits, elevating the sensory experience of enjoying desserts.
- Develop a holiday cookie exchange guide with recipes, packaging ideas, and hosting tips for organizing festive cookie swaps with friends, family, or coworkers.
- Create a cultural baking ebook showcasing recipes from around the world, celebrating diverse culinary traditions and flavors while introducing readers to new and exotic desserts.
- Produce a baking for beginners guide with simplified recipes, step-by-step tutorials, and troubleshooting advice for individuals new to the world of baking.
- Design a seasonal baking guide featuring recipes inspired by the flavors and ingredients of each season, capturing the essence of spring, summer, fall, and winter in delicious baked treats.

Podcasting for Bakeries

- Launch a podcast series featuring interviews with bakery owners, chefs, and industry experts, offering insights, advice, and inspiration for aspiring bakers and bakery enthusiasts.
- Create episodes highlighting the stories behind your bakery's signature products, sharing the history, ingredients, and techniques that make them unique and beloved by customers.
- Produce episodes focused on baking tips, tricks, and techniques, providing practical advice and demonstrations to help listeners improve their baking skills and achieve professional-quality results at home.
- Invite guest chefs or culinary professionals to share their favorite recipes and baking secrets on your podcast, providing diverse perspectives and expertise to enrich the content.
- Collaborate with local farmers, suppliers, and producers to explore the journey of ingredients from farm to table, highlighting the importance of sourcing quality ingredients for baking.
- Produce episodes showcasing the artistry and craftsmanship of bakery design and decoration, featuring interviews with cake decorators, pastry chefs, and confectionery artists.
- Create a series of episodes focused on seasonal baking, exploring the flavors, traditions, and celebrations associated with different holidays and occasions throughout the year.
- Invite customers to share their baking stories, experiences, and favorite recipes on your podcast, fostering community engagement and highlighting the role of baking in people's lives.
- Produce episodes highlighting the health benefits of baked goods made with wholesome ingredients, featuring discussions with nutritionists, dietitians, and wellness experts.
- Collaborate with local food bloggers or influencers to co-host episodes on your podcast, leveraging their audience and expertise to reach new listeners and attract followers.
- Create episodes featuring behind-the-scenes glimpses of your bakery's operations, including interviews with staff members, tours of the kitchen, and stories of daily life in the bakery.
- Produce episodes focused on the intersection of baking and culture, exploring traditional recipes, rituals, and customs from around the world and their significance in different communities.
- Invite cookbook authors or food writers to discuss their latest publications and share recipes from their books on your podcast, offering valuable content and promoting their work to your audience.
- Create episodes featuring interviews with local food entrepreneurs and artisans, highlighting collaborations, partnerships, and cross-promotional opportunities within the community.
- Produce episodes on sustainability and environmental stewardship in baking, discussing topics such as reducing food waste, sourcing eco-friendly ingredients, and implementing

green practices in the bakery.
- Invite guests to share their baking successes and failures on your podcast, providing a platform for honest and relatable conversations about the joys and challenges of baking.
- Collaborate with local historians or culinary experts to explore the rich history and heritage of baking in your community, uncovering stories, traditions, and recipes passed down through generations.
- Create episodes featuring baking competitions or challenges, inviting listeners to participate and share their creations for a chance to be featured on the podcast.
- Produce episodes focused on baking for special dietary needs, such as gluten-free, dairy-free, or vegan baking, offering tips, recipes, and resources for individuals with dietary restrictions.
- Invite listeners to submit their baking questions and dilemmas for a Q&A segment on your podcast, providing expert advice and solutions to common baking challenges.
- Collaborate with local musicians or artists to create original music or artwork inspired by baking themes, incorporating these elements into your podcast episodes for a unique and immersive experience.
- Produce episodes featuring interviews with customers sharing their favorite bakery memories, experiences, and recommendations, providing testimonials and social proof of your bakery's quality and reputation.
- Create episodes highlighting the science behind baking, exploring topics such as fermentation, leavening agents, and flavor chemistry to educate and inform listeners about the technical aspects of baking.
- Invite listeners to join a baking book club on your podcast, selecting a different cookbook or baking-themed book each month to discuss, review, and share recipes from with the community.

CONTENT MARKETING IDEAS

Implementing SEO Best Practices in Content

- Conduct keyword research to identify relevant and high-traffic keywords related to baking, pastries, and desserts that your bakery can target in its content.
- Optimize your bakery's website structure and navigation to ensure it is user-friendly and easy for both visitors and search engines to navigate.
- Create high-quality and informative content that addresses the needs, interests, and questions of your target audience, incorporating targeted keywords naturally throughout your text.
- Optimize your website's meta titles and descriptions with relevant keywords to improve visibility and click-through rates in search engine results pages (SERPs).
- Utilize schema markup to provide search engines with additional context and information about your bakery, such as location, hours of operation, and customer reviews.
- Optimize your bakery's Google My Business listing with accurate information, high-quality images, and positive customer reviews to improve your local search visibility and attract more customers.
- Implement internal linking strategies to connect related content within your website, helping search engines understand the structure and hierarchy of your site and improving overall SEO.
- Create a blog or resource center on your bakery's website to regularly publish fresh and relevant content that targets specific keywords and provides value to your audience.
- Optimize your images with descriptive filenames, alt tags, and captions to improve accessibility and enhance your website's SEO performance.
- Monitor your website's performance using tools like Google Analytics and Google Search Console to track key metrics such as traffic, engagement, and keyword rankings.
- Conduct regular SEO audits of your website to identify and address technical issues, broken links, and other factors that may negatively impact your search visibility.
- Leverage the power of local SEO by optimizing your bakery's listings on online directories, review sites, and social media platforms to increase your visibility in local search results.
- Develop a content calendar to plan and schedule your SEO-focused content creation efforts, ensuring a consistent and strategic approach to publishing.
- Optimize your website for mobile devices to provide a seamless and user-friendly experience for mobile users, which can positively impact your search rankings.
- Monitor and respond to customer reviews and feedback on platforms like Google My Business, Yelp, and social media to build trust and credibility with both customers and search engines.
- Build high-quality backlinks from reputable websites in the food, baking, and culinary industries to improve your website's authority and credibility in the eyes of search engines.
- Utilize social media platforms to promote your content and engage with your audience, driving traffic and increasing visibility for your bakery's website.

- Conduct competitor analysis to identify opportunities and gaps in your SEO strategy, allowing you to refine and improve your approach based on industry best practices.
- Optimize your website's page speed and performance to provide a fast and seamless browsing experience for users, which can positively impact your search rankings.
- Utilize long-tail keywords and natural language phrases in your content to capture more specific search queries and attract highly targeted traffic to your website.
- Incorporate user-generated content, such as customer reviews, testimonials, and photos, into your website to enhance authenticity and credibility, which can positively impact your SEO.
- Regularly update and refresh your existing content to keep it relevant and up-to-date, signaling to search engines that your website is active and authoritative in its niche.
- Develop partnerships and collaborations with other businesses and influencers in your industry to expand your reach and attract more traffic and backlinks to your website.
- Stay informed about changes and updates to search engine algorithms and SEO best practices to ensure your bakery's website remains optimized and competitive in the ever-evolving digital landscape.

CONTENT MARKETING IDEAS

Analyzing Content Performance and Engagement

- Utilize web analytics tools such as Google Analytics to track key metrics like website traffic, page views, and bounce rates, providing valuable insights into the performance of your bakery's content.
- Monitor engagement metrics such as time on page, scroll depth, and click-through rates to assess how effectively your content is capturing and retaining the attention of your audience.
- Analyze conversion metrics such as leads generated, email sign-ups, and online orders attributed to your content, measuring its impact on driving desired actions and business outcomes.
- Segment your audience data by demographics, interests, and behavior to identify patterns and trends in content consumption and engagement among different audience segments.
- Track the performance of individual pieces of content over time, identifying top-performing assets and opportunities for optimization or repurposing to maximize their impact.
- Conduct A/B tests or split tests to compare different versions of your content, such as headlines, images, or calls-to-action, to determine which variations resonate most with your audience.
- Monitor social media engagement metrics such as likes, shares, comments, and retweets to gauge the reach and virality of your content on social platforms.
- Use social listening tools to monitor brand mentions, sentiment, and conversations related to your bakery, allowing you to identify opportunities for engagement and reputation management.
- Analyze email marketing performance metrics such as open rates, click-through rates, and conversion rates to evaluate the effectiveness of your email content and campaigns.
- Measure the impact of influencer collaborations and partnerships on your content performance, tracking metrics such as referral traffic, engagement, and conversions attributed to influencer content.
- Monitor user-generated content and customer reviews to assess sentiment, feedback, and satisfaction levels with your bakery's products and services, informing future content strategy and product development efforts.
- Use heatmaps and scrollmaps to visualize user behavior and interactions on your website, identifying areas of high engagement and potential barriers to conversion or navigation.
- Conduct customer surveys or feedback polls to gather qualitative insights into content preferences, interests, and satisfaction levels among your audience.
- Benchmark your bakery's content performance against industry standards and competitors, identifying areas of strength and opportunities for improvement based on comparative analysis.
- Analyze search engine rankings and organic traffic for targeted keywords related to your bakery's products and services, assessing your content's visibility and effectiveness in attracting organic traffic.

- Monitor trends and shifts in content consumption habits and preferences among your target audience, adapting your content strategy accordingly to stay relevant and competitive.
- Use attribution modelling to analyze the contribution of different touchpoints and channels to overall conversions and revenue generated by your bakery's content marketing efforts.
- Implement event tracking and goal tracking in Google Analytics to measure the completion of specific actions or milestones on your website, such as form submissions or product purchases.
- Create custom dashboards and reports in your analytics platform to visualize and communicate key metrics and performance trends to stakeholders and decision-makers within your organization.
- Conduct content audits at regular intervals to assess the quality, relevance, and effectiveness of your bakery's content assets, identifying opportunities for optimization, consolidation, or retirement.
- Monitor customer retention and loyalty metrics, such as repeat purchases and lifetime value, to assess the long-term impact of your content marketing efforts on customer engagement and loyalty.
- Analyze customer journey data to understand how different touchpoints and interactions with your bakery's content contribute to the overall customer experience and path to purchase.
- Use sentiment analysis tools to assess the tone and sentiment of customer feedback and conversations related to your bakery's content and brand, identifying areas for improvement or intervention.
- Continuously iterate and refine your content marketing strategy based on data-driven insights and performance analysis, testing new ideas, and tactics to optimize engagement and achieve your business objectives.

CONTENT MARKETING IDEAS

Refreshing Old Content for New Engagement

- Review your bakery's existing blog posts, articles, and guides to identify evergreen content that remains relevant and valuable to your audience.
- Update outdated information, statistics, and references in old content to ensure accuracy and reliability, providing fresh insights and perspectives for your audience.
- Refresh headlines, titles, and meta descriptions of old content to make them more compelling, engaging, and optimized for search engines and social media platforms.
- Add new visuals, graphics, and multimedia elements to old content to enhance its visual appeal and engagement potential, making it more shareable and attractive to audiences.
- Incorporate new data, research findings, and case studies into old content to provide additional credibility and depth, supporting your claims and assertions with the latest evidence.
- Repurpose old blog posts and articles into different formats such as infographics, videos, podcasts, or slide presentations to reach new audiences and expand your content's reach.
- Create roundup posts or compilation articles featuring curated lists of your best-performing or most popular content from the past, showcasing your bakery's expertise and authority in the field.
- Rewrite and expand upon old content to provide more comprehensive coverage of topics, addressing frequently asked questions, addressing new trends, or exploring related subtopics.
- Update old recipes with new variations, adaptations, or improvements based on customer feedback, culinary trends, or personal experimentation, offering fresh inspiration to your audience.
- Incorporate user-generated content, customer testimonials, and success stories into old content to add authenticity and social proof, showcasing real-life experiences and feedback from satisfied customers.
- Translate old content into different languages to reach international audiences and expand your bakery's global reach and presence in new markets.
- Create seasonal or themed content bundles featuring related old content grouped together around specific holidays, occasions, or themes, providing comprehensive resources and inspiration for your audience.
- Optimize old content for voice search by incorporating natural language queries, conversational tone, and long-tail keywords that align with how users speak and search using voice assistants.
- Create interactive quizzes, polls, or surveys based on old content to engage your audience and encourage active participation and feedback, driving new engagement and interaction.
- Conduct outreach and promotion campaigns to reintroduce refreshed old content to your audience through email newsletters, social media posts, and targeted advertising campaigns.

- Collaborate with influencers or industry experts to co-create and promote refreshed old content, leveraging their expertise and networks to increase visibility and reach.
- Host live events or webinars based on old content topics, offering interactive discussions, Q&A sessions, and demonstrations to engage your audience in real-time and foster community interaction.
- Create downloadable resources or guides based on old content topics, offering additional value and utility to your audience in a convenient and accessible format.
- Host virtual workshops or cooking classes based on old recipes or baking techniques featured in your content, providing hands-on learning experiences for your audience.
- Share behind-the-scenes insights and updates on old content topics, showcasing ongoing developments, experiments, or innovations in your bakery's operations or offerings.
- Engage with comments, questions, and feedback on old content to foster conversations and connections with your audience, demonstrating your responsiveness and commitment to customer engagement.
- Optimize old content for social sharing by adding social media sharing buttons, click-to-tweet quotes, and visual elements that encourage users to share and amplify your content across their networks.
- Monitor analytics and performance metrics for refreshed old content to track engagement, traffic, and conversions over time, identifying areas of improvement and opportunities for further optimization.
- Continuously iterate and refine your approach to refreshing old content based on feedback, data, and evolving trends, adapting your strategies to meet the changing needs and preferences of your audience.

CONTENT MARKETING IDEAS

Storytelling Through Your Bakery's Brand

- Share the founding story of your bakery, detailing the inspiration, passion, and journey that led to its creation, providing a personal and relatable narrative for your audience.
- Highlight the unique heritage and traditions that inform your bakery's brand identity, celebrating the cultural influences, family recipes, and generational expertise that set you apart.
- Showcase the craftsmanship and attention to detail that goes into every product you create, telling the story of your dedication to quality, authenticity, and artisanal excellence.
- Introduce the team behind your bakery, featuring profiles and interviews with staff members, bakers, and artisans who bring your brand's vision to life with their talent and passion.
- Share behind-the-scenes glimpses of your bakery's operations, offering insights into the baking process, ingredient sourcing, and daily rituals that shape your brand's ethos and values.
- Highlight your commitment to sustainability and community engagement, sharing stories of environmental initiatives, local partnerships, and charitable efforts that reflect your bakery's social responsibility.
- Feature customer testimonials and success stories, showcasing the impact your bakery has had on people's lives, celebrations, and special moments with your delicious and memorable creations.
- Share stories of resilience and adaptation, documenting how your bakery has overcome challenges, embraced change, and evolved to meet the needs of your customers and community.
- Introduce your bakery's signature products and specialties, telling the stories behind their creation, inspiration, and unique flavor profiles that make them beloved by your customers.
- Share anecdotes and anecdotes from your bakery's history, highlighting memorable events, milestones, and milestones that have shaped your brand's identity and legacy over time.
- Celebrate seasonal traditions and holidays through storytelling, sharing recipes, memories, and cultural insights that evoke the spirit of the season and resonate with your audience.
- Feature collaborations and partnerships with local artisans, farmers, and producers, showcasing the shared values, craftsmanship, and authenticity that define your brand's collaborative spirit.
- Share stories of innovation and creativity, highlighting new products, flavors, and menu offerings that push the boundaries of traditional baking and delight your customers with fresh and exciting experiences.
- Document the process of recipe development and experimentation, sharing the stories behind your bakery's most popular creations and the inspiration that fuels your culinary creativity.
- Highlight your bakery's commitment to inclusivity and diversity, sharing stories of cultural exchange, culinary fusion, and global influences that enrich your brand's identity and

offerings.
- Share stories of customer loyalty and connection, featuring testimonials, reviews, and social media shoutouts from satisfied customers who have become loyal fans and advocates of your bakery.
- Showcase the role of storytelling in your branding and marketing efforts, highlighting campaigns, content series, and initiatives that leverage narrative storytelling to connect with your audience on a deeper level.
- Share stories of inspiration and aspiration, featuring profiles of individuals or organizations that embody your bakery's values and serve as sources of inspiration and motivation for your brand.
- Document the process of product creation and innovation, sharing the stories behind new menu items, seasonal specials, and limited-edition releases that captivate your customers' imaginations and taste buds.
- Highlight the role of tradition and nostalgia in your bakery's brand story, sharing memories, family recipes, and generational wisdom that evoke a sense of warmth, comfort, and familiarity for your audience.
- Share stories of community impact and engagement, documenting your bakery's involvement in local events, fundraisers, and initiatives that support and uplift your neighbors and customers.
- Feature stories of mentorship and apprenticeship, showcasing the role of mentorship in passing down baking skills, knowledge, and traditions from one generation to the next within your bakery.
- Share stories of passion and dedication, featuring interviews and profiles of individuals who have dedicated their lives to the craft of baking and embody the spirit of artisanal excellence that defines your brand.
- Invite your audience to become part of your bakery's brand story, encouraging them to share their own baking experiences, memories, and traditions that resonate with your bakery's values and ethos.

500+ Product Marketing Ideas for Bakeries

SECTIONS IN THIS CHAPTER:

1. Understanding Your Bakery Product Line – Page 188
2. Identifying Target Market for Each Product – Page 190
3. Pricing Strategies for Bakery Items – Page 192
4. Packaging Design that Sells – Page 194
5. Product Photography Tips – Page 196
6. Writing Compelling Product Descriptions – Page 198
7. Seasonal Product Launch Strategies – Page 200
8. Creating Product Bundles and Offers – Page 202
9. Setting Up an Online Ordering System – Page 204
10. Leveraging Social Media for Product Promotion – Page 206
11. Email Marketing Campaigns for Product Launches – Page 208
12. Utilizing Customer Reviews in Marketing – Page 210
13. Hosting Product Tasting Events – Page 212
14. Collaborations with Local Businesses – Page 214
15. Influencer Marketing for New Products – Page 216
16. Utilizing Pop-Up Sales and Markets – Page 218
17. Cross-Promotion with Complementary Products – Page 220
18. Creating Loyalty Programs for Repeat Purchases – Page 222
19. Implementing Flash Sales and Limited-Time Offers – Page 224
20. Educating Customers on Product USPs – Page 226
21. Tracking Product Sales and Feedback – Page 228
22. Adjusting Strategies Based on Analytics Insights – Page 230

PRODUCT MARKETING IDEAS

Understanding Your Bakery Product Line

- Conduct a thorough analysis of your bakery's current product line, including sales data, customer feedback, and market trends.
- Identify any gaps or areas for improvement in your product offerings, considering factors such as variety, pricing, and customer preferences.
- Utilize customer surveys or focus groups to gather insights into which products are most popular and which may need adjustments.
- Consider introducing seasonal or limited-time offerings to keep customers excited and coming back for new experiences.
- Collaborate with your bakery team to brainstorm innovative product ideas that align with your brand identity and target market.
- Explore opportunities to expand your product line by introducing complementary items or new flavor variations.
- Highlight the unique selling points of each product in your lineup, whether it's made with locally sourced ingredients or follows a traditional family recipe.
- Create visually appealing displays in your bakery to showcase your product range and entice customers to make a purchase.
- Develop a pricing strategy that reflects the value of your products while remaining competitive in the market.
- Offer samples or tastings of new or featured products to encourage trial and boost sales.
- Leverage social media platforms to promote your bakery's product line through mouth-watering images, behind-the-scenes content, and customer testimonials.
- Collaborate with local influencers or food bloggers to increase visibility and generate buzz around your products.
- Host themed events or workshops centered around specific products or product categories to engage with your community and drive sales.
- Implement a loyalty program that rewards customers for repeat purchases and encourages them to explore different items within your product line.
- Partner with other local businesses or organizations to cross-promote your products and reach new audiences.
- Offer customization options for certain products to cater to individual preferences and dietary restrictions.
- Highlight the health benefits or nutritional value of select products to appeal to health-conscious consumers.
- Incorporate storytelling into your marketing efforts to create an emotional connection with your audience and differentiate your products from competitors.
- Monitor industry trends and consumer preferences to stay ahead of the curve and adapt your product line accordingly.

- Invest in packaging design that not only protects your products but also communicates your brand's personality and values.
- Showcase your bakery's commitment to sustainability by using eco-friendly packaging materials or sourcing ingredients from local suppliers.
- Provide educational resources or recipe ideas to inspire customers to experiment with your products at home.
- Solicit feedback from customers on new product launches or changes to your existing lineup to ensure you're meeting their needs and expectations.
- Continuously evaluate the performance of your product line and be willing to make adjustments as needed to stay relevant and profitable in the market.

PRODUCT MARKETING IDEAS

Identifying Target Market for Each Product

- Begin by analyzing your bakery's existing customer base to identify common demographics, preferences, and buying behaviors.
- Utilize market research techniques such as surveys, focus groups, or interviews to gain insights into the needs and preferences of your target audience.
- Segment your target market based on factors such as age, gender, income level, lifestyle, and location to tailor your marketing efforts more effectively.
- Consider the unique features and benefits of each product in your bakery's lineup and determine which segments of your target market they are most likely to appeal to.
- Develop detailed buyer personas for each product, including information about their demographics, interests, pain points, and purchasing motivations.
- Explore niche markets or specialized customer segments that may have specific needs or preferences that align with certain products in your bakery.
- Leverage data analytics tools to track customer behavior and purchasing patterns, allowing you to refine your target market strategies over time.
- Conduct competitor analysis to identify gaps in the market or areas where your bakery's products can offer a competitive advantage to specific customer segments.
- Use social media listening tools to monitor conversations and sentiment around your bakery's products, helping you identify potential target markets or areas for improvement.
- Collaborate with local businesses or organizations that cater to your target market segments to expand your reach and attract new customers.
- Customize your marketing messages and promotions to resonate with each target market segment, addressing their unique needs and preferences.
- Offer incentives or promotions targeted specifically at certain customer segments to encourage trial and repeat purchases.
- Develop partnerships with influencers or brand ambassadors who have a strong following within your target market segments to increase brand awareness and credibility.
- Create targeted advertising campaigns using online platforms such as social media, search engines, or display networks to reach your desired audience segments.
- Participate in community events or sponsorships that align with the interests and values of your target market segments to enhance brand visibility and reputation.
- Monitor feedback and reviews from customers within each target market segment to identify areas for improvement and address any concerns or issues promptly.
- Experiment with different marketing channels and strategies to determine which ones resonate most effectively with each target market segment.
- Develop content marketing initiatives such as blog posts, videos, or podcasts that provide valuable information or entertainment tailored to the interests of your target audience segments.

- Offer personalized experiences or customization options for certain products to appeal to the individual preferences of different customer segments.
- Provide exceptional customer service and support to build loyalty and trust with each target market segment, encouraging repeat business and positive word-of-mouth referrals.
- Continuously monitor market trends and consumer preferences to ensure your bakery's products remain relevant and appealing to your target audience segments.
- Seek feedback from customers within each target market segment to understand their evolving needs and preferences, allowing you to adapt your product offerings and marketing strategies accordingly.
- Collaborate with industry experts or influencers to create educational content or experiences that resonate with your target market segments and position your bakery as a trusted authority in your niche.
- Regularly review and update your target market strategies based on changes in consumer behavior, market dynamics, or competitive landscape to maintain a competitive edge and drive sustained growth for your bakery.

PRODUCT MARKETING IDEAS

Pricing Strategies for Bakery Items

- Conduct a thorough analysis of your bakery's production costs, including ingredients, labor, overhead, and other expenses associated with each product.
- Consider your target market's willingness to pay and the perceived value of your bakery items when determining pricing strategies.
- Evaluate pricing strategies used by competitors in your market to ensure your bakery remains competitive while still maintaining profitability.
- Implement dynamic pricing strategies that take into account factors such as time of day, day of the week, seasonality, and demand fluctuations.
- Offer tiered pricing options for certain products, providing customers with choices that align with their budget and preferences.
- Bundle complementary items together to create value-added packages that encourage upselling and increase the average transaction value.
- Utilize psychological pricing techniques such as charm pricing (e.g., pricing items at $4.99 instead of $5.00) to make products appear more affordable and attractive to customers.
- Experiment with promotional pricing tactics such as discounts, BOGO offers, or limited-time specials to drive sales and attract new customers.
- Implement a loyalty program that rewards customers for repeat purchases or higher spending levels, incentivizing them to return to your bakery regularly.
- Offer volume discounts for large orders or catering services to attract business from corporate clients, event planners, or other bulk buyers.
- Provide special pricing incentives for customers who pre-order or subscribe to recurring deliveries of your bakery items.
- Consider implementing a value-based pricing strategy that reflects the unique qualities and benefits of your bakery's products compared to competitors.
- Utilize price anchoring techniques by prominently displaying premium-priced items next to lower-priced options to influence customer perceptions and increase sales of higher-margin products.
- Adjust pricing strategies based on seasonality, market trends, and other external factors that may impact consumer behavior and purchasing power.
- Monitor customer feedback and sales data to evaluate the effectiveness of pricing strategies and make adjustments as needed to optimize profitability.
- Offer flexible pricing options for custom orders or personalized products, taking into account factors such as design complexity, specialty ingredients, and production time.
- Conduct A/B testing or market research studies to assess the impact of different pricing strategies on customer perceptions, purchase intent, and overall sales performance.
- Collaborate with suppliers or distributors to negotiate better pricing terms or discounts on ingredients or packaging materials, allowing you to reduce costs and maintain competitive pricing for your bakery items.

- Implement seasonal pricing adjustments to capitalize on peak demand periods or holiday seasons when customers may be more willing to pay premium prices for festive or specialty items.
- Leverage data analytics tools to track pricing trends, monitor competitor pricing changes, and identify opportunities to optimize your bakery's pricing strategies for maximum profitability.
- Offer special promotions or discounts to loyal customers as a token of appreciation for their continued support and patronage.
- Provide transparent pricing information to customers, clearly communicating the value they receive with each purchase and building trust in your bakery's brand.
- Regularly review and adjust pricing strategies based on feedback from customers, changes in market conditions, and shifts in competitive dynamics to maintain relevance and profitability in the long term.
- Seek input from your bakery team and key stakeholders when developing pricing strategies, leveraging their expertise and insights to make informed decisions that benefit your business and customers alike.

Packaging Design that Sells

- Begin by understanding your bakery's brand identity, values, and target market to inform the design direction for your packaging.
- Consider the practical aspects of packaging design, such as functionality, durability, and ease of use, to ensure your products remain fresh and intact during transportation and storage.
- Develop packaging that reflects the unique qualities and artisanal craftsmanship of your bakery's products, conveying a sense of quality and authenticity to customers.
- Utilize high-quality materials and printing techniques to enhance the visual appeal and tactile experience of your packaging, making it stand out on the shelf and leave a lasting impression.
- Incorporate branding elements such as your bakery's logo, colors, and typography consistently across all packaging designs to reinforce brand recognition and build brand equity.
- Leverage packaging as a storytelling tool to communicate the heritage, inspiration, or special features of your bakery's products, creating a deeper connection with customers.
- Design packaging that showcases the freshness and deliciousness of your baked goods through enticing imagery, appetizing descriptions, and mouth-watering visuals.
- Explore innovative packaging formats or structural designs that differentiate your bakery's products from competitors and provide added convenience or functionality for customers.
- Incorporate eco-friendly materials and sustainable packaging practices into your design process to align with growing consumer demand for environmentally conscious products.
- Customize packaging for seasonal or holiday-themed promotions to create excitement and anticipation among customers, encouraging impulse purchases and repeat business.
- Implement personalized packaging options for special occasions such as weddings, birthdays, or corporate events, offering customers a unique and memorable gifting experience.
- Utilize packaging design as a platform for cross-promotion by featuring QR codes, social media handles, or website URLs that drive engagement and encourage customers to connect with your bakery online.
- Collaborate with local artists, designers, or illustrators to create custom artwork or designs for your packaging, adding a distinctive and memorable touch to your brand.
- Conduct market research or consumer testing to gather feedback on potential packaging designs and identify preferences, pain points, and opportunities for improvement.
- Invest in professional photography or food styling to capture high-quality images of your bakery's products for use on packaging, marketing materials, and online channels.
- Incorporate interactive elements or gamification features into your packaging design to engage customers and create memorable experiences that encourage repeat purchases.
- Design packaging that is resealable, reusable, or recyclable to enhance convenience for customers and minimize environmental impact.

- Use packaging as a platform for educational content or recipe ideas that inspire customers to explore creative ways of enjoying your bakery's products at home.
- Incorporate seasonal or thematic packaging designs that resonate with current trends, holidays, or cultural celebrations, capturing customers' attention and driving seasonal sales.
- Implement a cohesive packaging strategy across all product lines to maintain brand consistency and streamline production, distribution, and inventory management processes.
- Consider the practical considerations of packaging design, such as stackability, shelf space optimization, and transportation efficiency, to minimize costs and maximize convenience for retailers and distributors.
- Design packaging that reflects the premium quality and artisanal craftsmanship of your bakery's products, positioning them as desirable indulgences or special treats for customers.
- Leverage packaging as a marketing tool by including product information, nutritional facts, and serving suggestions that educate and inform customers while enhancing their overall experience.
- Continuously evaluate and evolve your packaging designs based on customer feedback, market trends, and competitive analysis to ensure your bakery's products remain relevant and appealing to consumers.

Product Photography Tips

- Invest in high-quality photography equipment, including a DSLR camera, tripod, lighting setup, and backdrop, to ensure professional-looking results.
- Familiarize yourself with the basic principles of photography, including composition, lighting, exposure, and depth of field, to capture stunning images of your bakery's products.
- Choose a clean and neutral backdrop that complements the colors and textures of your baked goods without distracting from them.
- Experiment with different angles and perspectives to showcase your bakery items from their most visually appealing angles, capturing details and textures that entice customers.
- Use natural light whenever possible to illuminate your products, positioning them near windows or in well-lit areas to achieve soft, flattering lighting that enhances their appearance.
- Consider investing in artificial lighting equipment, such as softboxes or LED panels, to supplement natural light and ensure consistent lighting conditions regardless of the time of day or weather.
- Pay attention to styling details such as garnishes, props, and serving utensils to create visually compelling compositions that tell a story and evoke emotion in viewers.
- Experiment with different props and accessories to add interest and context to your product photos, while ensuring they complement rather than overshadow your bakery items.
- Use a shallow depth of field to create a sense of depth and dimension in your photos, keeping the focus sharp on your main subject while blurring the background for a more polished look.
- Maintain consistency in your photography style and branding elements, such as color palettes, fonts, and image treatments, across all product photos to reinforce your bakery's visual identity.
- Pay attention to composition techniques such as the rule of thirds, leading lines, and negative space to create visually balanced and engaging images that draw viewers in.
- Capture a variety of shots for each bakery item, including close-ups, overhead shots, and lifestyle images that showcase different aspects of the product and its usage.
- Use props sparingly and strategically to enhance the story or concept behind your bakery items, ensuring they remain the focal point of the photograph.
- Experiment with different food styling techniques, such as layering, stacking, and drizzling, to add visual interest and dimension to your bakery products.
- Consider the context in which your bakery items will be consumed and photographed, incorporating elements such as table settings, serving dishes, and utensils to create a realistic and relatable scene.
- Pay attention to color balance and temperature settings to ensure accurate representation of your bakery's products, adjusting white balance settings as needed to achieve true-to-life colors.

- Shoot in RAW format whenever possible to retain maximum detail and flexibility during post-processing, allowing you to fine-tune exposure, color, and other settings without loss of quality.
- Experiment with different camera settings and shooting modes, such as aperture priority or manual mode, to achieve the desired level of control and creative expression in your photos.
- Take multiple shots of each bakery item from different angles and perspectives, allowing you to choose the best images during the editing process.
- Consider the intended use and platform for your product photos when determining aspect ratios, resolutions, and file formats, optimizing them for web, print, or social media as needed.
- Pay attention to detail and craftsmanship in your photography, ensuring that your bakery items are presented in the best possible light and accurately reflect the quality and care that goes into their production.
- Experiment with different post-processing techniques, such as cropping, color correction, and retouching, to enhance the visual impact and professionalism of your product photos.
- Seek feedback from colleagues, peers, or professional photographers to improve your photography skills and refine your approach to capturing images of bakery products.
- Continuously strive for excellence in your product photography, seeking inspiration from industry trends, artistic influences, and consumer preferences to create compelling and impactful images that drive engagement and sales for your bakery.

Writing Compelling Product Descriptions

- Begin by understanding the unique features, benefits, and selling points of each bakery product you wish to describe.
- Consider your target audience's preferences, needs, and aspirations when crafting product descriptions that resonate with them on a personal level.
- Use vivid and descriptive language to paint a picture of the sensory experience customers can expect when enjoying your bakery items, appealing to their emotions and imagination.
- Highlight the quality and craftsmanship of your bakery products, emphasizing factors such as freshness, authenticity, and artisanal techniques to differentiate them from mass-produced alternatives.
- Showcase the key ingredients and flavors that distinguish each product, tantalizing customers' taste buds and piquing their curiosity to try them for themselves.
- Incorporate storytelling elements into your product descriptions, sharing the inspiration, heritage, or special occasions behind each bakery item to create a connection with customers.
- Use persuasive language and compelling narratives to convey the value proposition of your bakery products, addressing customers' pain points and demonstrating how your offerings can enrich their lives.
- Focus on benefits rather than features in your product descriptions, highlighting how each bakery item solves a problem, fulfills a desire, or enhances a moment of indulgence for customers.
- Use sensory words and imagery to evoke the sights, sounds, smells, tastes, and textures associated with your bakery products, immersing customers in a multisensory experience that leaves a lasting impression.
- Incorporate social proof elements such as customer reviews, testimonials, or awards into your product descriptions to build credibility and trust with potential buyers.
- Keep your product descriptions concise and easy to read, using short sentences and paragraphs to maintain the reader's attention and facilitate quick comprehension.
- Use bullet points or numbered lists to highlight key features, benefits, or usage tips for each bakery product, making it easier for customers to scan and digest the information.
- Optimize your product descriptions for search engines by incorporating relevant keywords, phrases, and long-tail queries that potential customers may use when searching for bakery items online.
- Tailor your product descriptions to suit the platform or channel where they will be displayed, adapting the tone, length, and formatting to align with the expectations and browsing habits of your target audience.
- Create a sense of urgency or exclusivity in your product descriptions by highlighting limited-time offers, seasonal specials, or exclusive promotions that encourage customers to act quickly.

- Address common objections or concerns that customers may have about your bakery products in your product descriptions, providing reassurance and overcoming barriers to purchase.
- Use calls to action strategically throughout your product descriptions to prompt customers to learn more, explore related products, or make a purchase.
- Incorporate visual elements such as product images, videos, or interactive media into your product descriptions to enhance engagement and provide additional context for customers.
- Test different variations of your product descriptions using A/B testing or multivariate testing to identify which messaging resonates most effectively with your target audience.
- Solicit feedback from customers on your product descriptions, asking them to share their thoughts, preferences, and suggestions for improvement to continuously refine your messaging strategy.
- Keep your product descriptions up to date with accurate information on pricing, availability, and any changes or enhancements to your bakery products to ensure consistency and reliability for customers.
- Collaborate with copywriters, designers, or marketing professionals to brainstorm creative ideas and develop compelling product descriptions that captivate and persuade customers.
- Leverage user-generated content such as customer photos, videos, or testimonials in your product descriptions to add authenticity and social proof to your messaging.
- Continuously monitor the performance of your product descriptions, tracking metrics such as click-through rates, conversion rates, and sales revenue to evaluate their effectiveness and make data-driven optimizations over time.

Seasonal Product Launch Strategies

- Begin by conducting market research to identify seasonal trends, holidays, and events that present opportunities for launching new bakery products.
- Analyze past sales data and customer feedback to determine which seasonal products have been successful in the past and which ones may need adjustments or improvements.
- Develop a calendar or timeline outlining key dates and milestones for each seasonal product launch, including ideation, development, marketing, and sales phases.
- Collaborate with your bakery team to brainstorm creative ideas for seasonal products that align with current trends, customer preferences, and your brand identity.
- Consider incorporating seasonal ingredients, flavors, and themes into your bakery products to evoke the spirit and essence of each time of year.
- Leverage seasonal packaging designs and branding elements to create excitement and anticipation around your new product launches, reinforcing their connection to specific holidays or occasions.
- Create promotional campaigns or marketing materials that highlight the unique features, benefits, and limited-time availability of your seasonal products, encouraging customers to try them before they're gone.
- Utilize social media platforms, email newsletters, and other digital channels to tease upcoming seasonal product launches, build anticipation, and generate buzz among your audience.
- Collaborate with influencers, bloggers, or local media outlets to spread the word about your seasonal product launches and reach new audiences within your target market.
- Host tasting events, pop-up shops, or sampling stations to give customers a chance to experience your seasonal products firsthand and provide feedback before they officially launch.
- Offer exclusive pre-order or early access opportunities for loyal customers or members of your loyalty program, rewarding them for their patronage and building excitement around your seasonal offerings.
- Create seasonal product bundles or gift sets that combine multiple items into a themed package, offering customers added value and convenience for their holiday shopping needs.
- Partner with other local businesses or organizations to cross-promote your seasonal products and reach new customer segments who may be interested in your bakery items as gifts or treats.
- Develop seasonal marketing campaigns that tell a story or evoke emotion, connecting your bakery products to cherished memories, traditions, or experiences associated with each time of year.
- Offer limited-time promotions, discounts, or incentives to encourage customers to try your seasonal products and make repeat purchases throughout the holiday season.
- Customize your marketing messaging and imagery to resonate with the cultural, religious, or social significance of each seasonal occasion, ensuring your product launches are

relevant and appealing to diverse audiences.

- Create seasonal-themed content such as recipes, decorating tips, or entertaining ideas to inspire customers and showcase the versatility of your bakery products for holiday celebrations and gatherings.
- Collaborate with local charities or community organizations to donate a portion of proceeds from seasonal product sales to support meaningful causes and give back to those in need during the holidays.
- Engage with customers on social media by encouraging them to share photos, reviews, and testimonials of your seasonal products using branded hashtags or tagging your bakery's account.
- Monitor customer feedback and sales data throughout the seasonal product launch period to evaluate the success of your marketing strategies, identify areas for improvement, and make adjustments as needed.
- Create limited-edition or specialty variations of your seasonal products to cater to different tastes, preferences, and dietary restrictions within your target market.
- Offer seasonal product samplers or tasting flights that allow customers to sample a variety of flavors or options within a specific product category, encouraging exploration and discovery.
- Host seasonal-themed workshops, classes, or demonstrations at your bakery to engage with customers and provide educational opportunities related to your seasonal products and holiday traditions.
- Plan ahead for post-seasonal marketing initiatives such as clearance sales, repackaging or repurposing leftover inventory, and soliciting feedback from customers to inform future seasonal product launches and marketing strategies.

Creating Product Bundles and Offers

- Begin by analyzing your bakery's product lineup to identify complementary items that can be bundled together to create value-added packages for customers.
- Consider the preferences, needs, and purchasing behaviors of your target audience when developing product bundles and offers that resonate with them and provide meaningful benefits.
- Leverage seasonal themes, holidays, or special occasions as opportunities to create themed bundles and offers that align with the spirit and essence of each time of year.
- Develop a variety of bundle options at different price points to cater to a range of customer budgets and preferences, offering both basic and premium packages to maximize appeal.
- Bundle together popular or bestselling items with slower-moving products to increase their visibility and encourage customers to try new products they may not have considered otherwise.
- Create themed bundles based on customer lifestyles or interests, such as breakfast bundles for busy weekday mornings, afternoon tea bundles for relaxing weekends, or celebration bundles for special occasions.
- Offer exclusive or limited-time bundles and offers to create a sense of urgency and drive immediate sales, encouraging customers to take advantage of the opportunity before it's gone.
- Customize bundle options for different customer segments or demographics, tailoring the selection of products and pricing to meet the specific needs and preferences of each group.
- Incorporate cross-promotion strategies into your bundle offers by featuring complementary products from other local businesses or partner brands, expanding your reach and attracting new customers.
- Highlight the value proposition of each bundle offer, emphasizing the savings, convenience, and variety that customers will enjoy by purchasing the bundle instead of individual items.
- Use persuasive messaging and calls to action in your marketing materials to encourage customers to take advantage of your bundle offers, emphasizing the limited-time nature or exclusive benefits of the promotion.
- Create themed bundle offers for holidays and special occasions, such as Valentine's Day, Easter, Mother's Day, or Thanksgiving, that include a selection of seasonal treats and desserts perfect for gifting or sharing.
- Offer bundle options for different customer occasions, such as birthday parties, office gatherings, or family celebrations, providing all the essentials needed to make the event memorable and delicious.
- Develop bundle offers that cater to specific dietary preferences or restrictions, such as gluten-free, vegan, or nut-free options, ensuring that all customers can enjoy your bakery's products.

- Create customizable bundle options that allow customers to mix and match their favorite items or select from a variety of flavors, sizes, or quantities to create a personalized package that meets their needs.
- Promote bundle offers through a variety of marketing channels, including your bakery's website, social media platforms, email newsletters, and in-store signage, to maximize visibility and reach.
- Collaborate with influencers or brand ambassadors to promote your bundle offers to their followers, leveraging their reach and credibility to increase awareness and drive sales.
- Create bundle offers that include additional perks or incentives, such as free shipping, complimentary gift wrapping, or exclusive access to future promotions or events, to sweeten the deal for customers.
- Host tasting events or sampling stations at your bakery to allow customers to experience the quality and variety of your bundle offerings firsthand, encouraging them to make a purchase.
- Offer bundle discounts or rewards for loyal customers or members of your loyalty program, incentivizing repeat business and fostering long-term relationships with your bakery.
- Monitor the performance of your bundle offers regularly, tracking metrics such as sales volume, revenue, and customer feedback to evaluate their effectiveness and make adjustments as needed.
- Solicit feedback from customers on your bundle options, asking them about their preferences, satisfaction levels, and suggestions for improvement to refine your offerings and better meet their needs.
- Experiment with different bundle configurations, pricing strategies, and promotional tactics to identify which approaches resonate most effectively with your target audience and drive the highest return on investment.
- Continuously innovate and refresh your bundle offerings to keep them relevant and appealing to customers, introducing new themes, products, and promotions to keep them coming back for more.

Setting Up an Online Ordering System

- Develop a user-friendly website that showcases your bakery's products and services, emphasizing the convenience and ease of ordering online.
- Implement a mobile-responsive design to ensure seamless browsing and ordering experience across various devices, including smartphones and tablets.
- Offer incentives such as discounts or freebies for customers who place orders through your online platform, encouraging them to try the convenience of online ordering.
- Provide detailed product descriptions, high-quality images, and pricing information to help customers make informed purchasing decisions.
- Integrate a secure payment gateway to instill trust and confidence in your customers when making online transactions.
- Enable options for customization, allowing customers to personalize their orders according to their preferences, such as choosing flavors, toppings, or special dietary requirements.
- Implement a loyalty program tied to online orders, rewarding repeat customers with exclusive discounts, special offers, or points redeemable for future purchases.
- Utilize social media channels to promote your online ordering system, sharing engaging content, customer testimonials, and behind-the-scenes glimpses to generate excitement and interest.
- Partner with local delivery services or invest in your own delivery fleet to offer convenient delivery options for customers who prefer to have their orders brought directly to their doorstep.
- Provide multiple delivery time slots to accommodate varying schedules and preferences, ensuring flexibility for your customers.
- Optimize your website for search engines (SEO) to improve visibility and attract more potential customers searching for bakery products online.
- Offer a user-friendly and intuitive interface for the online ordering process, minimizing friction and streamlining the customer journey from browsing to checkout.
- Implement a real-time order tracking system to keep customers informed about the status of their orders, enhancing transparency and reducing anxiety about delivery times.
- Showcase customer reviews and testimonials prominently on your website to build trust and credibility, reassuring potential customers about the quality of your products and service.
- Leverage email marketing campaigns to promote your online ordering system, sending targeted messages to segmented customer groups with special offers, new product announcements, or seasonal promotions.
- Collaborate with local influencers or food bloggers to create buzz around your online ordering system, leveraging their reach and influence to attract new customers.
- Offer exclusive online-only deals and promotions to incentivize customers to explore your digital storefront and make repeat purchases.

- Provide seamless integration with popular third-party apps and platforms, such as social media channels or food delivery aggregators, to expand your reach and accessibility.
- Implement a robust inventory management system to ensure accurate stock levels and prevent overselling, minimizing disappointments and order fulfillment delays.
- Offer convenient pickup options for customers who prefer to collect their orders in person, providing designated pickup locations and streamlined pickup processes.
- Create engaging video content showcasing your bakery's products and the online ordering experience, sharing it across your website and social media channels to capture attention and drive conversions.
- Monitor and analyze key metrics such as website traffic, conversion rates, and customer feedback to continuously optimize and improve your online ordering system.
- Provide exceptional customer support through various channels, including live chat, email, or phone, to address any questions, concerns, or issues that may arise during the online ordering process.
- Stay responsive and adaptable to evolving customer preferences and technological advancements, regularly updating and refining your online ordering system to deliver the best possible experience for your customers.

Leveraging Social Media for Product Promotion

- Develop a comprehensive social media strategy tailored to your bakery's target audience, including platforms like Facebook, Instagram, Twitter, and Pinterest to maximize reach and engagement.
- Create visually appealing content showcasing your bakery's products, such as mouth-watering photos and videos highlighting the craftsmanship and quality ingredients used.
- Utilize Instagram Stories and Facebook Live to provide behind-the-scenes glimpses of your bakery's operations, including baking processes, staff interactions, and special events, fostering authenticity and connection with your audience.
- Encourage user-generated content by hosting photo contests, challenges, or hashtags campaigns, inviting customers to share their favorite bakery treats and experiences on social media, thereby increasing brand visibility and social proof.
- Collaborate with local influencers, food bloggers, or community organizations to amplify your bakery's reach and credibility, leveraging their networks and expertise to introduce your products to new audiences.
- Engage with your audience through interactive features like polls, quizzes, and Q&A sessions, encouraging participation and fostering a sense of community around your bakery brand.
- Leverage social media advertising tools to target specific demographics, interests, and locations with tailored promotions and sponsored posts, maximizing the impact of your marketing budget.
- Showcase seasonal and holiday-themed offerings through dedicated social media campaigns, tapping into festive occasions and cultural celebrations to drive excitement and sales.
- Share educational content related to baking techniques, ingredient sourcing, or flavor pairings, positioning your bakery as a trusted authority and resource within the culinary community.
- Offer exclusive discounts, promotions, or giveaways to your social media followers as a reward for their loyalty and engagement, incentivizing repeat purchases and word-of-mouth referrals.
- Incorporate user-generated reviews and testimonials into your social media content, highlighting positive feedback from satisfied customers to build trust and credibility among potential buyers.
- Monitor social media channels for customer feedback, inquiries, and mentions, responding promptly and professionally to comments, messages, and reviews to nurture positive relationships and address any concerns.
- Collaborate with complementary businesses or local establishments to cross-promote each other's products and services on social media, expanding your reach and fostering mutually beneficial partnerships.

- Create interactive experiences such as virtual tastings, recipe demonstrations, or online workshops, inviting followers to participate and engage with your bakery brand in meaningful ways.
- Share stories and anecdotes about your bakery's history, values, and community involvement to humanize your brand and forge emotional connections with your audience.
- Use social media analytics tools to track key metrics such as engagement rates, click-through rates, and conversion rates, gaining insights into the effectiveness of your marketing efforts and identifying areas for improvement.
- Experiment with different content formats and posting schedules to optimize your social media presence for maximum visibility and engagement, staying flexible and adaptable to evolving trends and algorithms.
- Partner with micro-influencers or brand ambassadors who align with your bakery's values and aesthetics, leveraging their authenticity and niche audiences to drive targeted traffic and conversions.
- Create themed content series or challenges around popular topics like #ThrowbackThursday or #FoodieFriday, encouraging regular interaction and anticipation from your social media followers.
- Harness the power of user-generated content by resharing customer photos, testimonials, and stories on your bakery's social media channels, showcasing real-life experiences and building a sense of community around your brand.
- Offer exclusive sneak peeks and behind-the-scenes access to upcoming product launches or menu updates on social media, generating excitement and anticipation among your followers.
- Host virtual events such as Facebook Live baking classes, recipe competitions, or online tasting sessions, providing interactive and immersive experiences that foster engagement and brand loyalty.
- Implement a consistent brand voice and visual aesthetic across all social media channels, maintaining cohesive messaging and branding elements to reinforce your bakery's identity and appeal.
- Continuously monitor social media trends, industry insights, and competitor strategies to stay informed and inspired, adapting your approach to product promotion on social media to remain relevant and competitive in the market.

PRODUCT MARKETING IDEAS

Email Marketing Campaigns for Product Launches

- Craft personalized email invitations to build anticipation and excitement for your bakery's upcoming product launches, highlighting the unique features, flavors, or benefits of the new offerings.
- Segment your email list based on factors such as purchase history, engagement levels, or demographics to tailor your messaging and promotions to specific audience segments, maximizing relevance and impact.
- Create teaser campaigns leading up to the product launch, sending a series of emails with sneak peeks, behind-the-scenes footage, or exclusive previews to pique curiosity and generate buzz among your subscribers.
- Offer early access or VIP perks to subscribers who opt in to receive exclusive email updates about the upcoming product launch, rewarding their loyalty and incentivizing them to stay engaged with your bakery brand.
- Implement countdown timers or urgency-inducing language in your email subject lines and copy to create a sense of anticipation and encourage recipients to act quickly to be among the first to try the new products.
- Showcase user-generated content or testimonials from beta testers or influencers who have had early access to the new products, leveraging social proof to build trust and credibility with your email subscribers.
- Incorporate interactive elements such as polls, surveys, or quizzes into your email campaigns to engage recipients and gather feedback or insights about their preferences and expectations for the upcoming product launch.
- Highlight the story behind the new products, including any inspirations, innovations, or special ingredients that differentiate them from existing offerings in the market, fostering emotional connections and storytelling.
- Offer exclusive discounts, promotions, or limited-time offers to email subscribers as a reward for their loyalty and engagement, providing additional incentives to participate in the product launch event.
- Create a sense of FOMO (fear of missing out) by emphasizing the limited availability or exclusivity of the new products in your email communications, motivating recipients to act quickly to secure their purchases.
- Leverage email automation tools to schedule a series of follow-up emails after the initial product launch announcement, reminding subscribers about the availability of the new products and prompting them to make a purchase.
- Provide detailed product descriptions, high-quality images, and pricing information in your email campaigns to help recipients make informed purchasing decisions and overcome any potential objections or uncertainties.
- Encourage social sharing and word-of-mouth referrals by including social media buttons or "share with a friend" options in your email campaigns, making it easy for recipients to spread the word about the new products within their networks.

- Incorporate user-generated reviews and testimonials into your email content, showcasing positive feedback from early adopters or beta testers to build trust and confidence in the new products among your email subscribers.
- Host virtual events or webinars to coincide with the product launch, inviting email subscribers to join live demonstrations, tastings, or Q&A sessions where they can learn more about the new offerings and interact with your bakery team.
- Offer incentives for subscribers to pre-order or reserve the new products ahead of the official launch date, such as exclusive gifts, discounts, or priority access to limited-edition variants or flavors.
- Provide sneak peeks or exclusive previews of the new products through email newsletters or dedicated landing pages, allowing subscribers to get a firsthand look at what's to come and generate excitement for the official launch.
- Collaborate with complementary brands or influencers to co-create content or joint promotions for the product launch, leveraging their reach and credibility to expand your email list and reach new audiences.
- Incorporate storytelling and visual storytelling elements into your email campaigns, such as videos, animations, or interactive graphics, to captivate recipients' attention and immerse them in the narrative of the new products.
- Encourage feedback and participation from email subscribers by inviting them to share their thoughts, suggestions, or ideas for future product developments or improvements, fostering a sense of co-creation and community engagement.
- Create dedicated landing pages or microsites for the new products, optimized for conversion and designed to provide additional information, testimonials, and purchasing options to email subscribers who click through from your emails.
- Leverage scarcity and exclusivity in your email marketing campaigns by offering limited-time promotions, early access, or special bundles for the new products, motivating recipients to take action before it's too late.
- Use A/B testing and performance analytics to optimize your email campaigns for maximum engagement and conversion rates, experimenting with different subject lines, visuals, and calls-to-action to identify what resonates most with your audience.
- Follow up with post-launch emails to thank subscribers for their support, gather feedback on their experiences with the new products, and keep them informed about any future releases, promotions, or events from your bakery brand.

PRODUCT MARKETING IDEAS

Utilizing Customer Reviews in Marketing

- Incorporate customer reviews and testimonials into your bakery's marketing materials, such as website content, social media posts, and email campaigns, to build trust and credibility with potential buyers.
- Showcase positive feedback and five-star ratings from satisfied customers prominently on your website's homepage or product pages, highlighting the quality and satisfaction associated with your bakery's offerings.
- Encourage customers to leave reviews and feedback by offering incentives such as discounts, freebies, or entry into a prize draw, motivating them to share their experiences and opinions about your bakery products.
- Respond promptly and professionally to both positive and negative reviews, demonstrating your commitment to customer satisfaction and willingness to address any concerns or issues raised by customers.
- Share customer testimonials and success stories through case studies, blog posts, or video testimonials, illustrating real-life examples of how your bakery's products have positively impacted customers' lives or special occasions.
- Leverage user-generated content from social media platforms such as Instagram, Facebook, and Twitter, resharing customer photos, reviews, and mentions to amplify your bakery's reach and engagement.
- Create a dedicated section on your website or blog featuring customer reviews and testimonials, organized by product category or occasion, to provide social proof and inspiration for potential buyers.
- Partner with review websites or food bloggers to generate third-party endorsements and authoritative testimonials for your bakery's products, tapping into their expertise and influence to reach new audiences.
- Use customer feedback to identify areas for improvement and innovation within your bakery's product lineup, soliciting suggestions and preferences from loyal buyers to inform future product development and marketing strategies.
- Highlight specific customer stories or anecdotes in your marketing campaigns, illustrating the emotional connections and memorable experiences that your bakery products can create for customers.
- Integrate customer reviews and ratings into your online ordering platform or e-commerce website, allowing shoppers to make informed decisions based on the experiences and opinions of previous buyers.
- Showcase customer reviews and testimonials in your offline marketing materials, such as printed flyers, brochures, or in-store signage, to reinforce your bakery's reputation and credibility among local customers.
- Feature customer reviews and testimonials in your email marketing campaigns, sharing snippets of positive feedback or success stories to engage subscribers and encourage them to explore your bakery's offerings.

- Create a loyalty program that rewards customers for leaving reviews and referrals, offering points, discounts, or exclusive perks in exchange for their ongoing support and advocacy for your bakery brand.
- Host events or tastings where customers can sample your bakery's products and share their feedback in real-time, fostering community engagement and building relationships with your most enthusiastic supporters.
- Use customer reviews and testimonials as social proof in your advertising campaigns, incorporating quotes, ratings, or endorsements into print ads, digital banners, or video commercials to persuade potential buyers.
- Showcase customer reviews and testimonials at your physical storefront or bakery counter, displaying printed cards or digital screens featuring quotes, photos, and star ratings from satisfied patrons.
- Monitor online review platforms and social media channels for mentions of your bakery brand, responding promptly to feedback and engaging with customers to show appreciation for their support and feedback.
- Create shareable graphics or visual testimonials featuring customer quotes and images of your bakery's products, making it easy for customers to spread the word about their positive experiences with your brand on social media.
- Incorporate customer reviews and testimonials into your sales presentations or pitches when reaching out to wholesale clients, distributors, or potential business partners, using social proof to strengthen your value proposition and credibility.
- Feature customer reviews and testimonials in your press releases or media pitches, highlighting the positive buzz and word-of-mouth endorsements surrounding your bakery's products to attract attention from journalists and influencers.
- Use customer reviews and testimonials to differentiate your bakery from competitors in your market, emphasizing the unique qualities, flavors, or experiences that set your products apart and resonate with your target audience.
- Share success stories and testimonials from corporate clients, event planners, or catering customers who have chosen your bakery for their special occasions or corporate events, showcasing your ability to deliver quality and satisfaction at scale.
- Continuously monitor and analyze customer reviews and feedback to identify trends, patterns, and areas for improvement within your bakery's products and services, using insights to refine your marketing strategies and enhance the overall customer experience.

Hosting Product Tasting Events

- Organize themed tasting events centered around specific products or flavors to create anticipation and excitement among customers.
- Collaborate with local influencers or food bloggers to host joint tasting events, leveraging their audience to expand reach and engagement.
- Offer exclusive sneak peeks of upcoming products during tasting events to incentivize attendance and foster a sense of exclusivity.
- Create visually appealing displays and decor that enhance the ambiance of tasting events, elevating the overall experience for attendees.
- Provide educational sessions during tasting events, such as demonstrations on baking techniques or the origins of ingredients, to add value and deepen customer engagement.
- Incorporate interactive elements like voting stations or feedback forms to encourage participation and gather valuable insights from attendees.
- Partner with complementary businesses, such as coffee shops or local breweries, to offer pairings that enhance the tasting experience and attract diverse audiences.
- Customize tasting events for different demographics or occasions, such as family-friendly events or themed date nights, to broaden appeal and cater to varied preferences.
- Leverage social media platforms to promote tasting events with enticing visuals, behind-the-scenes sneak peeks, and interactive contests to generate buzz and drive attendance.
- Offer special discounts or promotions exclusively available to tasting event attendees, incentivizing repeat visits and fostering loyalty.
- Showcase the craftsmanship and artisanal qualities of bakery products during tasting events through live baking demonstrations or storytelling sessions.
- Host charity or fundraising tasting events, where a portion of proceeds goes towards a meaningful cause, to engage with the community and demonstrate corporate social responsibility.
- Partner with local event venues or community centers to host off-site tasting events, reaching new audiences and establishing strategic partnerships.
- Create a loyalty program specifically for tasting event attendees, rewarding them with perks or discounts for their continued participation and support.
- Incorporate elements of entertainment, such as live music or interactive games, to enhance the overall atmosphere and make tasting events memorable experiences.
- Collaborate with other local businesses to co-promote tasting events through cross-promotional efforts, leveraging each other's networks and customer bases.
- Offer customizable tasting experiences where customers can create their own flavor combinations or tailor products to their preferences, enhancing personalization and satisfaction.

- Capture user-generated content during tasting events, such as photos or testimonials, to share on social media and amplify word-of-mouth marketing.
- Host VIP tasting events exclusively for loyal customers or members of a loyalty program, offering them early access to new products and special perks.
- Partner with food and beverage influencers to host virtual tasting events, reaching a wider audience beyond the local community and driving online engagement.
- Collaborate with local schools or culinary programs to host educational tasting events for students, fostering relationships with future customers and promoting culinary education.
- Offer guided tasting experiences led by knowledgeable staff members who can provide insights on flavor profiles, ingredient sourcing, and baking techniques.
- Create branded merchandise or gift bags for tasting event attendees, serving as memorable keepsakes and extending brand visibility beyond the event itself.
- Follow up with attendees after tasting events through personalized emails or surveys, soliciting feedback and expressing appreciation for their participation, while also encouraging future engagement.

PRODUCT MARKETING IDEAS

Collaborations with Local Businesses

- Forge partnerships with nearby coffee shops or cafes to cross-promote each other's offerings, attracting a wider customer base and encouraging repeat visits to both establishments.
- Collaborate with local farmers or artisanal producers to source high-quality, seasonal ingredients for bakery products, highlighting the importance of supporting local suppliers and emphasizing freshness and sustainability.
- Organize joint events with nearby wineries or breweries, pairing bakery products with complimentary beverages to create unique tasting experiences and capitalize on synergies between food and drink.
- Partner with fitness studios or wellness centers to create special bakery items tailored to health-conscious consumers, promoting balance and indulgence without compromising on taste or quality.
- Collaborate with neighborhood grocery stores or specialty food shops to feature bakery products in curated displays or promotional campaigns, increasing visibility and driving sales through strategic placement.
- Establish alliances with local event planners or wedding vendors to offer customized bakery packages for special occasions, such as weddings, birthdays, or corporate events, catering to diverse customer needs and preferences.
- Team up with nearby hotels or bed-and-breakfasts to provide bakery items for guests' breakfast offerings or special events, enhancing their overall experience and fostering long-term partnerships.
- Partner with culinary schools or cooking classes to host workshops or demonstrations showcasing bakery techniques or specialty recipes, positioning the bakery as an authority in the culinary community and attracting aspiring bakers.
- Collaborate with local artists or designers to create limited-edition packaging or branded merchandise for bakery products, adding aesthetic appeal and enhancing brand identity through unique visual elements.
- Form alliances with nearby restaurants or eateries to feature bakery items on their menus as dessert options or accompaniments, expanding reach and introducing bakery products to new audiences.
- Work with local food delivery services or meal kit companies to offer bakery items as add-ons or standalone options, providing convenient access to freshly baked goods for busy consumers.
- Partner with community organizations or charities to sponsor events or initiatives that align with bakery values or support local causes, demonstrating corporate social responsibility and fostering goodwill within the community.
- Collaborate with local food bloggers or influencers to create sponsored content featuring bakery products, leveraging their online presence to reach a wider audience and generate buzz around the brand.

- Establish partnerships with nearby schools or educational institutions to provide bakery products for school events, fundraisers, or culinary programs, fostering relationships with future generations of customers and promoting the importance of balanced nutrition.
- Team up with neighborhood pet stores or animal shelters to create specialty treats for pets using bakery ingredients, tapping into the growing market for pet-friendly products and engaging with pet owners in the community.
- Forge alliances with local theaters or entertainment venues to offer bakery items as concessions or pre-show snacks, enhancing the overall experience for patrons and creating opportunities for cross-promotion.
- Collaborate with nearby spas or salons to offer bakery-themed pampering packages, combining indulgent treats with relaxing treatments to create unique experiences for customers seeking self-care and indulgence.
- Partner with local libraries or bookstores to host literary-themed events or book clubs featuring bakery-inspired refreshments, creating opportunities for intellectual engagement and community building.
- Form alliances with neighborhood associations or business improvement districts to participate in local events or festivals, showcasing bakery products and contributing to the vibrancy of the community.
- Collaborate with local sports teams or athletic organizations to sponsor events or provide bakery items for post-game celebrations, fostering a sense of camaraderie and supporting active lifestyles within the community.
- Work with nearby corporate offices or businesses to offer bakery products as catering options for meetings, conferences, or employee appreciation events, positioning the bakery as a preferred vendor for corporate clients and expanding business-to-business opportunities.
- Partner with local tourism boards or visitor centers to create bakery-themed experiences or tours for tourists, highlighting the bakery's unique offerings and attracting visitors to the area.
- Collaborate with nearby schools or youth organizations to offer bakery workshops or mentorship programs for aspiring young bakers, nurturing talent within the community and fostering a love for baking.
- Form alliances with local environmental organizations or sustainability initiatives to implement eco-friendly practices within the bakery, such as reducing waste or sourcing ingredients responsibly, demonstrating commitment to environmental stewardship and appealing to eco-conscious consumers.

Influencer Marketing for New Products

- Identify key influencers in the food and lifestyle niche whose audience aligns with the target demographic of the bakery's new products, ensuring relevance and maximizing the impact of influencer collaborations.
- Reach out to influencers with personalized pitches highlighting the unique features and benefits of the new products, emphasizing why they would resonate with their audience and offering incentives for partnership.
- Offer exclusive sneak peeks or early access to the new products to influencers, generating anticipation and excitement among their followers and driving traffic to the bakery upon launch.
- Collaborate with influencers to create engaging and authentic content that showcases the new products in creative ways, such as recipe tutorials, taste tests, or behind-the-scenes footage of the bakery.
- Provide influencers with branded promotional materials or product samples to incorporate into their content, ensuring consistent messaging and reinforcing brand recognition among their audience.
- Leverage the reach and influence of macro influencers with large followings to generate widespread awareness and buzz around the new products, complemented by collaborations with micro influencers for targeted engagement and authenticity.
- Host influencer events or tastings to introduce the new products to a select group of influencers, allowing them to experience the quality and taste firsthand and fostering genuine enthusiasm and advocacy.
- Encourage influencers to share user-generated content featuring the new products, such as photos, reviews, or testimonials, to amplify word-of-mouth marketing and showcase social proof to their followers.
- Partner with influencers to run contests or giveaways featuring the new products as prizes, leveraging their audience to increase brand visibility, drive engagement, and expand reach through viral sharing.
- Collaborate with influencers to create sponsored blog posts or articles highlighting the story behind the new products, including their inspiration, ingredients, and craftsmanship, to build emotional connections with consumers and enhance brand storytelling.
- Engage with influencers beyond one-time collaborations by fostering long-term relationships through ongoing partnerships, ambassador programs, or affiliate marketing arrangements, cultivating loyalty and advocacy over time.
- Utilize influencer-generated content across various marketing channels, such as social media, email newsletters, or the bakery's website, to extend the reach and impact of influencer campaigns and reinforce brand messaging.
- Monitor and analyze the performance of influencer marketing campaigns using metrics such as engagement rates, click-through rates, and conversion rates, to measure ROI and inform future strategies and optimizations.

- Leverage influencer endorsements or testimonials in advertising campaigns or product packaging to lend credibility and authenticity to the new products and sway purchasing decisions.
- Collaborate with influencers to host live streaming or virtual events showcasing the new products, allowing for real-time interaction with their audience and providing opportunities for product demonstrations and Q&A sessions.
- Partner with influencers to create sponsored content featuring the new products in various formats, such as Instagram Stories, TikTok videos, or YouTube reviews, to cater to different audience preferences and consumption habits.
- Offer influencers exclusive discount codes or affiliate links to share with their followers, incentivizing purchases and tracking the effectiveness of influencer-driven sales.
- Collaborate with influencers to co-create limited-edition product variants or special bundles, adding exclusivity and collectability to the new product launch and driving urgency among consumers.
- Invite influencers to participate in product development or flavor testing sessions for future product iterations, involving them in the creative process and fostering a sense of ownership and investment in the brand.
- Partner with influencers who have expertise in specific niches or dietary preferences, such as gluten-free, vegan, or keto, to showcase how the new products cater to diverse dietary needs and lifestyles.
- Leverage influencer partnerships to gain access to new distribution channels or markets, such as online marketplaces or subscription boxes curated by influencers, to expand the reach and availability of the new products.
- Collaborate with influencers to create educational content highlighting the nutritional benefits or unique selling points of the new products, addressing consumer pain points or misconceptions and positioning the bakery as a trusted authority.
- Engage with influencers in meaningful ways beyond transactional partnerships, such as featuring them in brand storytelling initiatives, inviting them to participate in community events, or supporting their charitable causes, to build genuine relationships and foster brand advocacy.
- Continuously evaluate and evolve influencer marketing strategies based on industry trends, consumer preferences, and influencer landscape changes, to stay ahead of the curve and maintain relevance and effectiveness in reaching target audiences.

PRODUCT MARKETING IDEAS

Utilizing Pop-Up Sales and Markets

- Identify high-traffic locations in the community, such as farmer's markets, festivals, or local events, where the bakery can set up pop-up sales to reach a larger audience and increase brand visibility.
- Create eye-catching signage and displays for pop-up sales to attract passersby and draw them in with enticing visuals of the bakery's products, highlighting key selling points and promotions.
- Offer exclusive discounts or promotions for customers who visit the bakery's pop-up sales, incentivizing purchases and driving foot traffic to the location.
- Collaborate with other local businesses or vendors to co-host pop-up markets or joint sales events, pooling resources and attracting diverse customer bases to the shared space.
- Customize pop-up sales based on seasonal trends or local preferences, offering themed products or limited-edition items that align with current consumer interests and maximize sales potential.
- Utilize social media platforms to promote upcoming pop-up sales, sharing sneak peeks of featured products, behind-the-scenes glimpses of preparation, and location details to generate buzz and anticipation.
- Offer samples or tastings of bakery products during pop-up sales to allow customers to experience the quality and taste firsthand, increasing confidence and encouraging purchases.
- Provide convenient payment options, such as mobile payment solutions or contactless transactions, to streamline the checkout process and enhance the overall shopping experience for pop-up sale attendees.
- Leverage the power of storytelling to engage customers during pop-up sales, sharing the bakery's history, craftsmanship, and commitment to quality through signage, packaging, and personal interactions.
- Partner with local influencers or food bloggers to promote pop-up sales to their followers, leveraging their influence and credibility to expand reach and attract new customers to the bakery.
- Create branded merchandise or promotional items to give away or sell at pop-up sales, serving as souvenirs and extending brand visibility beyond the event itself.
- Host interactive activities or demonstrations during pop-up sales, such as cookie decorating stations or baking workshops, to engage attendees and create memorable experiences tied to the bakery's brand.
- Offer loyalty rewards or incentives for repeat customers who visit the bakery's pop-up sales regularly, encouraging ongoing patronage and building long-term relationships with the community.
- Partner with local organizations or charities to host fundraising events or donation drives during pop-up sales, giving back to the community and reinforcing the bakery's commitment to corporate social responsibility.

- Collect customer feedback and insights during pop-up sales through surveys or comment cards, soliciting suggestions for improvement and gaining valuable insights into consumer preferences and behavior.
- Collaborate with nearby businesses or venues to host pop-up sales in unconventional locations, such as parks, museums, or office buildings, to attract new audiences and create unique experiences for customers.
- Incorporate elements of entertainment or live music into pop-up sales to enhance the atmosphere and draw in crowds, creating a festive and inviting ambiance that encourages lingering and exploration.
- Showcase the bakery's commitment to sustainability and environmental stewardship during pop-up sales by using eco-friendly packaging, minimizing waste, and promoting responsible sourcing practices.
- Partner with local schools or community centers to host family-friendly pop-up sales featuring kid-friendly activities or special promotions, catering to a wider range of demographics and fostering community engagement.
- Offer pre-order options for customers attending pop-up sales, allowing them to reserve their favorite bakery items in advance and ensuring availability while minimizing wait times and disappointment.
- Leverage the appeal of exclusivity and scarcity by introducing limited-time offers or special collaborations during pop-up sales, creating urgency and driving impulse purchases among attendees.
- Capture user-generated content during pop-up sales, such as photos or testimonials shared on social media, to amplify word-of-mouth marketing and extend the reach of the event beyond physical attendance.
- Establish partnerships with local media outlets or publications to secure coverage and publicity for pop-up sales, leveraging their platforms to increase awareness and drive attendance.
- Continuously evaluate the success of pop-up sales through metrics such as sales performance, customer feedback, and foot traffic analysis, refining strategies and iterating on future events to maximize impact and ROI.

PRODUCT MARKETING IDEAS

Cross-Promotion with Complementary Products

- Partner with local coffee shops or cafes to cross-promote bakery products alongside their beverages, offering bundled deals or special discounts for customers who purchase both items together.
- Collaborate with nearby ice cream parlors or dessert shops to create indulgent dessert combinations featuring bakery items as toppings or accompaniments, appealing to sweet-toothed customers and driving joint sales.
- Form alliances with artisanal cheese shops or gourmet food stores to offer bakery products as part of curated cheese boards or charcuterie platters, showcasing complementary flavors and textures for a complete culinary experience.
- Team up with local breweries or wineries to pair bakery items with craft beers or fine wines, hosting tasting events or creating special menus that highlight the unique flavor profiles of both products.
- Partner with health food stores or wellness brands to promote bakery products as part of balanced lifestyles, offering nutritious options such as whole grain breads, gluten-free treats, or vegan pastries to health-conscious consumers.
- Collaborate with floral shops or gift boutiques to offer bakery items as part of gift packages or special occasions, such as Mother's Day brunch bundles or Valentine's Day gift sets, adding a touch of sweetness to memorable moments.
- Form alliances with local farmers' markets or produce stands to showcase bakery products alongside fresh, seasonal ingredients, highlighting the farm-to-table concept and promoting the use of locally sourced produce.
- Team up with specialty tea shops or tea rooms to pair bakery items with premium teas or herbal infusions, creating elegant afternoon tea experiences or offering tea-inspired baked goods for a sophisticated touch.
- Partner with fitness studios or athletic brands to promote bakery products as post-workout treats or energy-boosting snacks, emphasizing the balance between indulgence and healthy living.
- Collaborate with kitchenware stores or cooking schools to offer bakery-themed cooking classes or workshops, showcasing innovative recipes or baking techniques using bakery products as key ingredients.
- Form alliances with local bookstores or libraries to host literary-themed events or book clubs featuring bakery-inspired refreshments, fostering intellectual engagement and community connections.
- Team up with pet stores or animal shelters to create specialty treats for pets using bakery ingredients, tapping into the growing market for pet-friendly products and engaging with pet owners in the community.
- Partner with outdoor equipment retailers or adventure companies to promote bakery products as on-the-go snacks for outdoor enthusiasts, emphasizing portability and convenience for active lifestyles.

- Collaborate with art galleries or creative studios to host bakery-themed art exhibitions or workshops, combining culinary and artistic experiences to inspire creativity and self-expression.
- Form alliances with local museums or cultural institutions to create themed events or exhibits featuring bakery items inspired by historical periods or cultural traditions, offering educational and immersive experiences for visitors.
- Team up with beauty salons or spas to offer bakery-themed pampering packages, combining indulgent treats with relaxing treatments for a luxurious self-care experience.
- Partner with local schools or educational institutions to provide bakery items for school events, fundraisers, or culinary programs, fostering relationships with future generations of customers and promoting the importance of balanced nutrition.
- Collaborate with travel agencies or tourism boards to create bakery-themed tours or experiences for tourists, highlighting the bakery's unique offerings and attracting visitors to the area.
- Form alliances with local theaters or entertainment venues to offer bakery items as concessions or pre-show snacks, enhancing the overall experience for patrons and creating opportunities for cross-promotion.
- Team up with event planners or wedding vendors to offer customized bakery packages for special occasions, such as weddings, birthdays, or corporate events, catering to diverse customer needs and preferences.
- Partner with local event venues or community centers to host bakery-themed events or pop-up markets, reaching new audiences and establishing strategic partnerships.
- Collaborate with local charities or nonprofit organizations to host fundraising events or donation drives featuring bakery products, giving back to the community and reinforcing the bakery's commitment to social responsibility.
- Form alliances with local businesses or startups to offer bakery items as corporate gifts or employee incentives, strengthening business-to-business relationships and tapping into corporate gifting opportunities.
- Team up with food delivery services or meal kit companies to offer bakery items as add-ons or standalone options, providing convenient access to freshly baked goods for busy consumers and expanding distribution channels.

Creating Loyalty Programs for Repeat Purchases

- Develop a points-based loyalty program where customers earn points for every purchase of bakery products, which can be redeemed for discounts, free items, or exclusive rewards based on their accumulated points.
- Offer tiered loyalty programs with escalating benefits for higher levels of engagement, such as VIP access to new product launches, personalized offers, or birthday rewards, incentivizing customers to reach higher tiers through increased spending or frequency of purchases.
- Create a digital loyalty app or mobile platform where customers can easily track their rewards, receive personalized recommendations, and access exclusive deals or promotions, enhancing convenience and encouraging ongoing engagement with the bakery brand.
- Implement a referral program where loyal customers are rewarded for referring new customers to the bakery, either through discounts, bonus points, or special incentives for both the referrer and the referred individual, leveraging word-of-mouth marketing to expand the customer base.
- Offer special perks or privileges for members of the loyalty program, such as priority access to limited-edition products, reserved seating at bakery events, or early access to seasonal promotions, enhancing the sense of exclusivity and recognition for loyal customers.
- Partner with other local businesses or brands to offer cross-promotional rewards or joint loyalty programs, allowing customers to earn points or benefits across multiple participating establishments and fostering strategic alliances within the community.
- Host exclusive events or VIP experiences for loyalty program members, such as behind-the-scenes bakery tours, chef-led tastings, or baking workshops, creating memorable interactions and strengthening emotional connections with the brand.
- Utilize data analytics and customer insights to personalize loyalty rewards and offers based on individual preferences, purchase history, or demographic information, delivering tailored experiences that resonate with each customer segment.
- Offer surprise rewards or gamified challenges within the loyalty program, such as bonus points for completing certain actions or making purchases during specified time periods, injecting excitement and spontaneity into the rewards experience.
- Provide members of the loyalty program with early access to sales, promotions, or special events, giving them a sense of privilege and exclusivity while also driving incremental sales and engagement.
- Leverage social media platforms to engage with loyalty program members, sharing exclusive content, sneak peeks of upcoming rewards, or interactive challenges to foster community and encourage ongoing participation.
- Incorporate elements of charitable giving or social impact into the loyalty program, allowing customers to donate their rewards points to support local causes or participate in fundraising initiatives organized by the bakery, aligning loyalty with social responsibility.

- Encourage customers to provide feedback and reviews as part of the loyalty program, rewarding them with bonus points or exclusive perks for sharing their opinions and experiences, while also gathering valuable insights to improve products and services.
- Offer flexible redemption options for loyalty rewards, allowing customers to choose from a variety of incentives that cater to their preferences and lifestyle, such as discounts, free products, or charitable donations, maximizing relevance and value.
- Create seasonal or themed promotions within the loyalty program, such as holiday-themed rewards, birthday surprises, or anniversary milestones, adding excitement and anticipation to the rewards experience throughout the year.
- Collaborate with local influencers or brand ambassadors to promote the loyalty program to their followers, leveraging their influence and credibility to attract new members and increase program awareness.
- Provide members of the loyalty program with exclusive access to online ordering or delivery services, offering convenience and flexibility for busy customers while also driving digital engagement and retention.
- Reward customers for engaging with the bakery brand beyond purchases, such as following social media accounts, signing up for newsletters, or participating in online polls or surveys, fostering deeper connections and brand advocacy.
- Offer personalized incentives for customers celebrating life milestones or special occasions, such as weddings, graduations, or anniversaries, creating memorable experiences that strengthen emotional ties with the bakery brand.
- Partner with local schools or community organizations to offer educational opportunities or youth-focused initiatives as part of the loyalty program, such as scholarships, internships, or mentorship programs, investing in the future while also building goodwill within the community.
- Create themed loyalty events or challenges centered around seasonal holidays or cultural celebrations, such as baking contests, recipe exchanges, or themed scavenger hunts, encouraging participation and fostering a sense of camaraderie among members.
- Reward customers for sharing user-generated content featuring bakery products on social media, such as photos, recipes, or reviews, leveraging the power of social proof and word-of-mouth marketing to amplify brand awareness and engagement.
- Offer bonus rewards or incentives for customers who opt into loyalty program communications, such as email newsletters or SMS alerts, ensuring ongoing engagement and communication while also respecting individual preferences for communication channels.
- Continuously evaluate and optimize the loyalty program based on performance metrics, customer feedback, and market trends, evolving the program over time to meet changing consumer needs and preferences while maximizing ROI and customer lifetime value.

PRODUCT MARKETING IDEAS

Implementing Flash Sales and Limited-Time Offers

- Launch flash sales or limited-time offers to create a sense of urgency and excitement among customers, encouraging them to make spontaneous purchases and take advantage of exclusive discounts or promotions.
- Utilize social media platforms to announce flash sales and limited-time offers, leveraging the immediacy and viral nature of social media to generate buzz and reach a wider audience quickly.
- Offer special discounts or promotions for a short duration, such as a few hours or a single day, to maximize the impact of scarcity and drive immediate action from customers.
- Create countdown timers or urgency-inducing messaging to highlight the time-sensitive nature of flash sales and limited-time offers, instilling a fear of missing out (FOMO) and compelling customers to act quickly.
- Partner with influencers or brand ambassadors to promote flash sales and limited-time offers to their followers, leveraging their influence and credibility to increase visibility and drive traffic to the bakery.
- Segment customer email lists and send targeted communications about flash sales and limited-time offers to specific customer segments based on past purchase behavior, preferences, or demographics, ensuring relevance and maximizing response rates.
- Offer exclusive access or early previews of flash sales and limited-time offers to loyalty program members or email subscribers, rewarding their loyalty and incentivizing them to engage with the bakery brand.
- Create themed promotions or bundles for flash sales and limited-time offers, tying the offer to seasonal holidays, special occasions, or trending topics to increase relevance and appeal to customers.
- Experiment with dynamic pricing strategies for flash sales and limited-time offers, such as tiered discounts based on purchase amount or personalized offers tailored to individual customer preferences, to maximize conversion rates and revenue.
- Collaborate with complementary businesses or brands to co-promote flash sales and limited-time offers through cross-promotional efforts, reaching new audiences and expanding brand visibility.
- Host flash sales or limited-time offers exclusively on the bakery's website or mobile app, driving traffic to digital channels and increasing engagement with online platforms.
- Create scarcity by limiting the quantity or availability of products for flash sales and limited-time offers, emphasizing that supplies are limited and encouraging customers to act quickly to secure their purchase.
- Offer bonus incentives or rewards for customers who participate in flash sales and limited-time offers, such as free samples, gift cards, or entry into exclusive giveaways, to enhance the perceived value of the promotion and drive participation.
- Leverage customer data and insights to determine the optimal timing and duration for flash sales and limited-time offers, taking into account factors such as peak shopping times,

seasonal trends, and competitor activity.
- Utilize retargeting ads or abandoned cart emails to remind customers about flash sales and limited-time offers they may have shown interest in but not yet completed, prompting them to return and complete their purchase.
- Create a sense of exclusivity by offering VIP access or early invitations to flash sales and limited-time offers for select customers or members of loyalty programs, enhancing their sense of value and appreciation for the bakery brand.
- Implement gamification elements, such as limited-time challenges or rewards for completing certain actions, to increase engagement and excitement around flash sales and limited-time offers.
- Highlight the savings or value proposition of flash sales and limited-time offers through compelling messaging and visuals, emphasizing the opportunity for customers to score a great deal or try something new at a discounted price.
- Monitor and analyze the performance of flash sales and limited-time offers using metrics such as conversion rates, average order value, and customer acquisition cost, to optimize future promotions and maximize ROI.
- Create buzz and anticipation leading up to flash sales and limited-time offers by teasing upcoming promotions through sneak peeks, teaser trailers, or cryptic clues, building excitement and curiosity among customers.
- Leverage scarcity marketing tactics, such as limited-time countdowns or low stock alerts, to create a sense of urgency and drive immediate action from customers during flash sales and limited-time offers.
- Experiment with different types of offers for flash sales and limited-time promotions, such as buy-one-get-one (BOGO) deals, percentage discounts, or free shipping, to determine which incentives resonate most with customers and drive the highest response rates.
- Encourage social sharing and word-of-mouth marketing for flash sales and limited-time offers by incentivizing customers to spread the word to their friends and followers, rewarding them with additional discounts or exclusive perks for referrals.
- Continuously innovate and iterate on flash sales and limited-time offers by testing new strategies, incentives, and formats to keep customers engaged and excited about future promotions while staying ahead of competitors in the market.

PRODUCT MARKETING IDEAS

Educating Customers on Product USPs

- Create visually appealing infographics that highlight the unique selling points (USPs) of your bakery products, such as freshness, locally sourced ingredients, or special dietary options.
- Host tasting events where customers can sample your products while learning about their unique features and benefits.
- Develop engaging video content showcasing behind-the-scenes footage of your baking process, emphasizing the quality and care put into each product.
- Offer workshops or classes where customers can learn about the ingredients used in your products and the health benefits they provide.
- Collaborate with nutritionists or dieticians to create educational materials that explain the nutritional value of your bakery items.
- Utilize social media platforms to share educational posts about the history and origins of different baked goods, connecting customers with the cultural significance behind your products.
- Design interactive quizzes or games that challenge customers to identify the key features of your bakery items, reinforcing their understanding of your USPs.
- Publish blog articles or newsletters that delve into the craftsmanship behind your products, highlighting the skills and expertise of your bakers.
- Partner with influencers or food bloggers to create sponsored content that educates their followers about the unique qualities of your bakery offerings.
- Host live cooking demonstrations or baking tutorials on platforms like Facebook or Instagram, demonstrating how customers can incorporate your products into their own culinary creations.
- Offer guided tours of your bakery facilities, giving customers a firsthand look at the production process and the attention to detail that goes into every batch.
- Create branded recipe cards featuring innovative ways to use your bakery items, showcasing their versatility and appeal.
- Develop loyalty programs that reward customers for engaging with educational content about your products, such as earning points for attending workshops or sharing informative posts on social media.
- Partner with local schools or community centers to deliver educational presentations on topics like the science of baking or the cultural significance of different types of bread.
- Organize themed events or seasonal promotions that tie into educational themes, such as a "farm-to-table" showcase highlighting the locally sourced ingredients used in your products.
- Design eye-catching signage or displays in your bakery storefront that highlight the unique qualities of your featured products, drawing customers' attention and sparking their curiosity.

- Collaborate with other businesses in your community to host joint educational events, such as a wine and pastry pairing workshop or a cooking demonstration at a nearby farmers' market.
- Develop downloadable resources, such as e-books or whitepapers, that delve deeper into the stories behind your bakery products, offering customers a deeper understanding of their origins and ingredients.
- Host Q&A sessions on social media where customers can ask questions about your products and receive informative answers from your team of experts.
- Partner with local libraries or bookstores to host book clubs centered around baking-themed literature, providing opportunities for customers to learn and discuss topics related to your products.
- Create interactive online quizzes or surveys that help customers discover which of your bakery products best align with their preferences and dietary needs.
- Collaborate with local artisans or craftsmen to create limited-edition packaging or merchandise that highlights the unique qualities of your bakery items, offering customers an additional incentive to engage with your brand.
- Develop educational resources specifically tailored to different customer segments, such as parents looking for healthy snacks for their children or fitness enthusiasts seeking post-workout fuel.
- Offer virtual cooking classes or baking workshops that allow customers to learn new skills and techniques while gaining a deeper appreciation for your bakery products.

Tracking Product Sales and Feedback

- Implement a customer feedback system within your bakery, such as suggestion boxes or online surveys, to gather insights on product preferences and areas for improvement.
- Utilize point-of-sale (POS) data analytics to track sales trends and identify which bakery items are the best-sellers, allowing you to optimize your product offerings accordingly.
- Create loyalty programs or rewards programs that incentivize customers to provide feedback on their purchases, such as offering discounts or freebies in exchange for completing surveys or reviews.
- Monitor social media platforms and online review sites to gather real-time feedback from customers about their experiences with your bakery products, addressing any concerns or negative feedback promptly.
- Implement a customer relationship management (CRM) system to track individual customer preferences and purchase history, enabling personalized recommendations and targeted marketing efforts.
- Conduct regular taste tests or sampling events in-store to gather direct feedback from customers about new or experimental bakery products, gauging their reactions and adjusting recipes as needed.
- Collaborate with local businesses or community organizations to host focus groups or feedback sessions, gathering insights from diverse perspectives and demographics.
- Leverage email marketing campaigns to solicit feedback from customers after their bakery purchases, encouraging them to share their thoughts and suggestions for improvement.
- Offer incentives for customers to leave reviews or testimonials on your bakery's website or social media pages, such as entering them into a monthly giveaway or offering exclusive discounts.
- Implement a ratings and review system on your bakery's website, allowing customers to provide feedback and ratings for each product they purchase, which can help inform future product development decisions.
- Analyze sales data and customer feedback to identify any seasonal or regional trends in product preferences, adjusting your marketing strategies and product offerings accordingly.
- Partner with local influencers or food bloggers to review your bakery products and share their feedback with their followers, increasing brand awareness and credibility.
- Create feedback cards or surveys that accompany each bakery purchase, prompting customers to rate their satisfaction with the product quality, taste, and overall experience.
- Monitor online discussions and forums related to baking or food enthusiasts to gauge sentiment and gather feedback about your bakery products from a wider audience.
- Implement a customer referral program that rewards existing customers for referring their friends and family to your bakery, providing an additional incentive for them to share their positive experiences.
- Track customer complaints or issues reported through various channels, such as social media, email, or in-store interactions, and use this feedback to identify areas for

improvement and address any recurring issues.
- Analyze sales data alongside customer feedback to identify any potential correlations between product popularity and specific marketing initiatives or promotions.
- Conduct competitor analysis to gather insights into customer preferences and perceptions of competing bakery products, identifying opportunities to differentiate your offerings and attract new customers.
- Use customer feedback to inform product labeling and packaging design decisions, highlighting key selling points and addressing any common concerns or questions raised by customers.
- Implement regular staff training sessions to ensure that frontline employees are equipped to gather and relay customer feedback effectively, providing them with the tools and resources they need to address customer inquiries and concerns.
- Offer customers the option to provide feedback anonymously, ensuring that they feel comfortable sharing their honest opinions without fear of repercussions.
- Use customer feedback to identify opportunities for product innovation or expansion, such as introducing new flavors or variations based on popular customer suggestions or requests.
- Analyze customer feedback alongside demographic data to identify any specific preferences or trends among different customer segments, allowing for targeted marketing efforts and product offerings.
- Implement a system for tracking and responding to customer feedback in a timely manner, ensuring that all inquiries and concerns are addressed promptly and effectively to maintain customer satisfaction and loyalty.

Adjusting Strategies Based on Analytics Insights

- Utilize website analytics tools such as Google Analytics to track visitor behavior, including which bakery products are most popular, how customers navigate your site, and where they drop off in the purchasing process.
- Analyze social media metrics to identify which platforms drive the most engagement and traffic to your bakery's website, allowing you to focus your marketing efforts on the channels that yield the highest return on investment.
- Monitor email marketing metrics such as open rates, click-through rates, and conversion rates to assess the effectiveness of your email campaigns and tailor future messaging based on subscriber behavior.
- Implement A/B testing for marketing campaigns, website layouts, and product offerings to experiment with different strategies and identify which variations perform best in terms of sales and customer engagement.
- Track customer demographics and purchase history through your CRM system to better understand your target audience and tailor marketing messages and promotions to their preferences and behaviors.
- Analyze sales data to identify seasonal trends and adjust your product offerings and marketing strategies accordingly, such as introducing seasonal flavors or promotions during peak periods.
- Monitor customer feedback and reviews to identify any recurring issues or concerns and address them proactively to improve customer satisfaction and loyalty.
- Use heatmaps and session recording tools to visualize how users interact with your website, identifying areas for improvement in terms of usability, navigation, and conversion optimization.
- Collaborate with influencers or brand ambassadors to promote your bakery products to their followers, tracking metrics such as engagement, reach, and conversions to measure the effectiveness of these partnerships.
- Conduct market research surveys or focus groups to gather insights into consumer preferences, attitudes, and behaviors, informing your product development and marketing strategies.
- Analyze competitor performance and market trends to identify opportunities for differentiation and innovation, ensuring that your bakery remains competitive and relevant in the marketplace.
- Implement customer segmentation strategies based on demographic, psychographic, or behavioral factors to personalize marketing messages and promotions for different audience segments.
- Monitor search engine rankings and keyword performance to optimize your website's SEO strategy and improve visibility in organic search results for relevant bakery-related queries.
- Track customer lifetime value (CLV) and retention rates to assess the effectiveness of your customer acquisition and retention efforts, adjusting your marketing strategies to maximize

long-term profitability.
- Utilize geolocation data to target customers in specific geographic areas with localized marketing campaigns and promotions, tailoring messaging and offers to their preferences and needs.
- Monitor referral traffic sources to identify which channels drive the most qualified leads and sales to your bakery, allocating resources accordingly to optimize your marketing mix.
- Analyze customer engagement metrics such as time spent on site, pages per visit, and bounce rate to assess the effectiveness of your website content and user experience design.
- Use predictive analytics to forecast future sales and customer behavior, enabling proactive decision-making and strategic planning to capitalize on emerging opportunities and mitigate potential risks.
- Implement retargeting campaigns to re-engage website visitors who have shown interest in your bakery products but did not make a purchase, encouraging them to return and complete their purchase.
- Track the performance of marketing promotions and discounts to assess their impact on sales and profitability, refining your pricing and promotion strategies based on data-driven insights.
- Analyze customer churn rates and reasons for attrition to identify opportunities for improvement in customer retention efforts, such as enhancing loyalty programs or addressing common pain points.
- Monitor customer satisfaction scores and Net Promoter Score (NPS) to gauge overall brand perception and loyalty, identifying areas for improvement and opportunities to delight customers.
- Use sentiment analysis tools to analyze social media mentions and customer reviews, identifying trends in customer sentiment and addressing any negative feedback or concerns promptly.
- Continuously monitor and evaluate the performance of your marketing efforts across various channels and touchpoints, iterating and optimizing your strategies based on real-time analytics insights to drive sustainable growth and success for your bakery business.

Thank You!

Dear Friend,

We wanted to take a moment to express our heartfelt gratitude for choosing Karlstein Publishing for your marketing practice. Your support means the world to us and our small publishing house.

We genuinely care about the well-being of each and every customer, and we're dedicated to providing valuable resources that can make a positive difference in your life. Your satisfaction and feedback are incredibly important to us.

If you've had a positive experience with your book, we kindly request that you consider leaving a five-star review. Your review not only helps potential customers make informed decisions but also supports our small business in a big way.

To leave a review, simply go to the product page for this paperback which you can find under Your Orders.

Thank you again for choosing Karlstein Publishing. Your trust in our shop is deeply cherished.

Sincerely, Benjamin Karlstein, Karlstein Publishing

www.ingramcontent.com/pod-product-compliance
Lightning Source LLC
Chambersburg PA
CBHW052147220526
45471CB00004B/1557